THE DERBY

*The Official Book
of the
World's Greatest Race*

The DERBY

The Official Book of the World's Greatest Race

ALASTAIR BURNET

TIM NELIGAN

MICHAEL O'MARA BOOKS
in association with
UNITED RACECOURSES LIMITED

First published in Great Britain by
Michael O'Mara Books Limited
9 Lion Yard, Tremadoc Road, London SW4 7NQ
in association with
United Racecourses (Holdings) Ltd
The Grandstand, Epsom, Surrey KT18 5LQ

A CIP catalogue record for this book is available from
the British Library

ISBN 1 85479 175 3

Designed by Yvonne Dedman

Typeset by Florencetype Ltd, Kewstoke, Avon
Printed and bound in Italy
by New Interlitho

*Frontispiece: The 1848 Derby finish – Surplice beats Spring
Jack and Glendower. Beyond the winning post, to the right,
is Prince's Stand, the first ever permanent racecourse
building. It was built around 1783 for the use of George,
Prince of Wales, who won the Derby in 1788 with Sir
Thomas. Prince's Stand was refurbished in 1879 and again
in 1993, when the original brickwork was found to be in
excellent condition.*

Contents

FOREWORD

by
The Marchioness of Tavistock

Derby Day 1791. Eager, ridden by F. Stephenson, wins in the colours of the Duke of Bedford.

The Derby at Epsom is purely and simply the greatest horse race in the world! Some people may find this statement contentious yet you won't find many breeders in the world who would pick any other race of which they would rather breed the winner. Wherever you go in the world, after breeding a Derby winner, people will always add to their introduction, 'He bred the English Derby winner, you know!'

There are many races in other countries that are more valuable in terms of prize money, that are certainly run on a more sensible race track, but I do not believe that any other race is as emotive or charismatic.

My husband's family has won the Derby three times and, indeed, the Oaks three times. Their first Derby winner was with a horse called Skyscraper – a word which has a very clear meaning today but I am not sure what it meant in 1789. The second winner was in 1791 with a horse named Eager and, in 1797, with a horse that was never named, beyond, 'Colt by Fidget'.

When we bought our first race horse in 1965, a filly foal by Sica Boy, winner of the Arc de Triomphe, we only had one thought in mind, to breed another Derby winner, one that would hopefully win in the purple and white stripes, black velvet cap and gold tassel that had won the world's greatest race three times before. As yet it has not happened, but I know that I would rather breed the Derby winner and have it win in another's colours than buy a horse and win the Derby with it.

The last few days before Epsom feel like the days before Christmas did when I was a child. The anticipation, the knowledge that whoever wins on Wednesday has a permanent effect on breeders all over the world. My favourite way to go to the Derby is by car on my own – enjoying the slow build-up to the race.

The first Derby I really remember is Tulyar's in 1952 and I am still very conscious that he was sold to America. Since then only six Derby winners have gone to America to stud and, for the moment, it seems less likely that a Derby winner would go to the USA. A bigger probability would be Japan, for many horses who win or are placed in the Derby are bought by Japanese breeders.

I first went to the Derby in 1961 – and it set the shape for the rest of my life, for I happened to go with the owners/breeders Etti and Arpad Plesch. Etti performed an amazing Derby double – she won it with Psidium, a horse she had bred out of the very first mare she had bought, and she did it again in 1980 with one of the first horses, Henbit, she had bought after her husband's death, when the stud and all the breeding stock had been sold. Etti has really experienced the ultimate in Derby victories by breeding one winner and buying, as a yearling, another. I hope that she will win it again for a third time and have the best result of all – a winner of the Derby who becomes a great sire, for that is all that eludes her.

As a breeder there is that great goal to breed a horse that sires a Derby winner. Paul Mellon has achieved even greater heights – Mill Reef won the Derby and sired Shirley Heights and Reference Point who both won Derbies; then Shirley Heights sired Slip Anchor – the next generation.

A name most closely associated with the Derby is that of the Aga Khan. Since 1925 horses running in either the chocolate and green or scarlet and green

have won the race eight times, been second seven times and third five times; most of these were home-bred.

When I first started breeding, very few Derby winners were bought, the majority were owner bred; then we went through a phase when many were bought. During the last decade the majority have been bred by their owners again.

I am glad as a breeder that, once again, yearlings may be entered for the Derby. I would prefer it to be even earlier, so that it was the breeders who had to nominate their horses and pay the first entry for, at the end of the day, it is the breeders' race. The owner of the winner may win the solid gold cup, the prize money, lead the horse in to that magical winner's circle at Epsom, but the real winner is the breeder for, without him, that champion racehorse would never have been born.

So much contributes to breeding a Derby winner and yet, if you try and study it to establish a pattern, all you realize is that there really is none. A Derby winner can be any size, although more seem to be under 16.1 hands. I believe that temperament and courage are paramount, for to survive the rigours of Derby Day the eventual winner will need to cope with many stressful things: the crowd, the noise, the parade, the long walk across Epsom Downs, the start and then the daunting racecourse. One-and-a-half miles of ups, downs, bends and, most extraordinary of all, the slope from one side of the course to the other in the finishing straight. Everyone who is thrilled by the Derby should walk the course at Epsom just once. It is an amazing experience!

In the years since 1965 when we bought our first filly, we have only ever entered two horses for the Derby, both colts that we had bred; sadly, neither ran. Now, with the new entry system, we will enter all the yearling colts we breed with pedigrees that could stay a mile and a half. If we have an exceptional yearling filly we will enter her too. Maybe then we will rejoin that elite of all elites, a breeder of an Epsom Derby winner.

INTRODUCTION

by

Alastair Burnet

The Derby runners sweep over and round Epsom Downs in the blink of an eye, through the din of incoherent sound, a cluster of scrambling colours resolving briskly into recognizable success and failure. It is all over in two and a half minutes, over for that conglomerated crowd and those winners and losers. But for all those who saw and heard them, the colours, shapes and sounds go on running in the mind for months and years. They join the history and mystery of the Derby, a race which is perpetual, unmatched, immortal. No fantasy is more unlikely, or more probable, than the Derby. Whether or not the spectral Richard the Lionheart began racing over Epsom Downs for horses from the East after the Crusades, putting up a purse of forty gold pieces for the first Arabians, Barbs and Turks on that turf, whether or not any or every one of the countless stories, memories, ghosts, heroes, angels, tricksters and buffoons of the downs are merely chimerical, next year's Derby will duly produce its own.

This is an account of a number of the men, women and horses, those who won and lost, those who tried and those who didn't, those whom fortune preferred and those she crushed in their lives, who were drawn into the Derby's fantasy and reality. Many are honest, professionals in the racing game, their eyes and efforts intent on success, on the highest prize; theirs are famous names. There are, too, the rogues and cheats, the sly and the desperate, whose names are despised and disparaged but are indispensable to the Derby's story; their crimes and sins are the greater in the public mind because they were committed for nothing less than the Derby. There are the royal figures who have stood imposingly in box and paddock, the politicians who have taken the Epsom train rather than the Westminster one confident that it was their constituents' as well as their own wish that they should,

and there are the international owners, trainers, jockeys and racegoers who have been trying their luck at Epsom for over two centuries now.

And there are, above all, the exploits of great horses and the pleasures of plain people which are both part, now and for always, of this green, bosky, hummocky stretch of country. Most of the 204 colts and fillies (counting one Derby dead-heat, ten 'Derbys' run in wartime at Newmarket) who have won at Epsom have deserved to do so. They were the best of their year; and the Epsom course brought out that best in them. There is no winning post that stands beside Epsom's in the world. The greatest among its winners – the Diomeds, West Australians, Blink Bonnys, Gladiateurs, Ormondes, Hyperions, Bahrams, Sea Birds, Mill Reefs, Nashwans and others – have meant more in many homes than the evanescent human figures of their day.

For the hundreds of thousands who, every year, have gone hopefully down the Epsom road from London or caught the train to Tattenham Corner, and gone home in the evening replete with their holiday and probably nearly skint by the bookies, the memory is simply of fun. For all the scanning of the *Sporting Life*, the figuring of the tipsters and their curious prose, and the remembered expertise of the Channel Four masters, the point of the Derby is having a day out, London's day out, the one true holiday before the politicians, the teetotallers and the social workers began to take over people's lives. It belongs to a long and strong tradition running unhindered through the decades in town and country, the day when, win or lose, it was right to be there, in the stands, on the hill, watching on television. Those who appear in this book are those, equine and human, who have made the Derby, warts and all.

THE DERBY STORY

by

Alastair Burnet

On the Toss of a Coin

The American War of Independence was being fought across the Atlantic when the Derby Stakes, with nine runners, entered racing history. The twelfth Earl of Derby, whose name was given to the race when it was first run in 1780, was a hospitable but otherwise largely unremarkable young man. Racing has counted itself lucky that it was his family's name, and not that of the distinguished Sir Charles Bunbury, which was chosen – apparently on the toss of a coin. The name Bunbury had a less auspicious ring than Derby, even in those days; it was not helped subsequently by Oscar Wilde's pleasantry in *The Importance of Being Earnest*.

But Bunbury was a very considerable man, besides being the racing authority of his day and the 'Perpetual President' of the Jockey Club. He forbade Sam Chifney, the jockey of the Prince of Wales (later George IV), from riding again after the noticeably inconsistent running of Escape in 1791. At this the prince took great umbrage, sold his horses and did not deign to go racing again for fourteen years. Bunbury was a Suffolk Member of Parliament for over forty years; he also served as Chief Secretary for Ireland. He married, and divorced, the delectable Lady Sarah

Lennox who took the eye of the young George III and might have caught him had she not fallen from her horse and broken a leg at a delicate moment. She left Bunbury because she thought he spent too much time racing. He also spent much time at Dr Johnson's Club, with the likes of Reynolds, Garrick, Boswell, Fox, Gibbon, Adam Smith and Sheridan.

It was Bunbury, rather than Derby, who was the moving force behind the concept of races of a mile and a mile and a half (following the example of the St Leger at Doncaster in 1776), as distinct from the laborious two-mile and four-mile contests. These were run in heats to the boredom of spectators and, increasingly, the riders themselves.

So it was only justice that Bunbury owned Diomed, the first winner of the Derby, run over a mile, for which he collected the prize money of 1075 guineas. He won two further Derbys with Eleanor (1801), the first filly to win, and Smolensko (1813), the first dual winner of the Two Thousand Guineas and the Derby. Diomed was twenty-one and thought to be of small account at stud when Bunbury sold him to the United States in 1798 for fifty guineas. But Diomed survived

Opposite: Thomas Rowlandson depicted the Derby in four scenes in 1785. 'Mounting' (above), is followed by 'A Bolter' (below). See page 12 for the third and fourth scenes.

'The Race' (above) and 'The Finish' (below). Aimwell just wins from the grey Grantham.

the crossing, was bought by Colonel John Hoomes of Virginia for 1000 guineas, and proved active enough to found an American racing dynasty, with Lexington its star, in his last ten years.

Lord Derby's home near Epsom was The Oaks, at Woodmansterne. Its name was given to the all-fillies race when it was first run in 1779, a year before the Derby itself. Derby won it with Bridget. The house itself had been an alehouse, but was bought and enlarged by Captain John Burgoyne who eloped with, and married, Derby's elder sister, Lady Charlotte Stanley. Burgoyne, promoted to general, was the commander whose surrender at Saratoga in 1777 was the first major American success in the War of Independence.

Derby bought the house from him in 1773. Burgoyne helped to lose the colonies but he had a knack as a dramatist. His *The Maid of The Oaks* was produced there – and later by David Garrick in Drury Lane – to celebrate Derby's first marriage in 1774.

Derby was a congenial man, given to breeding cock-fighting champions: Black Breasted Reds were his speciality. His first wife, Lady Betty Hamilton, had an affair with the Duke of Dorset (it began when she was playing cricket at The Oaks) and they separated. Derby then fell in love with the actress Elizabeth Farren. Miss Farren's appearance in Burgoyne's comedy *The Heiress* (dedicated to Derby) captured Derby's heart, but her greatest stage success was as Lady Teazle in Sheridan's *School for Scandal*.

When his first wife died Derby married again. He had courted Miss Farren for twenty years, named a filly, Lady Teazle, after her, and went on to win the 1787 Derby with his colt, Sir Peter Teazle. Theirs was

'The Constant Couple' – A contemporary engraving by Deighton in 1795, the year of the marriage of the twelfth Earl of Derby to Elizabeth Farren.

a successful marriage. She banned cock-fighting in her drawing room and dared to give elocution lessons to the eldest grandson of his first marriage who became the fourteenth earl and three times prime minister.

Try as the family did throughout the nineteenth century, their first Derby win after 1787 was not until 137 years later with Sansovino on an almost waterlogged course in 1924. The winning earl was the seventeenth. He won again with the great Hyperion, small, lethargic at home but brilliant on the big day, in 1933. He did have a wartime success at Newmarket in 1942 – which he did not go to see; Churchill did find the time to send him a congratulatory telegram. But there has not been a Derby-owned Derby winner since.

The Old Prize-Fighter

John Gully the prize-fighter, Champion of England for three years, was a distinctly unaristocratic member of racing's elite. But he managed to win the Derby twice in his own name – and the other classics too. He was an independent man, 'tall and finely formed . . . his face coarse, with a bad expression'. He was said to have 'strong sense, discretion, reserve and a species of good taste'. His conversation was slow and profound, 'every

word weighed a pound'. He became a Member of Parliament and a colliery owner, and to beat him at knowledge of form and deviousness in betting a man had to get up very early indeed.

Gully fought the reigning champion, Henry Pearce, the 'game chicken', in 1805 and was beaten in the fifty-ninth round. But the fight made his reputation and, when Pearce retired, Gully beat Bob Gregson twice, over thirty-six rounds and twenty-eight rounds. He then retired himself. For his first fight Gully earned £500, but the next year he still had to walk from London to Doncaster races. Racing and betting became his mètier. His first horse, Cardenio, he bought in 1812 when he went to live in Newmarket. The belief was that he became George IV's betting agent. But he had his setbacks.

In 1827 his horse Mameluke was cheated of victory in the St Leger before the race began. The horse had a nervous disposition and the other jockeys (and, it was said, the starter) conspired to bring about a series of false starts and delays. When the horses were sent off Mameluke was facing the wrong way. Gully lost £40,000.

Prize fighter John Gully, subsequently an MP, father of twenty-four children, and owner of Derby winners in 1846 and 1854.

By 1830 he had formed a racing confederacy with the artful Robert Ridsdale whose St Giles won the Derby in 1832. Most of the other horses had been 'made safe', as the saying went, one way or another. Gully's own Margrave finished fourth. But the partners quarrelled over the betting spoils and, though Margrave went on to win the St Leger, Gully was not placated. Next year when he met Ridsdale in the hunting field he struck him with his crop. The jury awarded Ridsdale £500 in damages.

Gully now moved above that sort of society. He was elected Member of Parliament for Pontefract as a Liberal and ardent reformer; in 1835 he topped the poll with 509 votes. (Despite the Reform Act, it was still a minuscule electorate.) The old prize-fighter was presented at the Court of St James. But he was a silent MP, dropped out of politics and, when persuaded to stand again in 1841, was badly beaten by two Tories. From then on his attention was centred on racing.

He sent his horses to the Days at Danebury and arranged for their training gallops to be on Salisbury Plain, high above the river Test. He himself moved to Marwell Hall near Winchester. The patriarch 'Honest John' Day contrived two Derby winners for the Gully colours: Pyrrhus the First (Sam Day up) in 1846 and Andover (Alfred Day up) in 1854. Gully's son-in-law won with Cossack, also trained by John Day, in 1847, the year the first low-level start was used.

Pyrrhus's success was attributed, in part, to the inebriated state of Bill Scott, on the favoured Sir Tatton Sykes, who was seen to sink a stiff brandy before the race. Scott was cautioned by the starter for causing a delay and later fined £5 for using improper language. Pyrrhus won by only a neck. Gully went on to win that year's Oaks with Mendicant.

Gully was helpful to Lord George Bentinck in defending an action brought by an informer under an antiquated law which forbade betting, except in small sums. Had the action succeeded, it would have been a damaging blow to racing. Gully gave all the right answers for its defeat.

He got the right answers from William Day in 1845 after haranguing the family at Danebury to discover who was behind the betting against Old England in the Derby. Eventually William Day confessed he had agreed to make the horse 'safe'. It finished third behind The Merry Monarch and Annandale.

Andover, which won in 1854, was owned by Gully in partnership with Henry Padwick, the moneylender. Gully had few scruples about the company he kept. He was no hero. But he had, it was said, 'an honest and substantial shrewdness'.

He was married twice, had twelve children by each wife, and died a respected and financially comfortable Durham colliery owner. He and his career were part of racing in a rough-and-ready age; and he, in his fashion, was a representative Derby owner.

The Weighing Room at Epsom before the 1845 Derby which was won by The Merry Monarch with John Gully's horse Old England third. The Clerk of the Scales checks the jockey's weight at 8 stones 7 pounds (54kg).

The Two Dead-Heats

The Derby has had many close finishes to test the judges' eyes, but only two dead-heats. In the first, in 1828, the two horses and their riders were sent back later in the afternoon and raced the mile and a half all over again. It was an age that still remembered much longer races, contested in heats. In the second dead-heat, in 1884, the two principals met in the weighing room and decided to split the prize money. At that time it was still not unusual to race horses on successive days, even after big races, and there was some grumbling about bad sportsmanship when the Epsom

crowds were deprived of another spectacle. The photo-finish camera put an end to all that in 1947.

There were fifteen runners in 1828, of which only two were really rated: the Hon. E. Petre's The Colonel, the 7–2 favourite, and the Duke of Rutland's Cadland, 4–1, who had won the Two Thousand Guineas. There was a good crowd. *The Times*'s man reported in the appropriate style that, London having roused itself like a leviathan, the course was 'rich and animated in the extreme' and the number of equipages 'superior to what we have seen for many years'. Minor royalty (two princes, two dukes), numerous nobility and aspiring gentry graced the proceedings.

After two false starts Cadland was seen going 'at a good bat'. Quite early, however, one horse, Scipio, and his 'excellent little jockey', Conolly, were knocked to the ground. Help was promptly at hand, Conolly being 'immediately bled and taken off the course in a gentleman's curricle' to have his broken rib seen to. The other colts got safely round Tattenham Corner and 'a very severe and interesting struggle' developed. But once Zinganee (6–1) had been beaten off, it was a contest between The Colonel and Cadland 'who finished a most beautiful race with a dead heat'. One punter was said to have landed a 100–1 shot on just that happening. It was certainly a novelty.

The sensation occasioned by the unlooked-for event did not subside for some time, and many would hardly credit that it was a dead-heat, such an event never having before occurred for the Derby or Oaks, or, we believe, at Epsom. It being decided that the second heat should be run after the Durdain's stakes, betting began anew.

The Colonel stayed favourite, 'having the call at 6 to 5, from an idea that he left off fresher, and was made of more lasting materials'. What added to the crowd's interest was that The Colonel was a Yorkshire horse, taking on the best from Newmarket and the south.

Distance added to rivalry between the training centres. Horses had to be walked by their grooms all the way from Malton or Middleham to Epsom, or from Newmarket to Doncaster, so toughness was essential. Lord George Bentinck did not invent his van to carry them along the roads until 1836; horses only began to go by train on the new railways from 1840. So The Colonel was a celebrity at Epsom in the way French and American horses were to be later in the century. With this north–south duel to come, there was little interest in betting on the intervening races. The match began at 4.40 p.m. Once again Cadland (ridden by Jem Robinson) set off at a good pace, but The Colonel (William Scott) was in close touch:

A desperate contest followed, and lasted to the last few strides, when Cadland got a-head, sufficient to win the Derby by half a length. Two finer races were never seen for either Derby, Oaks, St Leger, or any other stakes; we know not which most to admire, the excellence of the running or the admirable skill displayed in the riding.

The Duke of Rutland got £2,450; the Hon. E. Petre £100. It was the fifth of Robinson's six Derby victories, a record second only to Lester Piggott's and equalled only by Steve Donoghue's. It was the first run-off for the Derby – and the last.

The 1884 Derby needed excitement. The weather was cold, the wind blew clouds of chalky dust over the downs, there was a trade slump and half-filled places in the stands. Several good horses (St Simon among them) were not entered. The arrival of enclosed courses at Sandown Park, Kempton Park and provincial cities like Derby and Leicester, whose turnstile-paying customers encouraged big prizes and low entrance fees by owners, had put the Derby and Oaks in the shade. Six years later the Derby had only eight runners.

Even royalty stayed away in 1884. In its place were the dubious likes of the ex-Khedive Ismail, dismissed by the British and French from Egypt because of his extravagance (but welcomed to the Stewards' Stand by the soon-to-be discredited Sir George Chetwynd), and the Grand Duke Paul from Russia; both men had travelled to Epsom courtesy of the shareholders of the London, Brighton and South Coast railway.

The favourite was a filly, owned by Sir John Willoughby (to be enmeshed in the Jameson Raid in the Transvaal eleven years later); he was also running a colt, Harvester, which was unfancied at 100–7. John Hammond's St Gatien presented 'a hard, wear and tear appearance' in the paddock and started at 100–8. But while the cognoscenti yawned at the indifferent fare put before them, a real race was developing. Harvester, 'the despised stable companion of the favourite', was seen to pass her 'and fight out as desperate a finish as was ever witnessed'. Harvester was ridden by Sam Loates. St Gatien, ridden by Charlie Woods, accused three years later of pulling his mounts (with the approval of Chetwynd) but doing his utmost for his patrons that afternoon, was upsides.

In the last furlong Harvester got his head in front, but the hill began to tell on him and St Gatien just got his ahead, only for Harvester to come back for a dead-heat in the final strides. It had been so close that 'when the judge signalled a dead-heat the public almost forgot to cheer'. Fifty-six years after the first dead-heat, the rival camps were wary of risking studbook values by having an immediate rematch. Hammond told Captain James Machell, the trainer who was acting for Willoughby, Harvester's owner, that he would do whatever Machell proposed. Hammond had begun as one of Machell's stable boys and he had learned much from his old master's astuteness. There was no reason to make an unnecessary enemy now.

When Machell said, 'Then we'll divide,' he went along with it. Machell knew that Harvester had been slightly lame on the Saturday before the race so he may have felt he had no option. Machell was a skilful operator, moody but with his eye on the main chance. He had offered Fred Archer the ride on either Harvester or another of his horses, St Medard. Archer had picked the wrong one. If Archer had chosen Harvester a dead-heat would have been unlikely.

Coming of Age

John Bowes, a successful but increasingly eccentric owner, was of the Strathmore family to which Queen Elizabeth the Queen Mother belongs. He won the Derby four times and would have been the tenth Earl of Strathmore himself had not, as it was deftly put, his father and mother unduly postponed their marriage. So he was disinherited of the title, but his father made sure that he did not want for worldly income. He was the owner of Streatlam Castle and estates, near Barnard Castle in County Durham, a wealthy young man with an eye for a promising thoroughbred, and a betting man's mind.

Bowes was still up at Cambridge when he came of age in 1835. He owned a fancied horse, Mundig

Above: John Bowes, aged 49, owner of four Derby winners.

Daniel O'Rourke, a small horse of just under 15 hands, was John Bowe's third Derby winner, in 1852.

(German for 'of age'), which his trustees had entered for the Derby and on which they had placed judicious bets in their own names. This knowledge came from the Whitewall stables at Malton, North Yorkshire, where the trainer, John Scott, was the master of all he surveyed. Mundig did not run in public before the Derby, but his performance in trial gallops was outstanding. Bowes knew this, heard of his trustees' investments and intervened decisively.

Calling a special meeting, he forced them to transfer their more substantial bets to him, saying that, if they did not, he, as the legal owner, would have the horse scratched. He had his way. But it was feared that one of the lads in Scott's yard had been got at. So Mundig and a stable companion were sent away from Epsom on the eve of the Derby; the lad duly reported this to his conspirators and the market promptly responded. But Mundig had only been taken a short distance and,

when the horses returned, the whole stable was told they should be ashamed of themselves. Mundig duly won. Bill Scott, the jockey, and his brother won £20,000 between them.

So did Bowes. He chose a solitary celebration. That night he sat down at Crockfords on his own and entertained himself to dinner. Whatever doubts he might have had about the stable lads, he stayed with Scott. The two men agreed to lay down a tan training gallop on Langton Wold a mile long, an innovative training improvement. Bowes patronised the Whitewall stable until Scott's death in 1871.

Bowes's second Derby winner was Cotherstone in 1843. The colt had impressed Bowes and Scott in a trial, and Bowes at once backed him in London to win £23,000. There was close security and Cotherstone started the 13–8 favourite. For once the start was clean and straightforward. Lord George Bentinck had intervened, ensuring that each jockey was given a printed slip warning him that no false starts would be allowed, on pain of a £5 fine. Cotherstone won by a good two lengths.

In 1852 Bowes's entry was Daniel O'Rourke, a small horse, just 14 hands, 3 inches. Bowes, as usual, spotted him early and backed him at long odds. The best horse in the race was said to be Stockwell, later a successful stallion, but he went to post just having had a septic gumboil lanced. There was much chicanery about the running but Daniel O'Rourke, starting at 25–1, got home in a very slow time: three minutes, two seconds. As if to show where the true form lay, Stockwell went on to win the St Leger by ten lengths.

The very next year Bowes had a great horse, West Australian, which he had backed as a two-year-old the previous August to win £30,000 in the Derby. The West, as the punters called him, started at 6–4 against and did not let them down. He entered English racing history as the first triple crown winner. Bowes himself was apparently so confident that he did not bother to go to Epsom to see the race.

But this was now his way. He began to follow an increasingly isolated and reclusive life. He was married to an unsuccessful French actress, whose career he subsidised, and spent much of his time in Paris. For the last thirty years of his life (he died in 1885) he did not set foot on a racecourse again.

Running Rein's Derby

The 1844 Derby brought to light all the special skills that had been developed in the English racing community. It was the dirtiest Derby to be run – or at least to be found out. Two horses, Running Rein and Leander, were found to be four-year-olds, a physical difference that almost guaranteed their superiority to the three-year-olds conforming to the race's rules in early summer. The deception was far from new. Bird, the trainer for Lord Egremont, who owned five early Derby winners, was said to have admitted on his deathbed that he had succeeded twice with four-year-olds; he cannily did not divulge in which years.

There were strong suspicions about others, too. One was St Giles in 1832; his owner was the highly devious Robert Ridsdale. In 1840 Little Wonder, the only Derby winner Queen Victoria watched passing the post, was also suspected. In 1844, besides Running Rein and Leander, it transpired that Ratan, the second favourite, was not only doped ('his coat was standing like quills upon the fretful porcupine, his eyes were dilated and he shivered like a man with ague') but, to make fully sure, he was pulled by his jockey, Samuel Rogers, who was duly warned off by the Jockey Club later in the year. The 5–2 favourite, The Ugly Buck, was also pulled by his rider, John Day, jun. But that was a relatively simple bit of roguery.

The man who plotted the substitution of a four-year-old, Maccabeus, for the three-year-old Derby entrant, Running Rein, was Abraham Levi Goodman who lived on the edge of the racing world on betting coups based on secret stable information and outright fraud. With Maccabeus/Running Rein being first past the post in the 1844 Derby, he came close to landing the biggest gamble of his life.

It was, necessarily, a complicated deception. In 1841 he bought two horses. One, a yearling (Maccabeus), was 'a bright bay, no white, black legs and good eyes'. The other, a foal (Running Rein) was a slight bay who had 'four black legs and a few white hairs on his forehead'. There was the prospect that, with a little hairdresser's dye, a casual inspection might confuse the identity of the two animals.

His first action was to get the two out of the hands of the stable staff who worked with them and would remember them. So in 1842 Goodman contrived a baffling series of movements from stable to stable in an apparently pointless way that would bemuse anyone trying to keep track of the colts' whereabouts. As Maccabeus lacerated a leg, which left a scar on his knee, Running Rein had to have his leg damaged and receive a similar scar. Eventually, Maccabeus and Running Rein, with a third colt to complicate matters, were taken to an Epsom trainer, William Smith, and presented to a breaker there as yearlings. The breaker

The Warren, Epsom Downs: jockeys mount before the 1844 Derby.

related later that he suspected one of them might be older but, as the trainer had horsewhipped him for suggesting the same thing with a previous colt, he kept his mouth shut.

What Goodman needed to do next was produce Maccabeus/Running Rein to fulfill Running Rein's public engagements in the autumn of 1843. One appearance, at least, on the racecourse was needed to establish him as the two-year-old who would be qualified to run in the Derby next year. But Maccabeus had been entered for races in 1843 under his own name. As it would have been foolhardy to risk someone spotting that Maccabeus/Running Rein ran as a three-year-old at the start of the season and a two-year-old at the end, Goodman leased another colt, Goneaway, from Ireland

to impersonate Maccabeus. So Goneaway, having had his coat dyed and his tail docked, duly ran as Maccabeus at the Epsom spring meeting and finished second in his race at odds of 7–4 on. This suggested that part of the deception, at least, had reached the bookmakers and, in any event, Goneaway's owner turned up unexpectedly in England and might be expected to know his own horse whatever it was called. Goneaway was taken back to Ireland and it was announced that Maccabeus was dead.

Goodman kept his two, still unraced, colts away from prying eyes in his own private paddocks at Sutton until the autumn arrived. Then, at Newmarket in October, Maccabeus/Running Rein won a small sweepstake and finished third in another one. So far, so good for the plan. But to one knowledgeable pair of eyes at Newmarket it seemed highly probable that the colt Goodman ran was already a three-year-old. Lord George Bentinck, who had devoted himself over the years to becoming the scourge of all evildoers on the turf, encouraged the Duke of Rutland, whose colt had come second to Maccabeus/Running Rein, to lodge an objection. The difference in physical conformation between a three-year-old and a two-year-old is often plain enough without resorting to an inspection of teeth. Not even idle stewards could be relied on to miss it. Goodman was on the verge of being detected.

But he knew his stewards. Rather than put themselves out, they decided to hold their inquiry at the next Newmarket meeting – two weeks later. Lord George had gone to the length of bringing the lad who had seen Running Rein born to be interrogated. Experts examined the colt. But Goodman had simply used the time to replace Maccabeus with the real Running Rein, an obvious two-year-old whom the

lad recognised as the one he had known in his stable. The objection was overruled, Goodman got his prize money and Maccabeus/Running Rein had qualified to run in the Derby. But Goodman knew something was up. Lord George had got his number and the stewards indicated that they did not wish to see Running Rein at Newmarket again.

Goodman thereupon decided it was politic to detach his name from Running Rein. A new owner could have the honour and pleasure of leading in the Derby winner, but Goodman merely wanted to ensure that all his bets on the winner came up. He had taken the odds from 33–1 down and now, it seems probable, he moved the real Running Rein back to Smith's stables at Epsom and, with him, delivered a hard-luck story. He owed Smith £200 for previous fees but, he said, he couldn't afford to pay them. The trainer suggested helpfully that the colt could be sold in settlement and, indeed, he knew of a potential customer, Alexander Wood, a respectable Epsom corn merchant who rented the

Betting on the result of the 1844 Derby . . . 10 to 1 against Running Rein.

stables to him. Wood paid off the debt to Smith and gave Goodman another £200 for Running Rein. He was to remain a bewildered cipher to the end of the saga. Once the deal with him was complete, Goodman deftly replaced Running Rein in Smith's yard with Maccabeus.

Lord George Bentinck, however, had not forgotten Goodman or his dissatisfaction with what had happened at Newmarket. As 1844 drew on towards 22 May, Derby day, there were two strong contenders to be favourite: The Ugly Buck, who had won the Two Thousand Guineas, and Ratan, on whom Bentinck himself had put a lot of money. Bentinck was sure that The Ugly Buck did not stay, but even the possibility that Running Rein was a four-year-old might ruin Ratan's chances. So on the Saturday before the Derby he got two men above suspicion, John Bowes the owner and John Scott the trainer of another Derby colt, T'Auld Squire, to join him in stopping Maccabeus/Running Rein from taking part until the stewards were satisfied about his credentials. Two days

The letter to the stakeholders, Weatherbys, from the Epsom stewards, instructing them to withhold payment of the £4,450 purse to Mr. Wood, pending the inquiry into the real identity of Running Rein.

later, the stewards got another protest, this time against the horse Leander whom Lord Maidstone also believed was a four-year-old.

But Goodman knew his dilatory stewards, as did Leander's owners. The two stewards, Sir Gilbert Heathcote and Baron de Tessier, were honest men and sufficiently knowledgeable about racing to be aware of miscreants and rumours; but they merely asked to see certificates of the horses' breeding and warned that if either Running Rein or Leander won the Derby there would be investigations and the stakes would be withheld. So the horses could start. The chances of getting away with deceit had narrowed, but there was still everything to play for. Lord George was extremely displeased.

Running Rein started the 10–1 third favourite, Leander at 14–1, and the two four-year-olds set a fast pace, with which the three-year-olds struggled to keep up. Leander was leading at the top of the hill when Running Rein, sent up to join him, struck into his off hind leg, smashing it to pieces. Leander had to be destroyed. Running Rein ran on unperturbed and had the strength to see off Orlando and Ionian (both owned by Colonel Jonathan Peel, the Prime Minister's brother), the best of the rest. Peel, a wholly reputable man, may not have needed Lord George's encouragement to let it be known that he objected to the winner; he told the stake-holders not to pay the prize of £4250 to Wood, Maccabeus/Running Rein's unsuspecting owner. Wood wanted his money, but Peel proposed that the whole matter should be determined by a barrister selected by the Lord Chief Justice of the Queen's Bench. But before any decisions could be taken there was plenty of business to be got out of the way.

First, there was the dead Leander, owned by the brothers Lichtwald, two German horse-dealers. Leander's body was quickly buried at Ashtead, near the racecourse. On the evening after the Oaks a drunken supper party dug up the body and found, to its surprise, that Leander's lower jaw had been sawn off and taken away. The digging party then cut off the horse's head with the upper jaw and the next morning got a veterinary surgeon to examine the teeth in particular. The finding was that it was the head of a four-year-old. Meanwhile Leander's elderly trainer, John Forth, who had the teeth from the lower jaw, took them for a vet's opinion in London; where he learned, to his discomfi-

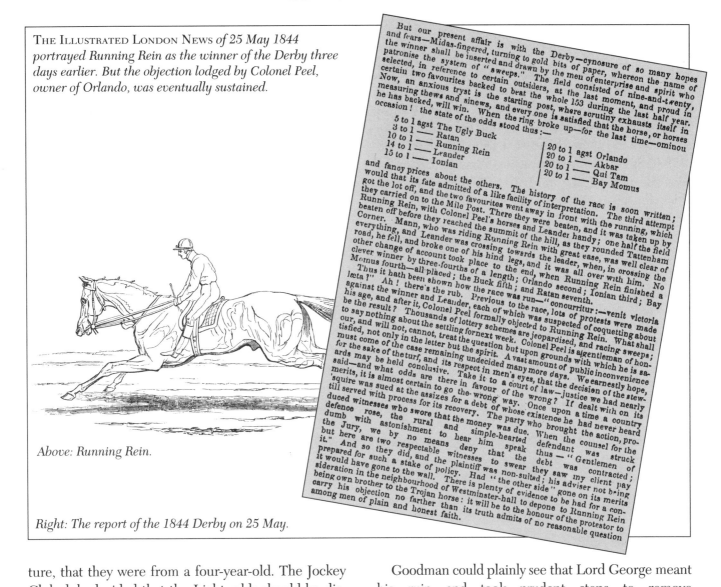

THE ILLUSTRATED LONDON NEWS *of 25 May 1844 portrayed Running Rein as the winner of the Derby three days earlier. But the objection lodged by Colonel Peel, owner of Orlando, was eventually sustained.*

Above: Running Rein.

Right: The report of the 1844 Derby on 25 May.

But our present affair is with the Derby—cynosure of so many hopes and fears—Midas-fingered, turning to gold bits of paper, whereon the name of the winner shall be inserted and drawn by the men of enterprise and spirit who patronise the system of "sweeps." The field consisted of nine-and-twenty, selected, in reference to certain outsiders, at the last moment, and proud in Now, an anxious tryst is the starting post, where scrutiny exhausts itself in measuring thews and sinews, and every one is satisfied that the horse, or horses he has backed, will win. When the ring broke up—for the last time—ominou occasion! the state of the odds stood thus:—

5 to 1 agst	The Ugly Buck		20 to 1 agst	Orlando
3 to 1 —	Ratan		20 to 1 —	Akbar
10 to 1 —	Running Rein		20 to 1 —	Qui Tam
14 to 1 —	Leander		20 to 1 —	Bay Momus
15 to 1 —	Ionian			

and fancy prices about the others. The history of the race is soon written; would that its fate admitted of a like facility of interpretation. The third attempt got the lot off, and the two favourites went away in front with the running, which they carried on to the Mile Post. There they were beaten, and it was taken up by Running Rein, with Colonel Peel's horses and Leander handy; one half the field beaten off before they reached the summit of the hill, as they rounded Tattenham Corner. Mann, who was riding Running Rein with great ease, was well clear of everything, and Leander was crossing towards the leader, when, in crossing the road, he fell, and broke one of his hind legs, and it was all over with him. No other change of account took place to the end, when Running Rein finished a clever winner by three-fourths of a length; Orlando second; Ionian third; Bay Momus fourth—all placed; the Buck fifth; and Ratan seventh.

Thus it hath been shown how the race was run—"concurritur:—venit victoria læta?" Ah! there's the rub. Previous to the race, lots of protests were made against the winner and Leander, each of which was suspected of coquetting about his age, and after it, Colonel Peel formally objected to Running Rein. What shall be the result? Thousands of lottery schemes are jeopardised, and racing sweeps; to say nothing about the settling for next week. Colonel Peel is a gentleman of honour, and will not, cannot, treat the question but upon grounds with which he is satisfied, not only in the letter but the spirit. A vast amount of public inconvenience must come of the case remaining undecided many more days. We earnestly hope, for the sake of the turf, and its respect in men's eyes, that the decision of the stewards may be held conclusive. Take it to a court of law—justice we had nearly said—and what odds are there in favour of the wrong? If dealt with on its merits, it is almost certain to go the wrong way. Once upon a time a country 'squire was sued at the assizes for a debt of whose existence he had never heard till served with process for its recovery. The party who brought the action, produced witnesses who swore that the money was due. When the counsel for the defence rose, the rural and simple-hearted defendant was struck dumb with astonishment to hear him speak thus:—"Gentlemen of the Jury, we by no means deny that the debt was contracted; but here are two respectable witnesses to swear they saw my client pay it." And so they did, and the plaintiff was non-suited; his adviser not being prepared for such a stake of policy. Had "the other side" gone on its merits it would have gone to the wall. There is plenty of evidence to depone to Running Rein being own brother to the Trojan horse: it will be to the honour of the protestor to carry his objection no farther than its truth admits of no reasonable question among men of plain and honest faith.

ture, that they were from a four-year-old. The Jockey Club duly decided that the Lichtwalds should be disqualified from racing in Britain.

The other business was Lord George Bentinck's unceasing search for more evidence against Goodman and Maccabeus/Running Rein. He was remorseless in pursuing his investigation to Ireland, in calling in the help of Harry Hill, the bookmaker with strong underworld connections, in tracking down the London barber who sold Goodman the dye, and even in indicting the Epsom stewards for partial and unfair conduct. A ruthless man in following his own interest he was ready to use the same tactics in what he saw to be the interest of the turf. This was soon necessary because the honest Wood liked the idea of being the owner of a Derby winner and accordingly sued Colonel Peel for the return of the Derby stakes which had been withheld from him.

Goodman could plainly see that Lord George meant his ruin and took prudent steps to remove Maccabeus/Running Rein from Smith's stables at Epsom, not to be seen again until any legal unpleasantness was over. He was naturally prepared to let a court see the true Running Rein, which could readily be proved to be a three-year-old again, as it had been shown to be a two-year-old at Newmarket, despite Lord George, the previous October. But this time Goodman had underestimated his opponent. Running Rein, the genuine one, was suddenly found to have disappeared as completely and mysteriously as Maccabeus had done from Smith's stables. The court case thereupon began.

It was not to last long. The judge, Baron Alderson, knew about racing and, when practising on the Northern Circuit in the past, had been a regular visitor to John Scott's stables at Malton. When Wood's counsel began calling evidence about Running Rein's identity, the judge cut him short by asking if the horse were available to be seen. On being told that permission had not been given, despite a court order, his reaction was brisk: 'I feel – and I am sure the jury feel too – that an examination and production of this horse are indispensable, and I should like to look at his mouth myself.'

Then Smith, the trainer, testified that the horse had been taken away from him five days before on a verbal order which he understood had come from Wood. The judge grew warm: 'Now I see the whole drift of it. This was the very day before my order reached the place, which order was contemptuously disobeyed.'

He repeated that justice demanded the production of the horse.

The next day Wood's counsel said his client felt it difficult to proceed without a Running Rein to produce. Wood had gone at once after the court had risen to Smith's stables at Epsom and Goodman's at Sutton, but the horse was at neither. Wood was now satisfied that there had been a fraud in which he had played no part but had, in fact, been the victim. He accepted that the court must find for Colonel Peel. The judge, having said that if the horse had been stolen he would try the parties who had done it and have them transported for felony, instructed the jury and told them how he felt about it all:

It has produced great regret and disgust in my mind. It has disclosed a wretched fraud, and has shown noblemen and gentlemen of rank associating and betting with men of low rank and infinitely below them in society. In so doing they have found themselves cheated and made the dupes of the grossest frauds. They may depend upon it that it will always be so when gentlemen associate and bet with blackguards.

Goodman had already left the country for France where he could escape both the law and his creditors. Nothing was ever seen of Running Rein in public again. One Ignatius Coyle, described in the court as 'a tall man with a red face', who had taken the colt away from Smith's stable, claimed long afterwards that he had done it by riding his own hack into the yard, throwing a saddle on Running Rein's back and riding away on him without anyone noticing. But Maccabeus, the four-year-old who ran in the Derby and did pass the winning post first, did not sink wholly out of sight. In 1845 Colonel Peel objected to a horse, called

Zanoni, who had been entered in the Chester Cup by a Reading vet called Parry. It turned out to be Maccabeus under yet another nom de course. How Parry had got him never came out. The stewards duly stopped the horse running at Chester, but he did start in races at both Ascot and York that summer – without success.

Lord George was the hero of the hour, whether the full part he had played was known or not. Subscriptions of £25 were invited by the Jockey Club and a presentation of £2000 was made to him with thanks for the 'energy, perseverance and skill' he had shown 'in detecting, exposing and defeating the atrocious frauds' at Epsom. He used the £2000 to set up a fund for trainers and jockeys who had fallen on hard times. He continued to harry the criminals he came across but, despite all his efforts over the years, he never won the Derby himself. In 1846 he joined Disraeli in opposing Sir Robert Peel's reform of the corn laws, which he believed would destroy the agricultural interest in England. He sold his stud to concentrate on his work in the House of Commons. Two years later one of the colts he sold, Surplice, won the Derby in Lord Clifden's colours. Disraeli, commiserating as best he could with the distraught Bentinck, was told:

'You do not know what the Derby is.'

'Yes, I do, it is the Blue Riband of the Turf.'

'It is the Blue Riband of the Turf,' he slowly repeated to himself and, sitting down, he buried himself in a folio of statistics.

A week after seeing Surplice win that year's St Leger from Lord Derby's Canezou, Lord George died of a heart attack.

Opposite: In 1847 the new-fangled railway provided Londoners with easy access to Epsom for a few shillings, according to class. Traditionalists moaned that it was the beginning of the end for Derby Day.

THE RAILWAY—FIRST CLASS.

SECOND CLASS.

THIRD CLASS.

The Pocket Venus and Friends

The brief racing career – and life – of Harry, fourth and last Marquis of Hastings, and his rapid descent from riches to rags, made him the epitome of moral depravity and recklessness so useful for the admonitions of mid-Victorians. He was not the only peer of the realm whose wild gambling forced him to sell up and depart from society. But Hastings outdid them all. He carried off the young woman he loved, eloping with her from the grasp of her fiancé, and had the decency, too, to die, bankrupt and broken, in just four years.

Hastings was the grandson of the second Earl of Moira, a veteran of Bunker's Hill and other battles in the American War of Independence and a former Governor-General of Bengal and Commander-in-Chief in India. The boy's mother was Barbara, Baroness Grey de Ruthyn, known as 'the jolly fast Marchioness' with a mania for gambling which she passed on to her offspring. The son was spoiled as a child and did little at either Eton or Oxford where he was overshadowed by the heavy set which counted the Prince of Wales among its friends.

Above: Lady Florence Paget, the beautiful fiancée of Henry Chaplin, who eloped with the Marquis of Hastings just days before her planned wedding to Chaplin (owner of Hermit, the 1867 Derby winner).

One of that set was Henry Chaplin, son of a landed parson in Rutlandshire who was by way of being a railway promoter in the Eastern Counties, and heir to his uncle, the rich squire of Blankney, in Lincolnshire. Chaplin, called the 'Magnifico' at Oxford, was considered the embodiment of elegance and promise; a good catch for a young woman. But if Chaplin was rich, Hastings was rolling in it, with big estates at Donington, on the south bank of the Trent in Leicestershire, and in Scotland. Both of them were going to need all their money and more before they were through.

The object of their affections was Lady Florence Paget, daughter of the Marquis of Anglesey and granddaughter of the Earl of Uxbridge who had been Wellington's cavalry commander, both in Spain and at Waterloo where his knee had been shattered and his leg had to be amputated. Lady Florence was petite (she was known as the 'pocket Venus') and was celebrated for her good colouring, her dove-like eyes and her unrivalled charm. Those not under her spell thought her self-willed, and it was said that she had taken as her model Diana Vernon, heroine of Scott's novel *Rob Roy*. She was presented to the Queen, naturally, and had the social world at her feet. But she turned out to be a very poor judge of men.

It did not take Hastings long to buy his first horse, on the advice of the trainer John Day of Danebury, choose his colours (scarlet and white hoop, white cap), and get elected to the Jockey Club on his twenty-first birthday in July 1863. He did not, it was said, keep his horses to look at or to eat their heads off. Garotter, his first winner in a maiden plate at Newmarket, was sent out to run another seventeen times that season.

His great aim was to beat the betting ring and he believed he had the nerve and the resources to do it. When he fancied any horse he bet extravagantly, taking short odds, to the annoyance of owners who, thinking they might have a 10–1 chance arriving at the course, found themselves offered 6–4 at best. But he was a hero in victory and defeat to his admirers and to the bookies who had summed him up. At Epsom he favoured the Jockey Club balcony. There he would stand smiling at the wild tumult below, wearing his hat jauntily on one side, a red flower in his buttonhole and his colours round his neck, and cool and calm while 'the talent' made his horse a 'hot favourite' at once.

But Hastings also began to get himself a reputation for being attracted to low life in the East End and other haunts. This did not make for popularity among aristocratic mothers who would not have approved, either, of his releasing a sackful of live rats in a West End ballroom. This censure might even have appealed to the maternal instinct of Lady Florence, but the drawing-room tittle-tattle preferred to link her name with Chaplin's. There were even rumours of an engagement.

That was not Chaplin's immediate plan. He went off big game hunting in the East with his friend Sir Frederick Johnstone (who was later to own two Derby winners himself). On going down from Oxford they had gone buffalo hunting in Canada. Now they spent the winter in India, returning in May 1864. It was noticeable right away that Chaplin became Lady Florence's regular escort at balls and parties.

At the Derby (won by Blair Athol) the two watched together in the royal box with the Prince of Wales and Sir Frederick. But Hastings was still pursuing the lady. He had named one of his fillies after her, and she went with him to the paddock at Ascot to see her run. She did not win. A fortnight later Chaplin and Lady Florence were engaged, after a ball given by the Marquis and Marchioness of Abercorn at Chesterfield House. She was just twenty. The engagement appeared in the better papers; the couple were congratulated by the Prince of Wales and by Hastings; the future bride was taken to Blankney to see the house, gardens, stables and kennels; and she bought her trousseau. On Friday, 15 July Chaplin, Lady Florence and Hastings went to Covent Garden together to see Adelina Patti singing in *Faust*.

The next morning Lady Florence rose in her father's town house at 70 Portland Place. She put her wedding dress on and showed it to him. She told him that she wanted to do more shopping before the wedding and went in his brougham to Marshall and Snelgrove's store in Oxford Street. Eye-witnesses gave the usual conflicting accounts to the papers. Some shop assistants claimed that she had actually left Chaplin waiting outside in the brougham and that they saw him later searching for her until he eventually called the manager. Some said she stopped at a haberdashery counter and bought a decoration for her wedding dress. Others declared that she had been met by a number of people but these may have been Hastings's friend Freddy Granville or his wife.

In any event she left, after a short conversation, by another door, and got into a cab which went down Bond Street and turned left to St George's Church, Hanover Square. There, by noon, she was married to Hastings.

Granville gave the bride away; Hastings's sister, Lady Edith, had been told of the wedding only at the last moment and just got to the church in time. The reception was at the Granvilles' lodgings in St James's Place. A special train had steam up at King's Cross and took the happy couple to Loughborough where Hastings's coach was waiting to take them to Donington Hall. The servants had been told by telegraph to be ready. It was a scene of excitement, happiness and triumph.

Lady Florence had not warned her father, or brothers or brother-in-law, and when they first heard of it they refused to believe it was true. Naturally, she had not given any hint to Chaplin, her fiancé. So while the reception in St James's Place celebrated noisily she had to sit down to write the most difficult letter of her life. However long, or briefly, she had thought about it, it made absorbing reading:

Henry. To you whom I have injured more deeply than any one, I hardly know how to address myself. Believe me, the task is most painful and one I shrink from. Would to God I had moral courage to open my heart to you sooner, but I could not bring myself to do so. However, now the truth must be told.

After apologising for treating him 'too infamously', she went on:

I know I ought never to have accepted you at all, and I also know I never could have made you happy. You must have seen ever since the beginning of our engagement how very little I *really* returned all your devotion to me. I assure you I have struggled hard against the feeling, but all to no purpose. There is not a man in the world I have a greater regard and respect for than yourself, but I do not *love* you in the way a woman ought to love her husband, and I am perfectly certain if I had married you, I should have rendered not only *my* life miserable, but your own also.

That apart, her excuses were slender:

And now we are eternally separated, for by the time you receive this I shall be the wife of Lord Hastings . . . You said one night here, a woman who ran away was not worth thinking or caring about, so I pray that the blow may fall less

Amusements on Epsom Downs in 1866. Coconut shies are still a feature of Derby Day today.

severely on you than it might have done. May God bless you, and may you soon find someone far more worthy of becoming your wife than I should ever have been. Yrs. Florence.

Chaplin did what she might have expected. He went off first to Reay Forest in the north-west of Sutherland, which he had rented for deer stalking. Then, in the spring of 1865, he went back to India, again with Sir Frederick Johnstone.

The Marquis and Marchioness of Hastings did not settle down to domestic bliss. He had promised to sell his whole racing stud at Brighton races to please her; but he insisted on excepting his best horse, The Duke, the second favourite for the next year's Derby. Romantic snapshots were taken of the two reclining on, or by, their chaise longue. The sceptical had no doubt he would break out again.

Chaplin, in India, had decided to take the racing game seriously himself. Johnstone was precisely the man to encourage him. It was said Chaplin began 'to buy horses as though he were drunk and to back them as though he were mad'. He went to the Scottish trainer William I'Anson, who had won in 1864 with Blair Athol, and bought two colts entered for the Derby for £11,500. He registered his colours (all rose). He took on a racing manager, Captain James Machell, who had been a friend of Hastings's but now changed sides. He, too, joined the Jockey Club.

Hastings's colt, The Duke, caught influenza, but Hastings was not to be outdone. He bought another one, Kangaroo, from the moneylender, Henry Padwick, for 12,000 guineas. It was, up to then, the

highest price ever paid for a three-year-old. Neither Chaplin nor Hastings got anywhere near the Derby winning post; it was the year of the French champion, Gladiateur.

After the Derby there was a sale of yearlings at William Blenkiron's Middle Park Stud. One, a chestnut colt, was bought by Chaplin and Machell for 1000 guineas. The colt was to be named Hermit and was to thrive into what was called 'a low and lengthy sort'. Hastings was the underbidder at 950 guineas. In 1866 Hastings's filly, Repulse, won the One Thousand Guineas, but he was already winning much less than he was spending and only a coup on his horse, Lecturer, which got home in the Cesarewitch, saved him. Hastings had, for reasons best known to him, taken strongly against the Derby prospects of Chaplin's Hermit, even though he was reckoned to be one of the best two-year-olds seen out; he backed steadily against him. It gave an edge to the coming 1867 season.

Hastings's view almost came true. Hermit broke a blood vessel in his nose during his final trial, and it looked nasty. The market got to hear about it and the colt was marked out to 66–1. *Bell's Life* was cheerless about the prospect:

> *Turn gentle Hermit doomed to fail*
> *Retrace your lonely way,*
> *To that seclusion all bewail*
> *You left a single day.*

It all encouraged Hastings to plunge still further, but Chaplin and Hermit's trainer, Old Bloss, who had been sleeping in the horse's box for weeks, were determined to run him.

Derby day was grey and bitterly cold. Snow and sleet fell. Hermit was seen 'pacing about, not only without the inconvenience of a mob at his heels, but absolutely disregarded and ignored'. Affectingly, 'his coat was rough and broken, and his eyes lacked the lustre characteristic of a horse in perfect condition'. Even so, Chaplin went so far as to warn Hastings that he thought Hermit still had a chance and Hastings still had time to cover his bets if he so wished.

There were ten false starts in the sleet, but Hermit's people were not altogether worried. The cold weather actually made them feel easier about the blood vessel and, as Hermit had been easy to train and was fresh, he might even have something in hand. Hermit surprised

Hermit, the 1867 Derby winner 'who ruined a Marquis . . .'

The front page of
THE ILLUSTRATED
LONDON NEWS
*showing the
Grand Stand in
snow, 1867.*

No. 1429.—VOL. L.

SATURDAY, JUNE 1, 1867.

WITH A SUPPLEMENT, FIVEPENCE

GOVERNMENT OF INDIA.

A VERY interesting and, as we presume to think, a very pregnant debate took place in the House of Commons towards the close of last week on a matter connected with the government of India, to the general drift and spirit of which we deem it a pleasant duty to call the attention of our readers.

We shall not trouble them with any summary of or criticism on the particular case which came under discussion on that occasion. We have no intention of recounting the history of the Maharajah of Mysore, nor of analysing the two treaties the negotiation of which, in 1799, followed upon the overthrow of Tippoo Sultan. Our object in adverting to the

debate of Friday se'nnight is simply to mark what appears to us to be the signs which it presents of a turning point in the administration of Indian affairs, which will be hailed with satisfaction by a vast majority of the native Princes and peoples comprised in that splendid dependency of the British Crown, and which, we think, will

THE GRAND STAND AT EPSOM ON THE DERBY DAY.

everyone else by showing his true turn of speed when needed at the finish – and winning by a neck. Chaplin had £120,000 in winnings coming to him, £20,000 of them from Hastings. In all, Hastings had to find over £120,000 to clear his book by Monday. Characteristically, Chaplin offered him time to find his £20,000. Now Hastings had a difficult letter to write. He wrote it thankfully:

I would sooner cut off my hand than ask anybody to do such a thing, but as you say it will not inconvenience you, I shall take advantage of your offer for a short time.

> With very many thanks, yours very sincerely,
> Hastings.

In fact, Hastings managed to appear at Tattersalls the next Monday and pay off £102,000 on the spot, with the moneylender Padwick's help. They cheered him. He said: 'Hermit's victory beat cock-fighting.' But his estates were now having to be sold off rapidly.

Hermit's jockey, Johnny Daley, won the Oaks on Hippia two days after the Derby. His career had peaked: he never won a classic again. *Punch*, noticing that among the Derby field had been Mr F. Pryor's Rake, improved Chaplin's shining hour by saying: 'Who will dare say that racing is a sinful amusement? Think

of £160,000 carried off from a Rake by a Hermit for the benefit of a Chaplin.' But nothing was funny any more for Hastings. By October Lady Florence had to approach Chaplin herself to ask if he could help with their unsettled debts:

'You told me the other day that if you could ever help me in any way you would do it. So I am going to take you at your word and ask you to do me a very great favour.'

So reduced were her finances that she wanted £1500 to stand over. She needed sympathy and sought it openly:

God knows, there is no sacrifice I would not make if I could only get some sort of affection in return. How I dread going home and how I dread the winter! You can have no idea. I feel as if I should never have the strength to go through it. But I will do my duty . . . for I am awfully worried about his health. What a miserable life mine is! I am quite disheartened.

It was plain that Hastings was suffering from serious kidney damage. In all, he needed to raise £300,000 and his Donington estate had to be mortgaged. His hopes rested on two remaining horses, and to keep them he had to borrow from Padwick. His two-year-old filly,

'The rush to see the finish'. An engraving of 1866.

Lady Elizabeth, was his pride and he came to think of her as a certainty for the next year's Derby. All she had to do was keep her form and his winnings were as good as in the Bank of England. She ran thirteen times in the 1867 season and won twelve of her races.

It was the practice then to insist on hard training and frequent racing, but Hastings had such faith in Lady Elizabeth and needed her to bring off his regular betting coups – and she responded so gamely – that he believed she could do even the impossible whenever he asked. His second Derby hope, The Earl, was also fancied, especially by those who understood what the filly had been asked to do. Certain bookmakers, especially, took The Earl very seriously and had plans for him.

When the 1868 season began there was an unspoken problem at the Danebury stables. Lady Elizabeth was no longer the brilliant filly she had been; she did not show the form, she did not even seem anxious to race. Day, the trainer, knew that she was finished, but he saw no point in telling Hastings and other innocents so. Hastings's enthusiasm was still unbounded and, as long as he had no doubts, the public had none either. Even though Lady Elizabeth was not brought out on a race-course before the Derby, because the Days had managed to fob Hastings off when he went down to see her, the big money was riding on her. She was sent off the 7–4 favourite.

She tried to buck her jockey, the highly experienced George Fordham, off at the start, tried to swerve out of the course in the first half-mile, and finished in the ruck. Hastings was devastated; his hopes had gone and so had the last of his money. When Lady Elizabeth was started again in the Oaks it was the same story. She had been raced out. The public, who had adored and fawned on Hastings the sportsman in his great days, did not take this well.

In particular, it was noticed that Hastings had withdrawn his other Derby runner, The Earl, after he had arrived at Epsom Downs, and sent him quickly over to France where he won the Grand Prix de Paris effortlessly. Back in England The Earl went on to win three more races. It looked all too obvious that Padwick and the bookmakers had used their hold on Hastings to scratch the colt that would have won the Derby and gull the public with the hopeless favourite. The ring had broken him.

The current scourge of miscreants, Admiral Rous, had been heard to say at the Derby that 'if he had taken as much laudanum as had been given to that mare he would be a dead man'. If that was how Day had managed to get Lady Elizabeth to race at all there would be repercussions. A letter from 'H.J. Rous, 13 Berkeley Square' duly appeared in *The Times* on Lady Elizabeth's failure:

The touters reported she was 'going like a bird.' Ten pounds will make any horse fly if the trainer wishes it to rise in the market! She has never been able to gallop the whole year. Lord Hastings has been shamefully deceived.

Rous then turned to The Earl's withdrawal and the part played by Padwick and the bookie Harry Hill:

With respect to scratching The Earl, Lord Westmorland came up to town early on Tuesday to beseech Lord Hastings not to commit such an act. On his arrival in Grosvenor Square he met Mr Hill going to Weatherbys with the order in his pocket to scratch The Earl, and Mr Padwick closeted with Lord Hastings.

In that company, he believed, Hastings was merely a pawn:

In justice to the Marquis of Hastings I state that he stood to win £35,000 by The Earl, and did not hedge his stake money. Then you will ask: 'Why did he scratch him?' What can the poor fly demand from the spider in whose web he is enveloped?

Bell's Life was simply incredulous:

It is really almost ludicrous to be gravely told that a horse like The Earl – who, be it borne in mind, was taken to Epsom one day, and away the next – that The Earl, who according to subsequent running could scarcely have lost the Derby, was scratched because, forsooth, Lady Elizabeth, who could scarcely raise a 'hand gallop,' had 'arrived safely at Epsom and was to run in the Derby.'

Padwick and Hill immediately remonstrated with *The Times*. Day told his lawyer to institute an action against Rous. This was bravado. It came to nothing.

But it was increasingly obvious that Hastings himself was now physically on his last legs. He went on a last cruise to Norway which did little or nothing to help his health. Then a last visit to Newmarket where he was said to be 'seated in a basket carriage' without the money to make anything of a bet and the bookmaker insisting he was paid first. A brief stay at Folkestone followed and then home to die. To a friend he admitted what had plainly been on his mind for over a year: 'Hermit's Derby broke my heart. But I did not show it, did I?'

The obituaries fastened on the story of 'that poor coronetted youth', as the *Daily News* put it. He had, it said, 'crowded into six years more Corinthian excitement, and weightier Turf cares, than many "fast men" know in a lifetime'. They played upon the 'nearly seven seasons' that had passed by 'since he first came a lad of nineteen fresh from Eton to Newmarket, and he left it a shattered man, only to die'. The balance was kind: 'His greatest faults were a love of excitement, a recklessness rather too bold, and an open-handedness that would have brought a Croesus to grief.'

Lady Florence's second choice of a husband was more conventional but, in the end, no more successful in the world's eye. Two years after Hastings's death she married Sir George Chetwynd of Grendon Hall in Warwickshire. He had just succeeded his father in possession of a substantial estate which would have provided a comfortable and quiet life while they brought up a son and three daughters, but her husband's ambitions, now he had the wherewithal, turned readily towards a life and expenditure sustained by regular betting coups.

He was an energetic sportsman, playing for Harrow against Eton at Lord's, hunting with the Leicestershire and Warwickshire, and shooting at the Gun Club at Shepherd's Bush and Hurlingham. George Lambton's shrewd eye summed him up:

A tall, slight, distinguished-looking figure, with, when he chose to exert it, a considerable charm of manner, but when success was at flood-tide inclined to be overbearing . . . He was determined to live as if money was no object, and in many ways he was the most extravagant man I have ever met. He was an extraordinary fine judge of racing, and it was well known that the Turf had to supply the money to support his style of life.

In fact, Lady Florence had done it again. She had married another young, well-off Midlands landowner ('owns about 6700 acres' was his self-description), educated at Christ Church, Oxford, who promptly put himself in the hands of the same Captain Machell who had left her husband to manage Henry Chaplin's horses. There was no one to blame but herself. Two years after they married he started a stud farm at Grendon, which was not a success. She must have seen the shifts her new husband was soon put to, moving from trainer to trainer in pursuit of success and money. From Machell's stables he went to Saunders's at Hednesford, then to Woolcot's at Beckhampton, and then to Sherrard's at Newmarket.

What he wanted was a compliant trainer, plus a jockey who was ready to ride as his betting required. Fred Archer, who bet heavily, rode for him, but in Charlie Wood he had someone he could rely on to do his bidding and share in his profits. As Lambton put it: 'Good as Sherrard was in the stable and on the training ground, about the form of horses and racing he knew little. But with George Chetwynd and his jockey, Charles Wood, this did not matter much, for what these two did not know was not worth knowing.'

When Chetwynd became senior steward of the Jockey Club he did not, and probably could not, change his dependence on his betting operations. These he managed to run with suitable discretion for years, although there were doubts, in 1883, about Wood's riding of the Derby winner, St Blaise, for Chaplin's friend, Johnstone. Chetwynd the steward turned a deaf ear to the suspicions. But in 1887 the protests grew strident about the in-and-out running of a number of horses.

That November the *Licensed Victuallers' Gazette* broke the silence, asking pointedly: 'How about the running of Success at Lewes and Alexandra Park, where Charlie Wood nearly pulled his head off on each occasion?' Worse than that, the upright Lord Durham, speaking at the annual Gimcrack dinner at York, levelled barely concealed charges at a 'fashionable stable'. This needed to be answered.

Chetwynd, as a Jockey Club member and one of the stable's patrons, 'challenged Lord Durham to prove his allegations'. Durham, confident in his knowledge, refused to withdraw so, as the report went, 'Sir George Chetwynd declared that the matter was an affair of honour and his brother, Captain Walter Chetwynd, on his behalf waited on Lord Durham with a challenge to a duel.'

This was anachronistic nonsense, and Durham just ignored it. The Jockey Club stewards had to take it up, however, and Wood also sued the *Licensed Victuallers'*

Gazette for £3000. After a court hearing that lasted twelve days Wood was awarded laughable damages of a farthing. Since the Jockey Club could not abide the idea of a senior steward appearing in court, it appointed arbitrators to hear Chetwynd's claim for £2000 libel damages against Durham. They awarded him precisely a farthing, too. He had no option but to resign from the club and protest in the strongest terms he dared: 'I look forward with confidence to the time when I shall be fully absolved from having acted in any way causing me to deserve the censure of honourable men.'

In its way, it was an even greater humiliation than Hastings's, although Chetwynd's friends duly spoke of his coolness and pluck in standing by his jockey. Eventually, it was Wood who was forgiven and got his licence back. Durham, to show that the past had been buried, gave him his first mount. Wood was soon back in form and won his third Derby on Galtee More in 1897. Chetwynd was not forgiven by his circle. He died at Monte Carlo during the First World War. He was sixty-five. Lady Florence had preceded him to the grave, dying almost unnoticed in 1907.

Henry Chaplin had a more successful life. Within a week of Hastings's death in November 1868, he became Conservative MP for Mid-Lincolnshire, a constituency he held until the great Liberal swing in 1906. He then transferred to the safe suburban seat of Wimbledon, campaigning with a magnum of champagne in his carriage and beating, in the by-election,

the youthful philosopher, Bertrand Russell, by 7000 votes.

Chaplin married comfortably into the aristocracy in 1876. His wife was Lady Florence Leveson-Gower, daughter of the third Duke of Sutherland. They had a son and two daughters, but she died after five years. He grew into a doughty and rotund defender of the agricultural interest, the epitome of the solid English country squire. Like Hastings, he knew how to spend money to the end. Although Hermit's annual earnings at stud (as much as £15,000) helped him for years, Chaplin lived well beyond his income. The great champion of mid-Victorian England got out of his depth. In 1892 he had to sell Blankney Hall itself.

In politics he rose with the party's patronage to be Chancellor of the Duchy of Lancaster and then President of the new Board of Agriculture. But he did not trust Lord Randolph Churchill or wish him to take over the party; Churchill, in return, kept Chaplin out of the cabinet until his influence faded. Chaplin got in then as President of the Local Government Board. He was a genial soul, even competing once with a portly Liberal to see who could lose most weight. (He got down from eighteen stones to sixteen – for a while.) But the big jobs passed him by until, in 1915, the Tory backbenchers who did not support Asquith's wartime coalition made him, surprisingly, a leader of the Opposition. It was, naturally, a loyal Opposition for which service Chaplin received a viscountcy. He died in 1923, a relic of a lost age.

The Grand Stand Children

The first Epsom Grand Stand (a more resplendent name than the modern grandstands that have succeeded it) housed in the 1840s two children whose names were to be household words. One was Isabella Mayson, the eldest daughter of her widowed mother, Emily; the other was Henry Mayson Dorling, one of Emily's sons by her second marriage – to Henry Dorling, the clerk of the course at Epsom. Isabella Mayson grew up to be the incomparable Mrs Beeton whose *Household Management* and its 1500 recipes taught Victorian housewives how to cook and run their homes and

servants; this encyclopaedia probably came to govern more people's lives (and stomachs) around the world than anything laid down by politicians and social reformers.

The other child did not earn so lasting and widespread a reputation but, in his day, he gloried in such titles as the 'Dictator of Epsom' and 'His Majesty Dorling', the man who controlled the Derby and its development for over forty years. It needed the Grand Stand (opened in 1830) and its saloons to house all the Dorling children. Both Henry Dorling and Emily

Mayson had four children in their first marriages and, when they eventually married (he had been her first husband's greatest friend), they went on to produce thirteen more.

The family lived in the stand for most of the year, only being evicted and placed with families around Epsom for the Derby meeting. Henry Dorling himself was a mild-mannered man and it is said that, when his brood was once being unduly obstreperous, he asked his wife what was going on. She replied, memorably: 'Your children and my children are fighting our children.' There could have been no better training for her eldest daughter to master the practicalities of household management for families of any size.

When Isabella Mayson was nineteen she met a young, ambitious, highly strung publisher, Samuel Orchard Beeton. He duly proposed. Wishing to be a good wife, she began a serious study of what she would need to know to bring up a family of her own. She always asserted that she had no expertise in cookery until their marriage in 1856, but her husband, recognizing her ability, encouraged her to set her hand to compiling what she had learned for a widening readership of aspiring young women intent on being part of respectable, and capable, middle-class society. He would do the publishing.

So she took on *The Englishwoman's Domestic Magazine*, voicing her own, often liberal, ideas to an approving audience. By 1859 she began writing her *Household Management* as a part-work, a prodigious effort. It came out as a complete book in 1860. It was a remarkable achievement, even in self-discipline, in an age that prided itself on such qualities, and all the more so for a young woman going through difficult pregnancies. Her first two children died in infancy. Had she known what the writing entailed, she said, she would 'have never been courageous enough to commence it'.

Mrs Beeton, admired and respected as the epitome of Victorian womanhood, the experienced, infallible manager and author of an international bestseller, died when she was only twenty-nine, after giving birth to her fourth child. Her own life story rivals any of the legends of the racecourse where she was brought up.

The Grand Stand in which Mrs Beeton's wedding reception was held in July 1856.

The author of MRS BEETON'S HOUSEHOLD MANAGEMENT *who lived in Epsom Grand Stand from 1843 to 1856.*

Above: 'What mustard is to roast beef, ice to Clicquot champagne, Chablis to oysters, that is Henry Dorling to The Derby . . .'

Below: The magnificent entrance foyer to the Grand Stand, 1886.

Her stepbrother, Henry Mayson Dorling, had determination and willpower in plenty too.

When his father died in 1873 he succeeded him as Epsom's clerk of the course; he held the job through thick and thin until his own death, just after the 1919 Derby, when he was eighty-four. He had inherited the responsibility of the Grand Stand and the ownership of the family print works in Epsom which turned out its own annual bestseller, the 'only Genuine Race Card Approved by Authority'. The card was certainly invaluable to racing men. 'Dorling's Correct Card' had an accuracy that not even Weatherbys could aspire to. Epsom was Dorling's empire and he ruled it pretty well as he liked.

Dorling flattered himself that he never cared whom he crossed. 'Everyone hates me – and I like it,' he would say. When a man asked him for a free pass to the racecourse, saying that his brother was a friend of Dorling's, the reply was crushing: 'I can count my friends on the fingers of one hand. All the rest of the world calls me an old bastard. Good day to you, Sir.' He battled remorselessly against anyone interfering with his domination of the downs, even Epsom residents claiming their rights of access; for him, no obstruction, no subterfuge was ignored if it got him his way.

The Dorling family had taken over, for the Grand Stand Association, the lease of the stand and the organization of the Derby, with the encouragement of Lord George Bentinck. It had seen off the challenge of

the rival Barnard family who ran their own, temporary stands – which had the closest view of the finishing line. It had reached arrangements with the owners of the paddock and the part of the course that ran briefly on Walton Downs. But Henry Mayson Dorling had set himself fresh fields to conquer.

In 1879 he got for the Grand Stand Association the leases of land to improve the course at Tattenham Corner and to establish the straight five-furlong course which, since the opening furlongs are steeply downhill, is the fastest in the world. In 1886 a new club stand was completed, adjoining the Grand Stand, for the 800 members.

This was all necessary. But these improvements were expensive and the Epsom finances have always depended on the return from a single annual meeting. Nothing was paid by the tens of thousands who jostled on the downs; the profits had to come from the relative few in the posh enclosures.

As the 1880s ended it became evident that the prize money, of no more than £5000, compared badly with what could then be offered by the new, enclosed courses, like Sandown Park (opened in 1875) and Kempton Park (opened 1878). Sandown's new Eclipse Stakes guaranteed an enviable £10,000, the biggest prize in the country. Money did not matter to owners like the Prince of Wales or Rosebery, the Prime Minister, but the Derby entries fell off. Dorling worked on to the end, still quarrelling (often with the stewards) to his heart's content. He lived to see the Derby return to Epsom after the 1914–18 War, still closely supervising the accuracy of the racecard. But something of his half-sister's organizing skills would have improved his management record.

Avenging Waterloo

The Derby had become the Englishman's favourite race and a prized possession. Englishmen had bred the thoroughbred and so knew themselves superior to every other nation. American horsemen who had been in England were said to have admitted that a first-class English horse was a stone better than a first-class American one – from the east or the west. It was not that mid nineteenth-century Englishmen were unusually complacent. They knew that the Emperor Napoleon III had got a taste for racing during his early exile in England, and he and the Duc de Morny worked to get French opinion interested in racing – with increasing impact. Money and effort went into developing racing and breeding, but success was slow in coming. The General Stud Book exemplified the English opinion: 'With the advantages this country already possesses, and so long as horse racing continues to be followed up with spirit by her men of rank and opulence, there can be little to apprehend.'

By 1864 there was much to be apprehensive about. The Comte Frédéric de Lagrange, son of one of Napoleon I's generals, won both the English and French Oaks with his half-English filly Fille de l'Air. As a successful industrialist Lagrange had money. He split his training effort in two: half at Compiègne in France, half under Tom Jennings at Newmarket. In 1865 he brought to England his wholly French-bred colt, Gladiateur, which won the Two Thousand Guineas when only half-fit. When Derby day came round Gladiateur was ready for the race of his life. The opposition was not top-class.

The Epsom crowd was visibly reinforced by the most fashionable of the French community in London, confident of success. They were spotted in the trains, in private carriages, in the refreshment rooms and on the roof of the grandstand. French voices were heard everywhere:

The emphatic roll of the letter 'r-r-r' betrayed the close proximity of our great allies, whose attachment to le sport has sometimes furnished occasion for mirth, but who must henceforward be recognised not only as worthy, but successful rivals.

Gladiateur had to survive a series of false starts in which one horse's rider (Teddy Sharpe on Joker) was thrown and broke his collar-bone. When the official off was signalled at 4p.m., Gladiateur's rider, Harry Grimshaw, soon found there were only two other colts of any quality: Christmas Carol and Eltham. But they did not last long: 'Before reaching the distance Gladiateur shot bang to the front, passed the two as though they were standing still, and, continuing in front, bounded away to the end.'

He won easily, by two lengths, at odds of 3–2. There were some English cheers, but not too many. National pride had taken a knock – it was not the Englishman's Derby any longer. Gladiateur was a great horse, the 'Avenger of Waterloo' (the race was run on almost the fiftieth anniversary of the battle); he went on to win the Grand Prix de Paris and the St Leger. His record has never been equalled. Lord Derby gave a big dinner for the Comte de Lagrange. But *The Times*, after its congratulations, felt a sermon coming on:

The Derby is but the climax of a disposition which pervades English life from the top to the bottom. The love of manly exercise, of racing in all its forms, of vigorous and friendly competition in trials of strength and skill, is one of the deepest and most influential of all the habits of this country.

Then the sting:

It educates that spirit of manly and generous rivalry which preserves our political struggles from the personal bitterness which marks similar contests in other nations. It teaches us how to respect one another, and how to accept defeat. It is just this rough moral frankness which, if we may on such an occasion observe a defect, is one of the chief wants of French society.

The *Morning Post* thought the same, but lied better:

The French will be exultant, for they invest these matters with an international interest, and look upon them as a positive struggle between the two countries . . . It must be acknowledged that fair play is ever the guiding principle of the English; and in accordance with its dictates the multitude at Epsom hailed with unanimous and enthusiastic acclamation the achievement of the best horse of 1865.

It was British policy, despite frights and rumours, to believe the best of the French. They had been on the right side in the Crimea, even if a steam navy might

Gladiateur – 'The Avenger of Waterloo', who won the Derby in 1865.

mean they could cross the Channel in a night. The *Morning Post* thought it best to look on the bright side of a national defeat:

This notable event will do as much for the *éntente cordiale* as diplomatic alliances or treaties of commerce. It will promote an immense good feeling between the two people. The English will respect French prowess, while the French will not fail to observe the honest cheerfulness with which we can meet defeat.

In fact, the French took it coolly. The English press said the news spread 'with wonderful rapidity' in Paris, and 'a national feeling of satisfaction prevailed'. True enough, there were celebrations: 'The Jockey Club at Paris illuminated the whole of its grand balcony, at the angle of which shone in large and brilliant letters, upon a white ground, the name of "Gladiateur." The Sporting Club did the same.'

So did several cafés. Lagrange had been a founder-member of the French Jockey Club. The newspaper *Débats* said the result had been 'received with but little sympathy on the ground by the populace' at Epsom, but 'loudly applauded by true gentlemen'. Of the other Paris papers, the *Temps, Siècle* and *Presse* said not a word. The *Figaro* was waspish. It reported that 20,000 silk scarves with a likeness of Gladiateur

had been sold in England but, apart from a *parfumier* in the Boulevard des Capucines, it found little enthusiasm in Paris and it doubted if even he would sell twenty-five. Whatever the Jockey Club did in Paris, it said, the English had taken the victory of a French horse as an affront; in addition, 99 per cent of the French population would always remain ignorant of the very name of Gladiateur.

Five years later, in 1870, Lagrange sent his stud to England on a three-year lease to escape the Franco-Prussian war. The Prussians occupied his estate in Normandy and drank their way through his cellars. After the war, English horses competing in France were highly unpopular with the crowds who thought Britain should have intervened on the French side. The jockey, Fred Archer, did not like the French crowds or the French jockeys. But the Epsom connection remained. French horses still came over. Some, like M. Edmond Blanc's Gouvernement (7–4 favourite in 1904), failed; others, like the American H.B. Duryea's Durbar II in 1914, succeeded. French supporters came regularly, the railway companies bringing them over 'on easy terms'.

After Gladiateur, England struggled to reconcile itself to defeat. It little suspected what the French were to inflict on it after the Second World War.

Fizz in New York

In 1881 it was the Americans' turn. In 1856 Richard Ten Broeck, the owner of the great American champion Lexington, moved to England to try his hand at winning the Derby with an American-bred horse. Ten Broeck, said to be a prototype of the Mississippi river boat gambler, was disappointed but he persisted. So did other rich and aspiring American owners, anxious to establish the reputation of the American turf in English and French eyes. They had to be rich, for the effort required shipping a stable across the Atlantic and establishing it at Newmarket or Chantilly. The two most persistent Americans were Pierre Lorillard, a tobacco manufacturer, and James R. Keene, an English-born Wall Street banker and 'a gentleman who longs to accomplish the unaccomplished'.

The rivalry between them was, if anything, as great as between them and the Europeans. Although the English experts, who rated Lorillard's Iroquois at 100–1 during the winter, came to reckon his chances as an outsider, few of them gave him much of a prospect against the favourite, Peregrine, owned by Captain Robert Grosvenor, a relative of the Duke of Westminster. They were critical of the in-and-out running of Lorillard's colt.

Two papers thought differently. The *Pall Mall Gazette*, which prided itself on being opinionated, declared: 'There really do not appear to be any sound reasons why we should persist in the irrational clamour about the vast superiority of our race horses, as though we held a permanent patent of precedence.'

And, on the Saturday before the Derby, *Bell's Life in London* had, perspicaciously, tipped Iroquois in verse:

> *Flushed red are American faces:*
> *Hurrah! for old Leamington's son–*
> *You'll show the pale Britons how races*
> *Across the Atlantic are won.*
> *Dash on, as if life was at venture,*
> *And news shall unloosen the cork*
> *From seas of champagne at Newmarket,*
> *And oceans of 'fizz' at New York.*

The *New York Times* carried the Derby betting on its front page. It reported that Iroquois was not particularly fancied on the day: 'One old habitué of the turf made the remark that he looked as though he would do better over hurdles than on a flat course.' But Iroquois was 'in the hands of England's most famous jockey, Fred Archer', and between them they did it: 'The gallant colt, making one grand effort, passed his antagonist at the grand stand, and won the race by half a length, amid a grand outburst of applause from the enormous multitude in attendance.'

Archer had not been sure, just before the first race, if he would be released to ride, but his success meant he became 'the King of Jockeys' to the Americans. It was said Archer rode as if there were only one horse in the race, and that was Peregrine. Directly Peregrine went to the front Iroquois went after him. The whip was hardly used. The race was clearly won 100 yards from home.

Bell's man was properly generous to the winner:

It is sufficient that, after crossing the Atlantic to measure merit with the best horses of his year that this country could oppose to him, he has succeeded in the great task set him, and I think those Englishmen who waved their hats and cheered Iroquois lustily on Wednesday did well.

The *Sporting Times* (the 'Pink 'Un') showed it could break into verse too:

> *So one of fair Columbia's dreams*
> *Is realised. It really seems*
> *Almost romantic.*
> *Here, Uncle Jonathan, we end*
> *All jealousies, and, friend to friend,*
> *Our warm congratulations send*
> *Across the wide Atlantic.*

Uncle Jonathan was an earlier version of Uncle Sam. The paper was relieved by the crowd's behaviour:

Any fears that one might have had as to the greeting that the winner would receive were soon shown to be groundless, cheer following on cheer, given with a heartiness that makes

1881. Iroquois, the first American-owned and bred Derby winner, ridden by Fred Archer.

us rejoice in the sporting manliness of the crowd, and at the same time makes us more than ever deplore the disgrace that the Henley authorities have fixed upon us by the want of courtesy they have shown to the Transatlantic oarsmen.

That criticism of the Henley stewards referred to their efforts to keep the reputation of English rowing afloat by insisting that the Cornell University entry had arrived too late.

The *Pall Mall Gazette* was grudging, deserting its earlier cosmopolitanism: 'Iroquois, like the nation he represents, has sprung from English stock, and Englishmen can only rejoice that the breed improves rather than degenerates in the Western world.'

The American support on Epsom Downs, naturally, was elated. The *New York Times* man was almost ecstatic. Having mentioned the presence of the Waleses, the Connaughts and 'every Englishman within reaching distance', he continued: 'Very many Americans who are visiting London also went to the grounds by rail, and had the pleasure of seeing an American horse win the first Derby which they had ever attended.' He mentioned sixteen by name, among them 'John McCullough, the tragedian' and 'Bartley Campbell, the dramatist'. To the paper's distress the winning owner was not there. But his wife was:

Mr Lorillard said last evening that his wife has never taken much interest in his horses, and frequently has not even known his colours when they came in ahead. Yesterday, being in London, some of her friends persuaded her to go with them to Epsom, and she telegraphed that no one was more astonished than herself at the result.

Lorillard was suitably modest about his own winnings, putting them at $12,000, of which $5000 went as a present to Archer. The stable's celebrations were muted because most of its money had gone on Lorillard's more favoured Barrett which had had to be withdrawn at the last moment – the ante-post money being lost. Iroquois was returned at 11–2.

Lorillard's New Jersey factory was illuminated, he drove through New York in triumph, and his friends celebrated in style: 'Last evening the Madison-square front of the Turf Club was illuminated with Chinese lanterns from the second storey to the roof in honour of the event.'

The *New York Herald* sent a reporter down to the stock exchange where the enthusiasm was great,

although expertise was not universal. The reporter found himself shouting at one dealer:

'Iroquois has captured the Derby, don't you understand?'

'No, I do not, young man, but God help Derby and everybody in the place if the Indians have captured it. Is it near a military post?'

An investor had trouble keeping up:

'Say, buy me 200 Iroquois, quick, right away. New stock; just come with a rush; they've all gone mad over it.'

The paper had its own idea of what would be suitable to perpetuate the city's memory of an historic triumph:

Iroquois reproduced in bronze would make a picturesque figure at some well-chosen point in Central Park. There are a great many monuments there of all sorts of creatures, mostly men; but there is not one in the whole collection about which would gather more sympathetic and sincere admirers than would stand around a magnificent statue of the first American winner of the Derby.

For, as the *Herald* insisted, 'it shows that America is pushing to the front in everything'. It was astonishing the world:

There is scarcely a gentleman in England who would not rather have seen his colors leading that trailing group of madly ridden steeds, amid the cheers of a hundred thousand people, than to feel the garter of chivalry buckled around his knee.

It was certainly a matter for satisfaction that 'the whole world of London is asking itself what it all means'.

The paper that got it right at once was the *News* in London: 'The Derby is not only a national but an international prize, and the laurels won by America will not be grudged her by England.'

The Derby had finally been internationalized. But so had racing everywhere. The second Sunday after Iroquois's Derby, the Grand Prix de Paris – the French Derby – was run at Longchamp. J.R. Keene, who had had two unsuccessful runners at Epsom, had a much better chance in Paris with his Foxhall, foaled in Kentucky, which went to post the 2–1 favourite. Foxhall duly romped home, with the English George Fordham in the saddle, and not even Archer, on the second horse, could peg them back. It was another American first in European racing. There were to be many successors.

The Fate of Fred Archer

Fred Archer was the greatest jockey of his generation. Over a century after his death, he still has claims to be the greatest ever. He won the Derby five times in a riding career of only seventeen years (and his critics said he lost a sixth trying to help his brother, Charles, win a gamble in 1883). He could never have had the longevity in the saddle of Gordon Richards or Lester Piggott, because he subjected himself to the direst methods of wasting in order to ride at the necessary weights. He was 5ft 8½ins tall. When he first became

Fred Archer, 'The Tinman', so-called on account of his predilection for cash, rode five Derby winners.

champion jockey in 1874 his body weight was just 6 stones, but those days soon ended. He once told his trainer, Mat Dawson, that to get his weight down in a hurry 'I shall sit in the Turkish bath and no doubt elsewhere' until he succeeded. This led to his final illness when, his mind unhinged, he shot himself. He was twenty-nine.

Archer, like Piggott, knew how to ride Epsom as none of his rivals did. He had a will of iron. It was said he would come round Tattenham Corner with one leg over the rail if he had to. But his real genius was in understanding his horses, judging the pace impeccably and producing the driving finish that lifted their heads or even their noses across the finishing line. At least two of his Derby winners, Bend Or and Melton, beat better staying horses on the day – and he made the day. He was lucky in having behind him the skill and friendship of the trainer Mat Dawson, to whom he had been apprenticed, who thought of him as a son, and whose niece he married. Dawson is credited with training six Derby winners, two of them ridden by Archer.

Archer's father, William, had ridden the Grand National victor, Little Charley, in 1858. His parents' enthusiasm and pride were important in his life – as was their regular need for money. Through all his successes Archer stayed a modest man, except on the course where his will to win was paramount and he spared no one who got in his way. But Dawson, a dryly spoken, upstanding Scot of the old school, taught him discipline as well as how to snatch races out of the fire. Though Dawson bet modestly, he disdained wealth. If his owners annoyed him he told them to take their horses away.

There was another steadying influence: the sixth Viscount Falmouth, an owner with an integrity that equalled his resources. He had been born the son of a parson and qualified for the Bar before a cousin's death gave him the title. His marriage added the money. He was one of a new type of owners who did not gamble because they neither needed to nor approved of it. He required high standards and, for a brief, golden period, the alliance of Falmouth, Dawson and Archer dominated English racing. Horses bred by Falmouth at his stud at Mereworth, Kent, trained by Dawson

1870. The dramatic descent down Tattenham Hill – the true test of jockeyship on Epsom Downs.

and ridden by Archer seemed to be unstoppable.

Archer's first Derby win was with Silvio (100–9) in 1877. The race had been thought to be a certainty for the Comte de Lagrange's Chamant, winner of the Two Thousand Guineas. But Chamant broke down and Archer was left with a challenge only from the 50–1 outsider, Glen Arthur. He merely eased Silvio in order to have something in hand if a better horse than Glen Arthur put in an appearance, but nothing did. Archer's mother was in tears. Dawson's face was reported 'jolly'. The former American president, Ulysses S. Grant, missed the race. He turned up in time for the Oaks.

Archer's next win was in 1880; a modern trainer and owner would not have allowed him to be there at all. A month before the Derby Archer was exercising Muley Edris, a bad-tempered colt to whom Archer had given some severe thrashings to get him to run. The

horse did not forget. When Archer dismounted Muley Edris went for him, getting his teeth into his arm and savaging him on the ground. Archer was adamant that he would ride Bend Or at Epsom, but his arm was slow to heal, he was in pain and a London specialist, not knowing who Archer was, told him he could only go to watch the Derby if he were driven there.

Archer had his way. He rode with his arm bound up, came perilously close to the rail at Tattenham Corner, and seemed to have too much to make up to catch a big, wiry colt, Robert the Devil. But Archer did catch up, went for his whip (which then fell from his bad hand) and, by the sheer strength of his finish, got Bend Or ahead in the very last stride to win by a head. An objection that Bend Or's parentage had been given inaccurately (and he was really another horse) was eventually overruled.

Next year Archer got the late ride on the American Iroquois, urging the first American Derby winner home, by half a length, to great enthusiasm in New York (see page 42). For one tipster, Hotspur in the *Daily Telegraph*, the race had been decided when Archer was freed for the ride: 'When I heard on Sunday night that Lord Falmouth had very generously given his jockey up, I felt pretty well assured that his riding would be quite 7lb in favour of Iroquois more than that of any other jockey available.' It was an appropriate compliment to the champion jockey. Hotspur's readers had been let into the secret in good time.

In 1883 there were three horses that mattered: Galliard, the Two Thousand Guineas winner that Archer was riding; Highland Chief, on which Charles Archer had staked a small fortune; and St Blaise – which beat Highland Chief by a neck, with Galliard, half a length behind, third. The dissatisfied immediately said that Archer had not tried to ride one of his devastating, all-out finishes. The newspapers were filled with accusations. Archer's admirers said then, and have said since, that to throw a race went against both his instinct and his record. But it did not help when Falmouth soon announced that he had decided to give up racing and was putting his horses and studs up for sale. Falmouth had been considering this move for some time, but his decision seemed damning. Archer had ridden for Falmouth for an annual retainer of just £100 and had never asked for an increase. He had called the new home he had built for himself at Newmarket, Falmouth House. Loyalty had not been repaid.

Archer's wife died in childbirth in the autumn of 1884 and he was desolate for months afterwards. He paid his only visit to the United States to get his mind off such thoughts, though he did not ride there. When he came back Dawson had a Derby prospect for him, but Melton was one of the most difficult colts which even Dawson, who had a reputation for dealing with horses which required tender treatment, had had to train. When so many judges said Melton's legs were suspect his success was a crowning moment in Dawson's career. He also needed Archer to be there. Archer had ridden Paradox, Melton's chief Derby rival, and he knew Paradox's weakness. Like a number of horses, Paradox invariably faltered when he found himself in the lead.

Fred Archer on his last Derby winner – Ormonde, 1886.

Archer began the race slowly, he lingered, and he let Paradox get ahead of the other runners and start to get worried. When Paradox showed uneasiness Archer pounced with just fifty yards to go. It was said he seemed to push Melton's head in front within a foot of the winning post. It was a brilliant ride with a splendidly timed finish. Two resounding cracks with the whip had done it. Paradox, by common consent, was much the stronger and should have won. His jockey actually thought he had and was devastated when Melton's number went up.

Next year was less demanding. Archer's mount, Ormonde, was expected to win easily and started at 9–4 on. There was only one serious challenger, The Bard, who made his effort about half a mile from home. It was brave but vain. When Archer settled down to ride Ormonde drew away and won easily by a length and a half. The third horse, seven or eight lengths away, was little noticed. He was called St Mirin and he was to contribute to Archer's illness and death that November.

The one important race that Archer had never won was the Cambridgeshire, a big betting race run over a mile and a furlong. It was a challenge. Archer had had to live with his weight problem, but it was not getting any easier for him. Visitors to his home found that one small tumblerful of champagne had become his only nourishment until racing ended for the day. A weighing chair stood beside his study table. He lay and read for hours on end in his own Turkish bath. When the

Duchess of Montrose (who regularly pursued him, without success) asked him to ride St Mirin in the Cambridgeshire, he agreed. The horse's handicap weight was 8st 6lb and, to get within a pound of it, he went without food for three days, dosed himself with purgatives and lived in the bath.

He was too weak to ride at his best. St Mirin finished second. Weak, sick and now doubting his own judgement, he rode almost desperately, seeking winners. He had five in nine races at Newmarket but, at Brighton the next week, he had none in two days. He became feverishly ill and, when he got home to Newmarket, his doctor put him to bed, suspecting typhoid. On the afternoon of 8 November 1886, Archer seemed slightly better. He asked his sister to send the nurse away because he had something to tell her. She looked out of the window, waiting for him to speak. He said: 'Are they coming?' Turning round, she saw he was half out of bed and had a revolver in his hand. There had been burglaries locally. She tried to get it from him. He

put it to his head and, while she wrestled with him, he pulled the trigger.

The bullet severed his spinal column and passed out at the back of his neck. He died in his sister's arms on the hearthrug.

Mat Dawson continued to train. He was a robust character who had been brought up on the stories of racing in the days of George IV and William IV. He had walked a horse himself all the way from Middleham to Epsom, and was always his own man. He read solid and serious books in the winter and, though a Liberal 'almost to the verge of radicalism', was devoted to the Tory *Quarterly Review*, perhaps because it had been started by Sir Walter Scott. He found in Lord Rosebery an owner who spoke his language and enjoyed his conversation, 'rich with the spoils of time', and he trained Rosebery's first Derby winner, Ladas II (page 55), in 1894. The next year, he admitted he felt old age creeping up on him with Rosebery's second winner, Sir Visto. He died, aged seventy-eight, in 1898.

The Luck of the Rothschilds

Derby winners come from dedication, determination – and sheer luck. The three de Rothschild Derby winners were typical. In 1871 Baron Meyer de Rothschild, the builder of Mentmore in Buckinghamshire, won with Favonius, but that year he won everything: the Derby, Oaks, One Thousand Guineas and St Leger. This avalanche of fulfilled ambitions came only after prolonged effort. As *The Times* put it expansively: 'One of the largest supporters of racing in this country, breeding his own horses and running them for the pure love of the sport, and a small speculator (on the Turf at least) he has at length obtained the reward of every racing man's ambition – and for which he has waited so patiently and long.'

Favonius won easily at 9–1 by a length and a half, though not in a particularly fast time. The Prince of Wales watched from a private stand and, by the marvels of modern communication, the result was telegraphed to Bombay in only eleven minutes. For the happy owner there was the racing certainty of his great filly Hannah winning the Oaks later in the week.

The head of the family, Baron Lionel, had to wait until the year of his death, 1879, to win his Derby with Sir Bevys. He was used to getting his way in the end. The banker who raised the money to pay for the Crimean war, the funding of the United States

St Bevys, the 1879 Derby winner ridden by George Fordham.

national debt, and (to him) the mere £4 million to let Disraeli buy the Suez Canal shares for Queen Victoria, had conducted a lengthy struggle simply to be allowed to take his seat in the House of Commons as Member of Parliament for the City of London. He had refused, as a Jew, to accept the words 'on the true faith of a Christian' in the parliamentary oath and, as an unsworn member, he sat regularly just outside the bar of the House from 1847 to 1858 when, with the support of Gladstone, Disraeli and Lord John Russell, he had his way.

Winning the Derby should have been easier, but it was formidable. He raced under the nom de course of Mr Acton, insisting that it was a family endeavour. Sir Bevys went to post under two handicaps: he was a notoriously slow starter and his jockey, the clever George Fordham, had never won the Derby and was suspected of lacking the nerve to cope with the pace at Tattenham Corner. Sir Bevys, said to combine short legs with prodigious propelling power, duly began a dozen lengths (some accounts said 100 yards) behind everything, justifying the odds of 20–1 against him. But Fordham belied the tipsters' doubts and duly delivered the colt, cannily, on the stand side where the going was best after two days of heavy rain. Sir Bevys's staying power did the rest. It was Fordham's only Derby success. Tennyson, the Poet Laureate, struck by the Arthurian name, had put a modest fiver on the winner. He picked up his £100.

Baron Lionel's third son, Leopold de Rothschild, who was widely regarded as the true contriver of Sir Bevys's victory, had an almost interminable wait for a Derby winner in his own name. He was a kindly man, popular in the City and familiarly called 'Mr Leopold' by the racing public. His best horse was said to be St Frusquin, but the colt frequently suffered from lameness. St Frusquin was beaten by a neck by the Prince of Wales's Persimmon in the 1896 race; de Rothschild was not at Epsom himself that year since the race fell on an anniversary of his father's death.

But St Frusquin's son, St Amant, made good that reverse in 1904, in what came to be known as the Thunderstorm Derby. St Amant had won the Two Thousand Guineas and, with his tremendous speed, had a good Derby chance, but for a colt with a tricky temper the weather was wholly unhelpful. The race had to be run 'in a most terrific thunderstorm, deluges of rain and thunder and lightning'. St Amant was fitted out with a hood, however, which probably helped to save his nerves from the storm that terrified several of the other horses.

There was an unexpected problem. His jockey, Kempton Cannon, recalled afterwards that, when he got up on the horse in the Epsom paddock and was being led round the ring, St Amant kept on putting his ears back and turning his head round as if he were trying to catch Cannon by the leg. 'When Kempton asked the boy what on earth was the matter with the horse, he replied, "That's all right: I've been pinching him all the morning. He'll be fairly on his toes now."'

St Amant was. He showed his merit, winning by three lengths in a canter. His happy owner led him in as drenched to the skin as he was. It was a highly popular success for de Rothschild after thirty-four years' trying, for his family colours (dark blue, yellow cap), and for a racing policy that remembered the plain punters. He was once asked if he agreed with giving two-year-olds an easy start to let them gain confidence. He said: 'Yes, that is what I like too, but if I do it my horse gets a false reputation. When he runs, half the City of London is on him: he may be beat to the devil – and then where am I?'

It was said no one saw St Amant's Derby; there were too many umbrellas in the way.

Above: Mr Leopold de Rothschild's Derby winner, St Amant. Opposite: 'The Thunderstorm Derby' of 1904; (top right) Mr de Rothschild receives an ovation.

Monkeys on a Stick

The American invasion of British racing from the mid-1890s to the outbreak of the First World War in 1914 revolutionized the sport. It brought in a new riding style which English jockeys found they had to adopt or go out of business. American jockeys won the Derby eight times in the years 1901–14. This competition meant new tactics, new training methods, an increase in professional gambling – and the spread, and attempted prohibition – of doping. The English establishment resented being shown how out of touch its ways had become, and it was taken aback to find that Americans it had learned to admire, such as Pierre Lorillard, the owner of the first American Derby winner, Iroquois, and Richard Ten Broeck, the type of dry, humorous American whom it identified with the characters in Mark Twain novels, had been followed over the Atlantic by race-course crooks and scoundrels.

This was not surprising. In one of its puritanical cycles the United States had condemned and legislated against racing and gambling. Even honest American owners and trainers felt they had no option but to shift to Europe; this move was markedly to English and French racing's advantage. But there was a price: the other immigrants. The Hon. George Lambton, a gentlemanly English trainer, once said to the highly professional American John Huggins (leading trainer, 1899) that he supposed there were 'a good many rogues and thieves racing in America', only to be told: 'There is not one, they have all come over here.'

Tod Sloan riding in the American style. American riders won the Derby eight times between 1901 and 1914.

Huggins was credited with the development of the American style of race-riding. The English laughed when they first saw Tod Sloan up on what he called the forward seat and they derided as the 'monkey-on-the-stick' method. Sloan made them laugh on the other side of their faces. He first came to Britain for only one month at the end of the 1897 season and promptly won with twenty-one of his forty-eight mounts. He and others quickly saw the possibilities of making an easy living out of the old-fashioned English.

It was not Sloan who invented the style. Simms, a black American jockey, demonstrated it at the Newmarket Craven meeting in 1895, but he was soon forgotten. It was Huggins who realized it was the natural way to ride from the young black stable boys who had never been taught any other way. The light fully dawned when Huggins, having bought a promising horse up-country, was begged by the black lad to buy him too. He took him on. When the horse showed no form, the boy persuaded Huggins to let him ride, and it was as if a different horse was running.

Up to then, established American jockeys had, if anything, ridden with even longer stirrups and had sat up even straighter than English ones. Lambton was told why the up-country method developed. The boys were 'thrown up on some old broncho with only a rug instead of a saddle, and they used to catch hold of the mane and hang on the best way they could until they had found their balance'. This inborn skill helped the horses and got the best out of them. The crouching seat cut wind resistance and gave a better weight distribution amounting, it was said, to many pounds' weight advantage.

Sloan's own contribution was that he was a wayward virtuoso, a master in judging pace and adept in waiting at the front of his field. The English habit of trying nothing enterprising until the final, decisive dash for the line played into his hands. He was cocky and self-confident, and far from popular in the weighing-room or with anyone else except the punters. The English jockeys tried to wear him down with delayed starts, but they were unlucky. The barrier start had arrived in 1897, and was made compulsory for two-year-old races in 1900 and for three-year-old ones in 1901. Sloan was already an expert. He had a reputation for trying to beat the starter and prided himself on being the first away.

He was a trail-blazer, and he paid for it. Lambton called him 'that wonderful little jockey' and the cartoonists delighted in him, always drawing him with a jaunty cigar stuck in his mouth. But he fell foul of authority. In Lambton's view,

It was Sloan's misfortune to be always surrounded by a crowd of the worst class of people that go racing . . . He was a genius on a horse; off one, erratic and foolish. He threw away a career that was full of the greatest promise . . . When he was full of life and confidence he could do anything, but when he was down he could do nothing, and would get beaten on the best thing in the world.

Sloan hated riding gallops. He turned up for races when he thought it right and not when his trainers and owners thought right, even trusting to the transatlantic liners to get him from holiday to the course just on time. He was no respecter of persons, telling Edward VII (when Prince of Wales) in the paddock: 'You can be a plunger here and have a bit on me.' Not that it put the prince off; Sloan was asked to ride for him in the 1901 season and was offered a retainer of 6000 guineas to do so by the royal racing manager, Lord Marcus Beresford. He accepted, knowing it would infuriate his English critics. But they were closing on him. He was certainly careless with his friends, many of them Americans who stayed, as he did, at either the Savoy or the Cecil Hotel in London – and had come over expressly to gamble.

Sloan betted habitually and heavily. He enjoyed it and his style of life required him to make a success of it. He thought English jockeys badly underpaid and he set out to ensure that, by his coups and his owners' presents, he was not. He insisted that he put money only on his own mounts but there were growing suspicions that he and the professional American backers did not seek each other out simply for the pleasure of their mutual company. Sloan was reported to have had big bets on the Cambridgeshire in 1900 and the stewards reprimanded him the next day. He thought that was the end of the matter, but he was told there was no point in his applying for a licence to ride in the next season. He did not stop trying or hoping, but the ban was never lifted.

Sloan won only one English classic (the One Thousand Guineas in 1899), although it seems probable – and he certainly believed it – that he had the beating of Flying Fox in the 1899 Derby when Holocause broke a leg with a furlong and a half to go. But through the door that Sloan opened other Americans entered to conquer Europe.

Lester Reiff was the top jockey in England in 1900, and next year went on to ensure an American triumph, riding Volodyovski to victory in the Derby for an American owner (William C. Whitney, Navy Secretary under President Grover Cleveland) and trainer (the pioneering John Huggins). Reiff himself was warned off at the end of the year for not trying in a race at Manchester. Reiff's younger brother, Johnny, won the 1907 Derby on Orby, Irish-trained and Irish–American owned. The owner was the redoubtable Richard Croker, born in Ireland in 1841; he had emigrated to the United States and raised himself to be a boss of Tammany Hall, the Democratic Party's political machine in New York.

Croker, like racing, had been forced out of America to Britain by the reformers. English racing duly observed him and found him clean of Tammany excesses. He proved, in fact, to be an agreeably shy man who left the socializing to his wife. Johnny Reiff, however, was thought to be part of the doping crowd. He preferred to ride in France, although he came over for big occasions, riding the grey filly Tagalie to victory in the Derby in 1912; he was brought over again to ride Craganour in the disastrous finish of 1913. The American that the English admired was Danny Maher who arrived in 1900, having been champion jockey in the United States in 1898. His reputation proved to be incorruptible, and he was liked and admired by such racing stalwarts as Rosebery and Derby. With these backers and credentials he even applied for British nationality.

Maher, like Sloan, was said to have dubious acquaintances but was scrupulous about betting himself. His waiting tactics, too, were brilliantly executed. He won the Derby three times in four years with Rock Sand (1903), Rosebery's Cicero (1905) and Eustace Loder's Spearmint (1906). In a sense, even the 1904 Derby was won under American influence, the winning jockey, Kempton Cannon, being one of the first English riders to emulate the American style of riding.

Maher himself was thought to have amalgamated the American and English riding styles to perfection. As George Lambton put it, the American style was all very well on American courses which were as level as a billiard table but, on British ones, 'with their ups and downs, and inequalities of ground, it was impossible to get horses balanced again if once they changed their legs and rolled about'. Maher got this right: 'His seat was the perfect mixture of the old and new style. His

highest praise for him: 'When Joyner made up his mind to leave England and return to America there was no more popular man in Newmarket.' The Americans had brought new skills and new technology. They taught the English that open doors and cool stables were far better and more hygienic for the horses and their performance than the hothouse atmosphere that had previously been the fashion. They also brought over new, improved racing plates for the horses.

Champion American jockey, Danny Maher, on Spearmint, 1906.

patience was wonderful, and nothing would induce him to ride a horse hard unless he had him going as he wanted.'

The severest criticism of Maher was that he was burning the candle at both ends. This may have been because he knew he was tubercular. His professional record was remarkable in its consistency: in the fifteen years he rode in Britain he had 1331 winners, an average of 25.3 per cent success. He left Britain in 1914 and died two years later.

Other American incomers were also as highly regarded. Among the trainers, besides Huggins, Andrew Joyner was widely liked. Lambton had the

These were better made and, above all, lighter than English ones. It was reckoned that having American, and not English, plates fitted could make the difference of at least four lengths in a mile race. All this was to the good.

But another able American trainer, Enoch Wishard, brought another new technique with him: doping with cocaine. At that time doping horses was not banned by the English authorities. Nor was Wishard particularly concerned with winning the Derby and other classics. He was chiefly interested in betting, and so concentrated on indifferent horses which had lost their form but could be decisively improved in handicaps. Wishard was so spectacularly successful that the Jockey Club had to make doping an offence. This did not end the coups, but it was noticeable that the success-rate of Wishard and other trainers and jockeys fell off. Huggins and Joyner, and even jockeys like Sloan, all naturally denied having anything to do with dope.

But sheer talent, too, showed through. For years the top five winning jockeys were American. J.H. (Skeets) Martin won the 1902 Derby on Ard Patrick; in 1912, when Johnny Reiff won on Tagalie, there was also in the race the American-bred Tracery which went on to win the Eclipse and the St Leger. In 1914, on the eve of war, the American Matt MacGee, a natural comedian, won the Derby on Durbar II. That gave the Jockey Club another headache because the horse had an American-bred dam, a status that British practice determinedly refused to recognize for the General Stud Book as other than a half-bred.

Durbar II's owner, H.B. Duryea, was American; he had shipped his mares over to France to escape from the anti-betting laws. Durbar's dam, Armenia, had been bred in America by W.C. Whitney. It made no difference. The British thoroughbred business had felt itself threatened, like British jockeys, by the American competition. It had forced through a change that said horses would not be accepted for the stud book unless they could be traced – on both the sire's and dam's side – to a strain that had been accepted in earlier volumes. This infuriated American breeders and owners and eventually had to be rescinded – although not until 1949 when two wars and growing American political influence managed to alter the insular British approach.

Still, after the First World War, English racing came back into its own without too many unwelcome trans-atlantic challenges. When the American Frank O'Neill, who rode in France, won the 1920 Derby on Spion Kop it was the last shot in the jockeys' Anglo-American conflict. The breeders still thought themselves safe until the American competition returned from the 1950s onwards – in unconquerable strength.

The Winning Prime Minister

Archibald Primrose, fifth Earl of Rosebery, was Prime Minister for just two years, 1894–95, and he won the Derby in both of them. It was his best success at 10 Downing Street where he struggled to lead a divided and unhappy Liberal Party. It did not help him politically that he was Gladstone's heir and was also isolated in a minority in the House of Lords. But fortune favoured him at Epsom with Ladas II and Sir Visto, and did so again with Cicero in 1905.

Queen Victoria, who did not follow racing, attempted to congratulate him at one of her audiences but spoiled the effect by assuming that his consecutive victories were with the same horse. His nonconformist voters hated racing and betting. But his Conservative opponents feared that each Derby was worth 100,000 votes to him.

Roseberry was up at Oxford in 1867 when he went to the Derby for the first time and, by prudent betting, made a profit of £10. His grandfather's death the next year made him a wealthy man. He could readily afford to lose £165 on the Oaks. He became an owner, and his colours of primrose and rose were to become famous around the country, carried by his and his son's horses.

His heart was set early on winning the Derby and he had high hopes of Ladas, a horse which had had some success; but his friends, Lord Randolph Churchill among them, were disparaging. Lord Randolph called it 'a brute of a beggar', but the proud owner was prepared to make any sacrifice to succeed. The authorities at his college, Christ Church, promptly put him to the test.

The very possession of a racehorse was, they said, unacceptable. It was not what young men were sent to Oxford to study. Either the horse went, or he did. Rosebery was not prepared to cave in. He wrote succinctly to his mother, the Duchess of Cleveland: 'Dear Mother, I have left Oxford. I have secured a house in Berkeley Square; and I have bought a horse to win the Derby. Your affectionate Archie.' So he departed without a degree.

Lord Rosebery, Matt Dawson, and Jack Watts with the 1894 Derby winner, Ladas II.

Ladas, by Lambton out of Zenobia, was naturally heavily backed at Christ Church (though not by the dons); its owner proceeded to address the supporters in verse:

> There was wailing in the Common Room,
>   the Censors tore their hair,
> Some scraped themselves with potsherds,
>   and some began to swear,
> They damned the race of Lambton,
>   and cursed Zenobia's womb,
> And wished the race of racehorses
>   a universal tomb.

Rosebery was the guest of Henry Chaplin (whose Hermit had won – to the ruin of the Marquis of Hastings – two years before) for Epsom week, but it brought him no luck. Ladas came in last. It was not his defeat that prompted Rosebery to put his horses up for sale at Tattersalls in November, but the failure of another horse, Mavela, in a selling plate at humble Stockton. The local punters had assumed that a wealthy young peer would not enter rubbish, and so backed it heavily. Accusation, rumour and suspicion went about and Rosebery read criticism of himself in the press. He reacted angrily against racing and its followers.

A public apology changed his mind, he went back to the game and was elected to the Jockey Club in 1870. Two years later he bought The Durdans, in Epsom, and started a stud there. It was to become his favourite home.

He recalled, years later, how Epsom was 'a little sleepy town' whose slumber 'was broken twice a year by race meetings, when the followers and camp followers of the Turf stormed the neighbourhood during a few agitated days, and then struck their tents and left the town, sodden and exhausted'. He quite approved of the licentious outbreaks because he thought they discouraged speculative builders and their suburban clients.

He began to win good races, too, among them the Gimcrack and the City and Suburban; his family, however, were appalled by this way of life. He remonstrated with them: 'Even a Scottish peer cannot be ruined by four racehorses, especially when they win:' In the end Rosebery won the Two Thousand Guineas three times, the One Thousand three times, the Derby three times and the Oaks and St Leger once each.

When he married Hannah de Rothschild in 1878, he married into not only one of the wealthiest families in the country but a racing one as well. His wife's father, Baron Meyer Amschel de Rothschild, had had one highly successful year in 1871, known as 'the Baron's year' thereafter, when he won the Derby with Favonius and the One Thousand Guineas, Oaks and St Leger with the filly Hannah, named after his daughter. He also won the Cesarewitch with Corisande. At the wedding the Prime Minister, Disraeli (by then Earl of Beaconsfield), gave the bride away and the Prince of Wales signed the register.

When Rosebery was Prime Minister in 1894 his colt Ladas II won the Two Thousand Guineas and was 9–2 favourite for the Derby. This time the omens were good and Ladas II came home an easy winner. The success was highly popular with racing people and his friends were delighted for him; one, Chauncey Depew, telegraphed from America, 'Only Heaven left'. Rosebery celebrated by circulating an updated series of verses for those who had suffered with him in the disappointment of 1868:

Another moral yet there is, if moral can be found
In what is so immoral and obviously unsound;
To bet may be unlawful, to race may be a sin,
Still in racing, as in everything, it's always best to win.

Ladas never won again. Rosebery told his Liberal critics that even Oliver Cromwell had owned racehorses, but it did not silence them. Three years later,

out of office, he declared acidly: 'Although without guilt or offence I might perpetually run seconds or thirds, or even run last, it became a matter of torture to many consciences if I won.'

Sir Visto's unexpected victory in 1895 came only when Rosebery's administration was disintegrating and he was preoccupied. Within a month the Liberals' Irish allies in the Commons rebelled (refusing to vote funds for a statue of Cromwell at Westminster) and his time as Prime Minister was over.

When Cicero won in 1905 the King proposed Rosebery's health at a Jockey Club dinner. There was a big party at The Durdans and three bands played in the gardens. He said simply he was ashamed to win the Derby thrice when so many owners had never won it once. He had some cause for modesty because the chief French challengers were coughing and one of them, Val d'Or, later beat Cicero in the Eclipse. But he kept on winning classics into the 1920s. He was one of the many who refused to accept the Derby and Oaks run at Newmarket during the First World War as

The Prime Minister, Lord Rosebery, leads in Ladas II after his 1894 Derby triumph.

genuine classics and opposed their inclusion in the numerical order of fame.

His son Harry Rosebery, the sixth earl, was not much of a politician. He was a Liberal MP for four years (he did not admire Lloyd George) and, briefly, Secretary of State for Scotland. But he was a statesman of the Turf for over forty years, imposing his views on discipline, condemning the Aga Khan for selling his bloodstock abroad, and championing the cause of staying horses against the growing fashion for two-year-old races. He won the Derby twice, with Blue Peter in 1939 and Ocean Swell (at a wartime Derby at Newmarket) in 1944. He did not win the Oaks until Sleeping Partner succeeded in 1969.

Among the Also-Rans

Rosebery apart, only one Prime Minister won the Derby. The Duke of Grafton, First Lord of the Treasury, 1766–70, actually won the Derby three times. He did it with Tyrant (1802), Pope (1809) and Whalebone (1810) towards the end of his life. By that time he had become mildly eccentric, writing religious books. His sons ran the horses.

Grafton's earlier life had been more exciting. He resigned hastily from being George III's first minister when his relationship with Nancy Parsons (who was painted by Gainsborough), the daughter of a Bond Street tailor, became too notorious even for those times. He appeared with her at the opera and took her racing at Ascot and Newmarket. This attracted the attention of the pamphleteer Junius; however, Grafton's indolence in office more likely brought him down than his choice of companion.

Horace Walpole summed him up, saying Grafton believed 'the world should be postponed to a whore and a horse race'. Even so, Grafton's own knowledge of bloodstock is well attested. His elder son, who succeeded him, won the Derby with Whisker (1815), when not even Napoleon's activities before Waterloo interrupted more serious Epsom business.

Charles James Fox, who certainly thought he should be Prime Minister and was three times Foreign Secretary, had a Derby runner, Grey Diomed, which came fifth in 1788. Fox and his racing confederate, the second Lord Foley, owned Vermin, perhaps an unlucky second to Eager in 1791. Foley was said to have lost a million on cards and horses. His heir, the third baron, won the Derby with Paris in 1806, the year of Fox's death.

Fox was a better judge of a gamble than he was of a horse. Travelling on the continent with his mistress, Mrs Armistead, in the summer of 1787, he left no address and only opened a newspaper once to see how his bets had worked out. It was news to him when he found George III had been adjudged insane; he returned to London expecting to be Prime Minister. He was not asked.

Colonel Jonathan Peel, brother of Sir Robert Peel (twice Prime Minister) and himself MP for Huntingdon for thirty-seven years, won the Derby with Orlando in 1844 on Running Rein's disqualification (page 19). It was his hour of glory. He was commissioned in the army three days before Waterloo, but never saw active service in his life. He ended as a General and Secretary for War in two cabinets of the fourteenth Earl of Derby.

Derby himself, despite over twenty years' effort, never managed to win the race, although he won the Two Thousand Guineas, the One Thousand and the Oaks. The closest he came was with Toxophilite, the favourite in 1858. *Bell's Life in London* tipped Tox, as the punters called it, in rhyme:

> *I give the fruit of many an anxious night,*
> *My fixed opinion is – Toxophilite!*

Tox set off at 100–30 against, but Beadsman, a 10–1 chance, was more than a match for him. For half a dozen strides opposite the grandstand Toxophilite got to Beadsman's shoulder, but no further. He was beaten 'very easily' by a length. But the winning jockey, John Wells, weighed in light – it was a very hot day – and his bridle had to be brought and added to the scales before he passed. 'It was,' said *Bell's*, 'a moment of awful suspense for all parties'.

Derby was a classical scholar (he wrote a version of the Iliad) and could be a difficult man, as Disraeli found, especially with inferiors. When told that Charles Greville, clerk to the Privy Council, failed to attend Council meetings when he was Prime Minister, Derby replied: 'Is that the case? I had not observed it. When I order coals to be put on the fire, I do not notice whether it be John or Thomas who does it.' But he had a sense of humour ('Gladstone's jokes are no laughing matter') and he was a racing enthusiast, at his best with racecourse crowds. He often left the House of Lords to catch the night-mail train to John Scott's yard at Malton to see his horses at the gallops in the morning.

When telling the Jockey Club to warn off an owner, James Adkins, who fleeced a youth of £25,000 using loaded dice, he regretted in *The Times* that an increasing number of horses in training were 'in the hands of persons in an inferior position who keep them not for the purposes of sport but for the purposes of

'The Stock Exchange out for the Day.' Cartoon by John Leech from PUNCH, 1847.
Jones: 'I say, Brown, things are deuced bad in the City!'
Brown: 'Then I'm deuced glad I'm at Epsom.'

gambling'. He sold his stud and left the turf, a disappointed man, in 1863.

Lord Palmerston, Prime Minister, 1855–8 and 1859–65, kept horses in training most of his life, although usually racing them at small meetings and seldom going himself, except in his own constituency, Tiverton. His Derby chance, when he was Prime Minister, was in 1860. His Mainstone, a bay colt trained by John Day at Danebury, was for a time third favourite. But Mainstone's chance seemed to disappear when he suffered an enlargement of a joint; training was interrupted and his odds went out to 40–1. Palmerston, still hopeful, met Derby in the Epsom paddock on the Wednesday afternoon. The rival party leaders' conversation was overhead.

They had something to talk about. There had just been a series of votes in the Lords in which the Tory peers, led by Derby, had inflicted five defeats on Palmerston's efforts to repeal the excise duties on paper. The Tories were intent on keeping these duties which prevented the expansion of a cheap popular press.

After cordially shaking hands and passing the ordinary compliments, Lord Palmerston asked Lord Derby if he expected to win today with Cape Flyaway, to which Lord Derby replied in the negative, adding that he had 'done pretty well lately, having won five times out of six'.

To this Lord Palmerston rejoined:

'Yes, and you cannot expect to win on Mondays and Wednesdays too!' Lord Derby: 'No, but I expect you would rather win on the Wednesday!'

So they passed the time. Besides being a political Derby it was also an early international one, with Comte Frédéric de Lagrange's Dango, bred in France, and the American Richard Ten Broeck's Umpire both running. The race was won by none of them. Thormanby did it, with the French horse fourth, just ahead of the American, with Palmerston's and Derby's nowhere. *Bell's* did not waste much sympathy on the politicians' trouncing (though Palmerston was very disappointed), but it was not unhappy at Umpire's defeat either:

For the present his hollow defeat must silence the boastings and expose the ignorance of American sporting writers, whose 'bunkum' respecting 'Our horses in England' that has appeared week after week in the New York prints, must have been most distasteful to Mr Ten Broeck.

As for Palmerston, his big race victories remained the Cesarewitch and the Ascot Stakes.

Lord Randolph Churchill and his son, Winston, both tried their luck racing – when their great days in politics were over. When, impetuously, Lord Randolph resigned as Chancellor of the Exchequer and Leader of the Commons in 1886, he began buying yearlings and boasting about his inevitable success: 'Nearly all you people who go racing are fools, and no really clever man has ever taken it up seriously, but now that I have done so I shall succeed.' That was his style. He won the Oaks and other races with a good filly, L'Abbesse de Jouarre. As he was more and more deserted by his former political friends, he was happy to find her remembering him, trying to put her nose into his pocket for sugar and apples. Tears rolled down his cheeks. But the Derby eluded him.

Winston Churchill had some useful horses picked out for him by the Epsom trainer, Walter Nightingall, after the Second World War; it did no harm with the betting voters. Churchill's grey three-year-old Colonist II won three minor races in 1949, and then six in 1950 and two stakes at Hurst Park in 1951. He was the sire of the steeplechaser, Stalbridge Colonist, which once defeated the great Arkle.

Churchill's one chance of the Derby was in 1960 when his colt, Vienna, had its supporters, but the colt's foot was pricked by the blacksmith when being plated and had to be withdrawn. Vienna did run in the St Leger and came third, behind St Paddy (the Derby winner) and Die Hard. Vienna then went on to sire Vaguely Noble, so backward when a foal that his trainer did not think of entering him for the Derby but who won the Arc de Triomphe (beating Sir Ivor) in 1968. Also bred at Churchill's Newchapel Stud, near Lingfield, was High Hat, who once beat Petite Etoile herself at Kempton Park. The Derby has yet to be won by a great politician.

The Unluckiest Colt

The 1913 Derby had no equal – which was just as well. The horse that was favourite and first past the post was disqualified by the stewards although, as only two of them took the decision, officially there was no quorum. The second horse, Aboyeur, which was placed first, started at 100–1 against and never won again. In many spectators' minds he was the real culprit for the bumping in the race in the final furlong; his jockey and owner did not object to the first horse.

King George V's colt, at the back of the field, was brought down by a militant suffragette, demonstrating for women's votes. She died from her injuries. The official winner was sold quickly to the Imperial Racing Club of St Petersburg and was, it was said, seized by a White Russian officer in the revolution and subsequently died in the fighting with the Bolsheviks.

Aboyeur was a difficult, even a savage, horse, who had passed from owner to owner. But his fourth owner, Percy Cunliffe, saw promise in him and began betting on him in the winter. No one else saw ability but Cunliffe, a leading member of what was called the Druid's Lodge Confederacy, was used to going his own

way and backing his own judgement. He put £500 on each way on the morning of the Derby.

Craganour, the favourite, had everything going for him except, it seemed, luck. He appeared to have won the Two Thousand Guineas at Newmarket by a length at least, but the judge managed not to notice him and eventually placed him second. There were no photograph finishes in those days, and the judge's word was law. The American jockey Tod Sloan always believed the judge's box at Newmarket was set so low that it was almost impossible to judge a finish correctly. It happened that Craganour finished on the other side of the course from the official winner, Louvois. But Louvois's own trainer was heard to say that the judge had been wrong.

Others said that Craganour's jockey, William Saxby, had not ridden the horse out for some reason. In the two colts' next race Saxby was replaced by the American, Danny Maher, and Craganour beat Louvois by more than three lengths over ten furlongs. It seemed an injustice had been righted. But there was bad blood about. The senior steward at the Two

Thousand Guineas had been Major Eustace Loder, who had no time for Craganour's owner, C. Bower Ismay.

Ismay's family controlled the White Star line, the owner of the *Titanic* which had sunk with great loss of life the previous year. Ismay's elder brother, Bruce Ismay, the chairman of the company, had been rescued from the *Titanic* when 1500 died; he was given a hard time by the inquiry set up by the United States Senate and by the Hearst press, which openly accused him of cowardice. Although the later British inquiry exonerated him, there was a shadow across the family's reputation.

The two brothers were close. In 1900 Bower Ismay married the sister of Bruce Ismay's wife, both daughters of George R. Schiefflin of New York. Feelings ran high about them. Though nothing was said openly, even Bower Ismay was anathema to a certain type of Englishman; he was from a family in trade, with an American wife and a brother who had let the side down.

Besides that, Bower Ismay was believed to have had an affair with Loder's sister-in-law. It was noticed that Loder had not dissented from the Newmarket judge's inability to see Craganour, and Loder was senior steward at Epsom as well. Loder had a high reputation. He had earned the name of 'Lucky Loder' as the owner of Pretty Polly, winner of the One Thousand Guineas, Oaks and St Leger in 1904. He had then gone on to win the Derby with Spearmint in 1906 (Spearmint had cost him only 300 guineas). But Loder, of all people, was only too well aware that he had actually bred Craganour – and had sold him and his dam, a half-sister to Pretty Polly, because he did not think they were worth keeping. Whenever Loder was congratulated about Craganour's promise, his feelings may be imagined.

Ismay would have liked the honest Maher to ride Craganour in the Derby, but Maher was retained by Lord Rosebery; though Rosebery was willing to release him, Maher insisted on honouring the retainer. Craganour's trainer, Jack Robinson, then promptly sent to France for another American, Johnny Reiff, whose reputation was for riding determined finishes.

All this meant that Craganour and his owner had no reason to expect sympathy from the Derby officials, or from the unhappy English jockeys, like Saxby who was to ride Louvois, who resented being passed over for an American from Paris. The ill-tempered Aboyeur, given to biting lumps out of anything that displeased him, was going to be a factor; he had been steadily backed by a man who lived by coups. It promised to be a rough afternoon.

The other surprise factor was Miss Emily Davison. She was an Oxford graduate and, for seven years, had devoted herself to the cause of women's suffrage. She

Miss Emily Davison, a suffragette, threw herself in front of the King's horse, Anmer, near Tattenham Corner, during the 1913 Derby; she died of her injuries four days later.

had gone to prison nine times for her demonstrations, had been found hiding in the House of Commons three times, and had won release from prison three times by hunger-striking. She was a clever and determined woman. She went down by train to Tattenham Corner station, buying a return ticket. Although she had staged what appeared to be suicide attempts in prison, she had not come to real harm there; buying a return ticket was later held to show that she did not plan to come to grief at the Derby.

The King's horse, Anmer, had only two others behind him as the field began to come down the hill to Tattenham Corner. Miss Davison was waiting just inside the rail, with the suffragette colours inside her coat, and it has been thought wholly improbable that she had any idea of the particular runners passing her or that she could pick out the royal horse. It seemed to onlookers that her first lunge was actually at Aboyeur. By the time the early leaders had passed she was out in the middle of the course. She raised her arms and tried to snatch at Anmer's bridle. The horse sent her flying.

But Anmer fell himself and his jockey, Herbert Jones, was concussed and received fractured ribs. Miss Davison lay unconscious; she was taken to Epsom cottage hospital in a coma and died there of a fractured skull four days later. An early newsreel film showed the Derby scene to audiences in London. Miss Davison's middle-class friends and sympathisers naturally ensured that her death, her sacrifice as they put it, was widely remembered.

So the belief remained for years that she had meant to bring the royal horse down, but her true plans are uncertain. She left no suicide note. She was certainly intent on publicity, but she got minimal public sympathy, except from her devotees; the royal reaction was to find out first what had happened to the royal jockey. For her it was probably an unintended martyrdom.

Up ahead, in front of the grandstand, other curious things were happening fast. Aboyeur had been at the front for most of the race and his jockey, the little-known Edwin Piper, had sensibly kept him on the rails. Reiff then made his challenge with Craganour. Aboyeur had not seen another horse until then, and promptly lunged to savage this rival. Reiff was not the man to flinch. He kept at Craganour, apparently determined to do to Aboyeur what Aboyeur was plainly intent on doing himself.

In the scrimmage Craganour jumped towards Aboyeur and just got his head in front. In fact, four horses finished almost together, with two more only a stride behind. For the judge it was the most difficult of all decisions. He put Craganour ahead by a head and a neck from Aboyeur and Louvois.

At first, that seemed to be that. There were no immediate dissentients. Most of the jockeys in the finish knew they had been guilty of rough riding when it mattered; they feared disqualification and were not inclined to object. Piper, Aboyeur's jockey, told his owner there were no grounds for any objection. Even so Loder, descending from the stands, expected one and told a friend that Craganour 'has not won it yet'. The clerk of the scales, however, understood there was no objection and gave the instruction that the winner was 'all right'; the flag was hoisted, to the delight of the favourite's backers.

Still, Loder had only begun. He called for an inquiry himself and the flag was lowered after being up, it was said, for five minutes. Loder insisted that Craganour had jostled Aboyeur. This needed a stewards' adjudication but there happened to be only two stewards to make it. Rosebery, even though his horse had been unplaced, insisted that he had an interest and should take no part. Even so, he stayed in the stewards' room, heard the evidence and said afterwards that he agreed with the official decision. His silence actually meant there was no quorum, but no one apparently noticed.

Loder's chief witnesses were, naturally, the jockeys who were not well disposed towards Reiff and Craganour and, if there was to be blame, knew precisely where to direct it. The same judge, who had not spotted Craganour winning the Two Thousand Guineas, now turned out to be equally reluctant to let him have the Derby if he could avoid it. The accounts all made out that Reiff was in the wrong.

The verdict was that Craganour had bumped and bored Aboyeur and had interfered with other horses too, and was therefore disqualified. The bookies who had begun to pay out on the favourite leapt at the idea of a 100–1 outsider winning. Big sweepstake fortunes quickly changed hands. Ismay thought to appeal, but changed his mind. He gladly sold Craganour, so unlucky a horse, to Argentina for £30,000. Aboyeur, having given his owner a coup, was sold to the Imperial Racing Club of St Petersburg for a mere £13,000.

The Jockey Club tried to maintain the impression that normality had returned. But the expression 'all right' which had helped to cause confusion after the race was subsequently dropped from English racing (it continues in Ireland) to ensure that the Epsom clerk of the scales's initiative would not be easily repeated.

Loder was soon dead. His friends blamed the controversy; others said he had kidney trouble and a weak heart which might have clouded his judgement in any event. Bower Ismay was an unlucky man himself. He had run horses in the Grand National since 1905 and two of them, Jacobus (1915) and Bloodstone (1912) finished second. He liked hunting, often going out with the Pytchley, and big-game shooting in East Africa and the Sudan. He joined up at the outset of the First World War and went to France with the 12th Lancers; he survived. He took his misfortune in 1913 resignedly. He died in 1924. The winning jockey, Piper, died in obscurity in Epsom as late as 1951.

As for Aboyeur, conflicting legends grew up about his end. One story said he was last seen in Serbia after the Russian revolution; another had it his groom walked him all the way from St Petersburg south to the Crimea, hoping to find a ship to escape to England. But there one of the White General Denikin's officers took him for a cavalry mount. Whatever Aboyeur did to the Red Army, he had had a go at a few English horses in his day.

Come on, Steve!

Steve Donoghue, the idol of the 1920s, was a great Epsom rider with the same skills, instinct and determination as Fred Archer and Lester Piggott. He had six Derby winners (although two were at Newmarket in wartime). He understood Epsom and its demands; it had no problems, he once said, for someone who had served an apprenticeship in the French Midi. He spared nobody when cajoling owners to let him ride a good Derby horse, and he spared no owner in breaking any contract if another stable had a better prospect. So he won three Derbys in succession and four in five years. But owners and trainers did not forget or forgive, and Donoghue might have had even more Derby winners if his loyalties had been stronger.

Donoghue, though, was quicksilver. He enjoyed celebrity; he liked hearing the crowds shout 'Come on, Steve.' He dreaded becoming a trainer and not hearing the cry. He betted heavily, as Archer did. When the big wins stopped, bankruptcy advanced. He was affable, generous and revelled in the headlines and bright lights. Anything show business offered, he took. He was one of the first jockeys who liked flying to his meetings (despite one appalling crash) and the acclaim it brought. And, the classics apart, he had the good fortune to ride two great horses: The Tetrarch, scratched from the 1914 Derby, and Brown Jack, the indestructible champion hurdler who made

Steve Donoghue, Derby winner six times, and to be ranked with Fred Archer, Gordon Richards and Lester Piggott.

1921. Humorist and twenty-two other horses start the race.
Humorist died the same month he won The Derby.
    'He takes his rest on the further shore
    with Hermit and Ormonde and Galtee More
    Death called him forth in the pride of his power
    But he blazed his name on one splendid hour'

Royal Ascot's Queen Alexandra Stakes his own, winning it six times.

Donoghue was champion jockey ten times (four of them during the First World War). He had good hands, a sharp eye for an opening, and gave the stewards no trouble. The Epsom crowds loved him for his dash and courage. In 1920 his mount was brought down by another horse and most of the field seemed to run over him. He was concussed, but rose and walked away. He then went out and rode a winner and a dead-heat in the last two races.

In 1921 Donoghue was intent on riding Humorist, owned by Jack Joel who had made his fortune in South Africa. Humorist had flopped badly in the Two Thousand Guineas and was an unaccountable colt, but Donoghue thought him a better prospect than Glorioso, owned by Lord Derby, who retained Donoghue and expected him to honour his contract. Badgered and reluctant, Derby released Donoghue but stipulated that it would not happen again.

Humorist came down to Tattenham Corner on the rail, was pushed into the lead and held on to win by a short head at 6–1. The horse was exhausted after the race and was given no duties except posing for his portrait by the artist Alfred (later Sir Alfred) Munnings. After a champagne lunch, Munnings was woken to be told that Humorist was dead; he had had a major haemorrhage in his box. He was found to have suffered from consumption, both an explanation for his varying form and a measure of his courage in getting home at Epsom.

Next year, after more bargaining and drama, Donoghue got the ride on Captain Cuttle, owned by the whisky baron Lord Woolavington and trained by Fred Darling. Captain Cuttle lost a plate in the paddock and the blacksmith had an urgent job to do, but it was not a difficult victory (at 10–1) although Donoghue said afterwards he was sore with the effort of keeping so big a horse balanced round the curves and turns of the course. It was the first of two Derby victories for Woolavington (Coronach in 1926 was the other). For Donoghue it was just the start of his search for a third Derby winner in a row.

His choice fell on Papyrus, a colt owned by Ben Irish who ran a hotel in Peterborough and was flattered to have Donoghue riding for him. But Woolavington was forthright; he would never employ Donoghue again. Papyrus (100–15) duly won by a length, but he was beaten in the St Leger and again, in an Anglo-American challenge, at Belmont, where he could not cope with the dirt track which heavy rain had turned into a mudbath. Next year at Epsom torrential rain turned the course into a quagmire in which Lord Derby's Sansovino ended the family's 137 years of bad luck. Donoghue was not offered the ride.

In 1925, though, he had his fourth success – on Manna, a small colt but a game one on another wet day (it was a bad decade for Derby weather), winning at 9–1 by eight lengths. Donoghue had ridden with a moneylender's writ, handed to him in the paddock, in his breeches. It was over a loan that Donoghue had merely guaranteed, but his own finances were always shaky and in the coming years, as the good rides dried up and young jockeys like Gordon Richards and Charlie Smirke took the headlines, he lived from pillar to post financially. His betting debts mounted and in 1929 he was declared bankrupt.

But he was never a quitter. He found a new patron, Sir Victor Sassoon, who had made his money in India and had ambitions for the classics (although he had to wait until 1953 for the first of his four Derby victories). The housewives and other once-a-year punters who had put their shillings on Donoghue with routine trust found he was no longer a Derby talisman but, as late as 1937, when he was fifty-two, he won the Oaks at Epsom on Exhibitionist. He retired reluctantly, and the Second World War ended whatever chance he might have had to show his talent as a trainer. He died in 1945.

Lionel Edwards records the 1923 Derby finish when Steve Donoghue on Papyrus beats Pharos and Parth. This was the year of the first radio coverage at Epsom.

[63]

The Aga Khan and Family

The racing ambitions of the third Aga Khan made him, in his day and way, a pioneer of the international game. Sultan Sir Mohammed Shah, descendant in the direct line from the Prophet and forty-eighth head of the Ismaili sect of the Shia Moslem community, won the Derby five times. His successes included those of Bahram, triple-crown winner in 1935, and Mahmoud, whose official time of 2min. 33.8sec. in 1936 (recorded by stopwatch) is still the fastest. The Aga's bulky figure, equipped with heavy glasses and baggy umbrella, leading his horses in to the winner's circle, was a familiar photograph on the front pages. An astute and realistic man, he conducted his racing strictly as a business. This cost him admirers.

The Aga was as recognizable at the League of Nations between the wars as he was at Epsom. He had been a moderating Moslem influence in Indian affairs, urged full cooperation with the Allies in the First World War, and took a leading part in the regular disarmament talks at Geneva. He met Hitler when president of the League Assembly, supported the Munich appeasement in 1938 and spent the war in Switzerland when Hitler overran France in 1940. His political credit much diminished, he still enjoyed celebrating his diamond and platinum jubilees in 1946 and 1954, being weighed against precious stones donated by enthusiastic followers.

When the Aga went into racing and breeding in the 1920s he did so spectacularly in both England and France, buying fillies of the calibre of Terasina, Cos and Mumtaz Mahal who were to be strong influences on European bloodstock. When he died in 1957 he owned five studs in Ireland and four in France, in partnership with his son, Prince Aly Khan. The Aga had firm views about what he wanted and how to get it, and switched his trainers (apart from the incomparable Frank Butters, who trained for him, 1931–49) whenever he wanted. Dissatisfied with English prize money, he moved all his horses to France in 1954. He actively disliked bookmakers.

His first Derby winner was Blenheim, ridden by Harry Wragg, at 18–1 – although his Rustam Pasha was

Above: Mahmoud, the Aga Khan's second string in 1936, still holds the Derby record hand-time, 35.11 m.p.h., over Epsom's 1½-mile course on going described as 'extremely firm'.

better fancied – in 1930. (The Aga did not stint in his entries.) Blenheim strained a tendon and never ran again. The Aga quarrelled with Dick Dawson, his trainer, in 1931 and then found in Butters a man he both respected and who brought him all the success and acclaim he looked for. Butters represented old-fashioned virtues: all his horses were expected to run for their lives.

The most successful was Bahram whom his owner bred and who won the triple crown in 1935 in the easy style of a true champion. He started at Epsom at odds of 5–4. His winnings that year amounted to £43,086, a remarkable total for the time. The Aga, leading the owners' table, won only another £3000 from all his other horses put together. Bahram was the first triple-crown winner (apart from the First World War years) since Rock Sand in 1903; and there was not to be another until Nijinsky in 1970. Butters considered him the best horse he trained. Bahram might have had a highly successful career as a four-year-old, but it was never the Aga's way to take the chance; the horse was promptly sent to stud after the St Leger.

A successor was already in place for 1936. Mahmoud, a smallish, greyish colt, sired by Blenheim, was only just beaten in the Two Thousand Guineas and he won the Derby, ridden by Charlie Smirke, at 100–8 in the record time that still stands. Mahmoud never won another race and his denigrators count him statistically lucky on two grounds. His record was hand-timed by stopwatch, whereas later potential record-breakers are electrically timed. In 1936, too, the course was exceptionally hard and did not have the good covering of grass that modern groundsmen's expertise provides. Kahyasi (owned by the present Aga Khan), who was returned at 2min. 33.84sec. in 1988, has a good claim to be the true record-holder.

When the Second World War came the Aga was said to have taken a poor view of it and sold all three of his Derby winners to the United States in 1940, attracting much-publicized odium to himself. Blenheim and Mahmoud were popular with American breeders, but Bahram, sold for £40,000, was soon sold on to Argentina. English breeders were vitriolic at the loss of such important bloodstock and the popular memory that the Aga had said he would never sell Bahram was long-lived. When, in quieter times, he wrote to the papers about the sale of the country's best horses to America, Rosebery at once reminded him of his own transgressions.

The Aga's two post-war Derby winners, My Love and Tulyar, were not allowed four-year-old careers either. My Love (1948) was French trained and also won the Grand Prix de Paris. He stood at stud in France for five years and was then sent to Argentina. Tulyar (1952) started favourite at 11–2 and went on to win the Eclipse, King George VI and Queen Elizabeth Stakes, and the St Leger – after which he was promptly sold to the Irish National Stud for £250,000.

The Aga had become disenchanted with English racing, and it with him, when he died. But his record has not been surpassed. His five Derby wins are equalled only by those of Lord Egremont in the very early years; besides them, he won the St Leger five times, the Two Thousand Guineas three times, the Oaks twice and the One Thousand Guineas once. He won the Arc de Triomphe twice.

His son, Aly Khan, kept up the tradition and was the leading owner in both England (where he ran Petite Etoile) and France in 1959. Like his father, he was an international diplomat, being elected a vice-president of the United Nations Assembly. Also like his father, he pursued the family's ambitions in breeding, but it was his social reputation that was remembered when he died in a car crash near Paris in May 1960. It was Prince Aly's son, Karim, who succeeded the Aga Khan as spiritual leader of the Ismaili Shias; the young Aga's initial racing interests were in France, but he eventually sent horses to be trained in England in 1979 and success followed quickly.

One of the first yearlings which he sent to England, Shergar (11–10 on), ridden by Walter Swinburn and trained by Michael Stoute, won the 1981 Derby by a comfortable and record ten lengths; then, ridden by Piggott because Swinburn had been suspended, he also won the Irish Derby. But he was beaten in the St Leger and did not contest the Arc. This disappointing conclusion to his racing career still allowed Shergar to be valued at £10 million at stud at Ballymany, alongside the Curragh course. There, apparently for intended blackmail or IRA publicity, he was kidnapped. He was never found and the real criminals have never identified themselves. He left just thirty-six live off-spring and an enduring Derby mystery.

The Aga Khan leads in Shergar, ten lengths winner of the 1981 Derby, ridden by teenager Walter Swinburn Jr. Twenty months later, Shergar was stolen from Ballymany Stud – a mystery that remains unsolved.

THE AGA KHAN AND FAMILY

The Aga Khan then began to rival his grandfather's triumphs in rapid time, with Epsom successes by Shahrastani (1986), also ridden by Swinburn and trained by Stoute, at odds of 11–2, and by the speedy Kahyasi (1988), ridden by Ray Cochrane and trained by Luca Cumani, at 11–1. It was widely thought that Shahrastani, a good horse, was a lucky winner because the second, Dancing Brave, was closing inexorably in the last strides, having been left a lot to do. Dancing Brave had won the Two Thousand Guineas and later won the Arc. He had to be ridden in the knowledge that he might not get a mile and a half, but what happened at Epsom will always haunt his jockey, Greville Starkey.

Kahyasi had made a suspiciously slow start going up the hill on the far side of the course and, despite his finish and his time, the usual excuse was offered for the horses he beat: that they needed a galloping course to show their true merit. Kahyasi duly beat the Epsom second, Glacial Storm, even better at the Curragh than he did at Epsom, but that was his last success. He finished sixth in the Arc and was retired to stud at Ballymany. For the Aga, that has turned out to be his last Epsom Derby, unless he and the Jockey Club can ever bury, if not forget, their differences over the substances which were found in the disqualified winner of the 1989 Oaks, Aliysa. He is not a man accustomed to losing in such litigation.

Shahrastani and Walter Swinburn give the Aga Khan his second Derby victory in 1986. Second home is Dancing Brave, considered by many to be unlucky not to complete the 2000 Guineas/Derby double.

France's Champions

English and French rivalry at Epsom has been one of international racing's highlights ever since Comte Frédéric de Lagrange brought Gladiateur over to win the triple crown in 1865. Durbar II's victory in the 1914 Derby, just before the First World War, was another warning that English hegemony would not be permanent. In 1938 Bois Roussel (owned by Peter Beatty, son of the great admiral), French-bred and English-trained, also won at Epsom. But not even a chauvinist would have supposed then that seven horses, trained in France, would carry off the Derby riband in the nineteen years between 1947 and 1965, when the Epsom crowds grew almost reconciled to French superiority.

Colts of the calibre of Relko and Sea Bird II would have been outstanding in any generation, but the English press would never accept that a French jockey could master Epsom's contours. Even Yves St-Martin had his perennial critics, and only the Australian Rae Johnstone, who rode three Derby winners for French owners and so lived down an unhappy reputation he had earned in the 1930s on his first efforts in England, was grudgingly thought to pass muster. And there were times, indeed, when some French challengers were taken on curious routes along the downs.

The first postwar French success, by Baron G. de Waldner's Pearl Diver in 1947, did take Epsom by surprise, as his odds of 40–1 showed. English racing after the war had not recovered with the alacrity that the French had shown. But this had been concealed by insular successes in all the 1946 classics, and by the looming presence of the undefeated Tudor Minstrel, ridden by the celebrated Gordon Richards, whose triumph was taken for granted at 7–4 on. Seldom has there been a greater downfall.

Tudor Minstrel fought for his head from the paddock onwards and destroyed his own chances. Pearl Diver was not even extended in a smooth run, winning by four lengths. His jockey, George Bridgland, had been born in France of English parents, and, although he came to Britain when France fell in the Second World War, he returned there to ride and, later, train. He was one of the distinctive Anglo-French community at Chantilly, in which the Head family has been

prominent, who have made a particular contribution to trans-Channel racing.

Next year, 1948, the French came over in strength. The Derby winner, My Love, was ridden by Johnstone and trained by Richard Carver for the joint owners, the Aga Khan and Léon Volterra. Carver was British, though he had been born at Chantilly and had never been to Epsom before. He also trained the second horse, Royal Drake, for Volterra; My Love won the Grand Prix de Paris a month later. There were four French-bred colts in the first six at Epsom. English racing was mortified. Explanations were demanded.

The Jockey Club eventually came to the conclusion that too much emphasis had been placed for years on breeding fast two-year-olds, while the French had given greater priority to colts that would be able to go a mile and a quarter. It was an English predicament that could not be quickly remedied, and English racing stayed at a disadvantage until French owners decided to capitalize on the high prices in the American market and began selling their better stallions. English prize money, of course, steadily became less attractive to French challengers.

In 1949 there was a remission. The Derby was won by an English colt, Nimbus, ridden by Charlie Elliott, and owned by an Englishwoman, Mrs M. Glenister, whose husband had given her the horse as a birthday present. (He was a Midland bank official and it transpired that he was expertly defrauding it to raise the cash.) Volterra's colt, Amour Drake, was placed second in the first Derby photo-finish, but Johnstone was strongly criticized for switching Amour Drake to the inside in the last 100 yards; the colt only got his head in front two strides after the post. Volterra himself, who had been in bad health after his internment by the Germans in the war, was on his deathbed in Paris when the Derby was run; his wife could not bring herself to tell him that Amour Drake had lost.

The 1950 race went to another French colt, Galcador, ridden by Johnstone and owned by Marcel Boussac, the industrialist who had invested heavily in racing to become the most prominent figure on the French racing scene. This time it was the English jockey, Harry Carr, on the second, Prince Simon, who was blamed for riding a bad race, going to the front too early and then not pushing the horse hard enough. Galcador was not a distinguished winner; he never raced again and was sold to Japan. Boussac became the first French owner since the Comte de Lagrange to be the top winning owner and breeder in Britain.

The next French success came in 1955 when Mme Suzy Volterra's Phil Drake, bred by her late husband, moved uncannily in and out through his field from Tattenham Corner onwards and got up with a length and a half to spare. The jockey, Fred Palmer, was French, though his father was English. It was the first of the two Derby winners trained by the great François Mathet. Phil Drake had had his hour. He was unplaced in the King George VI and Queen Elizabeth and was not risked again after that.

Rae Johnstone's last Derby winner, Lavandin, in 1956, was trained by Alec Head but was not thought particularly impressive then or after, although he started the 7–1 favourite. He, too, was packed off to Japan. But if Lavandin had little to recommend him, the runner-up was also French and there was no English horse in the first three. Still, the tide was turning and French luck was momentarily running out. The French favourite, Angers, broke a leg in 1960 coming down the hill to Tattenham Corner and had to be destroyed. But if Psidium, the surprise winner in 1961, was English trained, he was French bred and ridden by Roger Poincelet.

Relko was the next French winner in 1963, trained by Mathet and ridden by St-Martin. He was a long-time favourite (5–1) and easily won by six lengths. An English colt was second, but was the only English horse in the first four. Nine weeks later, Relko was said by the Jockey Club to be one of a number of flat and jumping horses to have 'shown positive evidence of doping' after routine tests. A reward was offered but without result. Eventually, in October, the Jockey Club declared that the trainer and his employees had no case to answer. The handling of the affair did not please French opinion which felt its suspicions of English prejudice had been justified.

There could be no possible doubt about the pre-eminence of Sea Bird II in 1965. He was a tall chestnut with a white blaze and two white stockings and, although he was beaten once as a two-year-old, no one who saw his power of acceleration had any doubt of his

Sea Bird II, led in by his French owner Jean Ternynck after his 1965 Derby triumph, ridden by Australian Pat Glennon.

distinction. Trained by Etienne Pollet and ridden by the Irish jockey Pat Glennon, he started the 7–4 favourite at Epsom and won by two lengths. He won the Arc de Triomphe by six. Among his offspring was the superb filly, Allez France. Of all France's champions Sea Bird II deserves to be mentioned in the same breath as Gladiateur.

The most recent French-trained winner was Empery (10–1), owned by N. Bunker Hunt and trained by Maurice Zilber, in 1976. Empery, a Vaguely Noble colt, was not at all of Sea Bird's quality, but with Piggott riding he won well enough by three lengths from Relkino; Wollow, the favourite, another Derby non-stayer, was fifth. Bunker Hunt had decided to stay in Texas for his silver wedding anniversary, but his daughter Elizabeth led the winner in. Empery ran in the Irish Derby at the Curragh but came second to Malacate. The French have been quiescent lately, but ought never to be underestimated.

The Master of Epsom Downs

Lester Piggott's record at Epsom is unrivalled and is recorded in more detail elsewhere in this book. Nine Derby winners (and six in the Oaks) mean that no one else has ridden the course with his success. Willie Carson (three Derby winners), Pat Eddery (three) and Steve Cauthen (two) have some way to go before, collectively, they catch up with him. In his fifty-seven years Piggott has managed to be the bane of everyone but the punters, the people who go racing to see him and win with him. Jockey Club stewards who tried to discipline him in his youth, owners and trainers who called him disloyal, other riders who found themselves jocked off for him, and even the Customs and Excise and the Inland Revenue have all had their own ideas. Through it all he has gone his own way, seemingly detached from the rows around him, and even now, grey-haired, dryly quizzical and successful again, he is seldom confused with an elder statesman of the turf.

Piggott is of racing stock; his grandfather rode two winners of the Grand National. It is bred in his bones. He was brought up on nothing but racing; he was only twelve when he had his first winner at Haydock Park. His uncertain hearing (deaf to sounds of a high frequency) drove him in on his own resources and on his innate ability at riding, the one thing he did well. He liked money even when he was young; from this liking grew the caricature of meanness, which he encouraged. Youthful prodigies do not get an easy time in racing. Young Piggott had a way with horses, precocious skill and fearlessness; these he hardened with relentless determination into a lifelong pursuit of being first.

His first Derby ride was on Zucchero, unplaced in 1951. But the next year, when Piggott was sixteen, he rode Gay Time into second place, three-quarters of a length behind the winner, Tulyar – and young Piggott firmly believed that Tulyar had hampered him, so an objection would give him the race. Derby objections are discouraged, but that would not have held Piggott back if he had not been embarrassingly without his own horse.

Gay Time had slipped and fallen (dislodging Piggott) between the winning post and the paddock. He then cantered off through the Durdans stables, taking the saddle and weight cloth with him, and so avoided all capture. His jockey, whatever his intentions, could not weigh in. Gay Time kept on running for quite a distance until a lad working in another stable was surprised to see a sweating, riderless horse come trotting up to him in the middle of the afternoon. Not guessing that it had come from a tight finish in the Derby, the lad rode it slowly back to the racecourse where Piggott reclaimed it. An hour had nearly passed and, by that time, the idea of an objection had come to seem meaningless.

Two years later, in 1954, Piggott left nothing to chance, getting Never Say Die, a 33–1 outsider, past the post by two lengths. He was eighteen and the youngest winning jockey since proper records had been kept. Piggott was as cool and as imperturbable then as he was to be after all his Derby successes: nerves never cost him a race or an unnecessary word afterwards. Never Say Die was owned by Robert Sterling Clark who had quarrelled with the New York Jockey Club and had decided to run his horses in England. He was actually ill in New York on Derby day, but did see Never Say Die win the St Leger (he later presented the colt to the National Stud). But Piggott was not riding him then.

He had been suspended for the remainder of the season, having seriously displeased the Jockey Club stewards by forcing his and Never Say Die's way out of a melee of horses at Ascot a fortnight after the Derby. The stewards were determined to censure the young man. They disliked what they said was 'his dangerous and erratic riding both this season and in previous seasons, and that in spite of continuous warnings he continued to show complete disregard for the Rules of Racing and for the safety of other jockeys'. They said he must be attached to a trainer other than his father for six months; he was sent to Jack Jarvis, a trainer of the old school, but as Jarvis was ill for much of the time he may not have been too effective a disciplinarian. But Piggott, the complete professional, was not going to be caught wasting his own time again.

In 1957 Piggott kept Sir Victor Sassoon's Crepello, a big chestnut colt, perfectly balanced round Epsom to win by a length and a half on firm ground. Crepello, the 6–4 favourite, needed the firm ground he got early

Sir Victor Sassoon's Crepello gives Lester Piggott his second Derby winner in 1957.

that summer. He was the first Derby winner Piggott rode for the great postwar trainer, Sir Noel Murless. Three years later it was another Sassoon-Murless-Piggott success with St Paddy (7–1). St Paddy won other good races but may have been lucky that the French favourite, Angers, broke a fetlock and had to be destroyed.

In 1961 the trio was widely expected to have another winner in Pinturischio, but the colt was drugged twice by a bookmakers' gang who broke into Murless's stables at Warren Place. Although nursed back to health after the first attack, the colt could not race again after the second. Piggott was then offered the ride on Psidium, trained by Harry Wragg, but as Psidium was wholly unfancied (he started at 66–1) Piggott turned the idea down. Psidium duly won and never saw a racecourse again.

Trainer Noel Murless leads in St Paddy after his 1960 Derby victory – the third in Lester Piggott's career.

The day before the 1972 Derby. Lester Piggott exercises Roberto in front of the empty grandstand at Epsom.

Lester Piggott discusses tactics with Robert Sangster, in whose colours The Minstrel won the 1977 Derby.

Piggott had had his differences with Murless and in 1966 he severed the retainer to ride freelance in search of big race winners. (He thereby lost the chance of riding Royal Palace, the 1967 Derby winner.) Piggott's main new connection was with Vincent O'Brien, on the understanding that he would ride the Ballydoyle horses outside Ireland. In 1968 that meant Sir Ivor, the personification of the American thoroughbred, a bay colt with great speed (he won the Two Thousand Guineas) who needed a first-class jockey to dispel some doubts about his stamina. Piggott duly delayed his challenge until it seemed as if he could not catch the dour front-running Connaught, but Sir Ivor's acceleration decided things in the final furlong by a length and a half. Sir Ivor was the 5–4 on favourite. In the subsequent Washington International at Laurel, Piggott again nursed Sir Ivor to win by three-quarters of a length – and was roundly criticized by the American papers for not making it more conclusive.

Two years later it was Nijinsky (11–8), the greatest Northern Dancer colt to run at Epsom, that Piggott got home by two and a half lengths from the French stayer, Gyr. Nijinsky went on to become the latest (and possibly last) triple-crown winner – all three ridden by Piggott. But he was beaten by a head in the Arc de Triomphe by Sassafras. Nijinsky was not the peerless horse he had been at Epsom, but most of the blame was directed at Piggott for trying to make up too much ground in the relatively short straight at Longchamp. Though Piggott twice won the Arc on Alleged, he has not seemed as safe or as confident there as at Epsom.

His hardest Derby was in 1972. As horses he favoured failed to show the form he wanted, he was highly uncertain about just what he would ride at Epsom. Roberto, another American-bred in a lengthening series, was to be ridden by Bill Williamson, a stylish Australian, but Williamson injured a shoulder and Roberto's American owner, John Galbreath, doubted if he could ride a punishing, all-out finish. Piggott was asked, and promptly agreed, to take the ride. It was the forcefulness with which he got the tiring Roberto's head in front in the last stride that won the day (at 3–1). It was not a popular victory because the crowd sympathized with the jocked-off Williamson, and Roberto was not an impressive champion. It turned out he only ran well on left-handed courses.

Nor was Empery, the 10–1 winner in 1976, a particular adornment to the Derby's reputation. His only victory before Epsom had been in a newcomers' race for two-year-olds the previous September, and he did not win again after the Derby. But Empery stayed over the course on the day that mattered and won by three lengths. The next year's hope from the Sangster-O'Brien syndicate was a tough, if smallish, colt, The Minstrel (5–1), who had a hard race before getting up by a neck. The Minstrel's courage and all Piggott's vigour were needed. Six years later, in 1983, Eric Moller's Teenoso, trained by Geoff Wragg, happened in a wet year to have endless stamina in soft going and had no difficulty in winning (9–2) by three lengths. He was Piggott's ninth winner in his first thirty Derby rides. Piggott himself was forty-seven.

No further Derby success has followed, either before or since his brief decision to retire in 1986, followed by his incarceration at Highpoint open prison in Suffolk for tax fraud. But his return to riding, and his impressive results, have put him back among the challengers again. His 1992 Two Thousand Guineas winner, Rodrigo de Triano, was not expected to stay the Derby's one and a half miles, yet such was Piggott's name and his reputation for getting speedy colts past the post, whatever the odds, that Rodrigo started the 13–2 favourite. He finished nowhere, but to many people it was fitting that the Lester they were used to backing – always essential in the Derby story – should be riding again, standing up in his stirrups and with his backside higher than everyone else's, above the downs that had seen his greatest triumphs.

A favourite that didn't win the 1992 Derby. Lester Piggott exercises Rodrigo de Triano before the race.

Irish Legends

Irish challengers are an essential, and often successful, element in the English Derby, just as many Epsom winners go over to the Curragh and complete the highly profitable double for their owners. But despite Epsom's long history it was not until as late as 1907 that Orby, owned by the expatriate American politician, Richard Croker, and ridden by another American, Johnny Reiff, became the first Irish-trained colt to win the Derby; he went on to win at the Curragh at 10–1 on. In those days Irish-bred horses had already begun to make a big impact on the flat in England. Two that did so in the Derby were Galtee More (1897), a triple-crown winner, and Ard Patrick (1902) who defeated the legendary filly, Sceptre, both bred by their owner, John Gubbins, at Bruree in the Golden Vale of Limerick. Even then, however, the first Irish trainer to dominate Epsom did not turn to flat racing until the late 1950s, and he did it with a succession of American-bred colts of high calibre. He was Vincent O'Brien, of County Tipperary, who had already conquered everything in sight over the jumps.

O'Brien has trained six Derby winners on his gallops at Ballydoyle, and he would have had a seventh in 1984 had his favourite, El Gran Senor, not been beaten by Secreto, trained by his son David next door. O'Brien's known success, his expanding reputation in America and his sheer perfectionism, built his establishment at Ballydoyle into one of the most formidable in the world. First among trainers in the British Isles he grasped the value of a major American connection; he also understood that his horses must be prepared to travel to be in the big league and air transport had opened the way.

O'Brien's first big venture in the style he made his own was by buying a group of yearlings at Doncaster for an American owner, John McShain, a building contractor from Philadelphia, and then persuading him to let them be trained at Ballydoyle. One of them was Ballymoss, a fine horse except on soft going, which went on to win the Irish Derby, the English St Leger and the French Arc de Triomphe; but starting at 33–1 on Derby day in 1957 he was beaten by Crepello. Still, by winning the St Leger, Ballymoss became the first Irish colt to take an English classic since Orby.

Next year an Irish trainer did saddle an Epsom Derby winner, but it was not O'Brien. It was Mick Rogers (who trained at the Curragh) who won it with Hard Ridden whose owner, Sir Victor Sassoon, thus had two Derby winners in succession; Rogers did it again in 1964 with Santa Claus. O'Brien's turn came in 1962. His colt Larkspur was sired by the American, Never Say Die, which had won the Derby in 1954. Larkspur was a capable, staying colt but was not greatly thought of. The idea of winning the Derby had attracted the American Ambassador to Dublin, Raymond Guest, a great owner of steeplechasers (he won four Cheltenham Gold Cups and three Grand Nationals). Larkspur was bought expensively to justify his enthusiasm, but the stable jockey, Pat Glennon, refused the ride and it took all Guest's confidence to keep up Ballydoyle's morale.

Larkspur was both game and lucky. Seven horses fell coming down the hill to Tattenham Corner, including the favourite, Hethersett. The Epsom stewards reported afterwards that too many beaten horses were already falling back; one horse, Romulus, was brought down in the scrimmage, and the other six fell over him. No one was blamed, except the owners and trainers who allowed horses 'not up to classic standard' to start at all. Larkspur's jockey, the Australian Neville Sellwood, was able to pull his mount away from the rails, jump over Hethersett's upturned legs, and get out of trouble. He won by two lengths at 22–1. The doubts about the Derby's quality were reinforced by Larkspur's subsequent record. He failed both at the Curragh and in the St Leger, where Hethersett beat him easily. But it was only the opening of two O'Brien decades.

His winner in 1968 was one of his greatest horses, Sir Ivor, also owned by Raymond Guest. Sir Ivor was American-bred, a calm, tough horse with especially good acceleration. Everyone who handled him remembered how untemperamental he was; and if any horse liked flying, he did. He was a brilliant two-year-old and, in the Two Thousand Guineas, ridden by Piggott, he had no trouble in beating a good field. But there was doubt, as so often at Epsom, about his ability to stay a mile and a half. He actually started at 5–4 on, and Piggott justified the odds by exceptional race-riding,

Vincent O'Brien, the Irish trainer of six Derby winners, at home at Ballydoyle with Lester Piggott.

holding the colt up until it seemed to be too late to overtake the sturdy Connaught. Then Piggott showed Sir Ivor's class and his own within a decisive furlong – a finish to live in the memory. It proved to be Sir Ivor's limit. He was beaten at the Curragh and his only other victory at a mile and a half was in the Washington International at Laurel Park, Maryland, where the tight corners helped to preserve his stamina in heavy going.

Two years later it was Nijinsky's turn at Epsom. Nijinsky, a Northern Dancer colt bred by E.P. Taylor in Canada, was an outstanding horse, although difficult and temperamental when he chose. He has been the only horse since Bahram in 1935 to win the English triple crown and, as his own experience suggested, the number of important races that now clash with the St Leger suggests that he may not have too many successors. The discovery of Nijinsky was a combination of chance and judgement. O'Brien had been urged by Charles Engelhard to go to Taylor's Windfields Farm to look over a Ribot colt, but the one that impressed him was by Northern Dancer, then little known as a sire. Engelhard was persuaded to buy.

Nijinsky's career was sharply divided. He was unbeaten as a two-year-old. He won the Derby comfortably by two and a half lengths at 11–8. He then won the King George VI and Queen Elizabeth Stakes easily. It seemed as if his career would be an uninterrupted success. But in August he had a bad attack of ringworm which made much of his hair fall out. It was difficult to train him and, although he won the St Leger, it may have taken more out of him than an ordinary preparation for the Arc de Triomphe. Again, Piggott may have left him too much to do at Longchamp. But he lost both there and in the Champion Stakes at Newmarket, when he was seen to be trembling with nerves before going down to the start. It was a doleful end.

The O'Brien horse in 1972 was Roberto, bred by his owner, John Galbreath, the owner of the Pittsburgh Pirates, in the bluegrass country. Roberto was not quite among the top class of O'Brien horses. He disliked right-handed courses, he hated soft going, and he was thought to be lazy at home. Once again Piggott could not be sure that he would go the distance, and once again Piggott made sure the horse did. He rode at his most forceful to win in a photo finish and survive an

inquiry. The starting odds were 3–1. The victory was heard in near-silence because Galbreath had insisted on removing the Australian jockey, Bill Williamson, from the ride because he thought Williamson was still unfit after falling ten days before at Kempton Park. The crowd gave Williamson a hero's welcome when he rode the winner of the Woodcote Stakes, the next race after the Derby. Roberto was greatly underestimated and was allowed to start at long odds in the Benson and Hedges Gold Cup at York. It was a left-handed track like Epsom; the jockey was the Panamanian Braulio Baeza, imported from the United States; and it was a record time. The horse Roberto beat was the incomparable Brigadier Gerard, then still undefeated.

In 1977 O'Brien had another Northern Dancer colt, The Minstrel. This time the head of the syndicate was Robert Sangster, the football pools millionaire. The Minstrel was a small and compact horse, but he was of the right stuff: besides having Northern Dancer as his sire, his dam was a daughter of Nijinsky's dam. Even so, he had his detractors. It was said he was only a flashy chestnut, with a white face and four white stockings. It was supposed he would not have courage or stamina, but he proved to be remarkably tough and resilient.

Indeed, O'Brien worried about his temperament only once; he plugged The Minstrel's ears with cotton wool to shut out the noise of the Epsom crowd in the parade before the start. The Minstrel was just in front at the finish, after another hard ride by Piggott. The odds were 5–1. He won the King George VI and Queen Elizabeth by inches after another severe race, and, though he seemed none the worse for either outing, he was quickly shipped back to the United States before the authorities there could impose an import ban because of an outbreak of equine metritis in Europe.

Golden Fleece in 1982 was a Nijinsky colt, bought at Keeneland and big enough to be considered as a potential steeplechaser if he failed on the flat. The Sangster syndicate was again the owner, but Piggott had ended his riding commitment and the new jockey was Pat Eddery. Golden Fleece was, like his sire, highly strung (he was liable to claustrophobia if kept too long in his box) but had the same brilliant speed.

Putting a sheepskin noseband on him seemed to settle him at Epsom and although he coughed a few times

Golden Fleece, son of 1970 winner Nijinsky, wins at Epsom in 1982. Both were trained by Vincent O'Brien.

on the Derby's eve he was not faced with particularly strong competition. He went through his field effortlessly and won unchallenged in a fast time at 3–1. It was only his fourth race and it was naturally assumed he had a great future before him, but he never raced again. The cough developed into a cold, which stopped training for the Curragh, and then a swelling developed on a hind leg. As the weeks passed so did the big races he could have been expected to dominate. He was retired to stud in Ireland where, a year later, it was found he had contracted cancer. A brilliant career was cut short.

O'Brien's prospect in 1984 was El Gran Senor, sired by Northern Dancer, a placid and affectionate colt of great ability, the best two-year-old in Europe and an impressive winner of the Two Thousand Guineas. Another inevitable Epsom victory was forecast. But there were doubts about El Gran Senor's stamina, and one doubter was O'Brien's son, David, now training on his own. David O'Brien had in his yard Secreto, another Northern Dancer colt, who had been bought by Luigi Miglietti, a Venezuelan businessman. The rival O'Brien camps made their separate ways to Epsom, each with their own thoughts on tactics. El Gran Senor seemed to have everything within his grasp with two furlongs to go, but his finishing strength just failed him on the final rise. Secreto, starting at 14–1, was just inches ahead. The son had beaten the father.

There has been no subsequent Derby winner from Ballydoyle, and David O'Brien announced that he was quitting training in 1988. But the memories of Vincent O'Brien's achievement are part of Epsom's, and Irish, legend.

Sons of Northern Dancer separated by a short head in the 1984 Derby. Secreto (left) beats the favourite, El Gran Senor.

The Arab Impact

The Arab impact on British racing made a delayed, but definite, impression on the Derby at the end of the 1980s. It was a revolution. For two decades the winning owners had been easily identified. They included familiar American anglophiles like Charles Engelhard (Nijinsky) and Paul Mellon (Mill Reef), such aristocrats as Lord Halifax (Shirley Heights) and Lord Howard de Walden (Slip Anchor), and continental Europeans like Dr Carlo Vittadini (Grundy) and Mme Armand Plesch (Henbit). Winners also included, of course, horses from the dominant stables of the Aga Khan (Shergar, Shahrastani and Kahyasi) and the Robert Sangster syndicate (The Minstrel, Golden Fleece). But, by 1989, Arab investment began to pay off in a spectacular way.

This was more than money talking. Sangster had found himself the underbidder at Keeneland and elsewhere, but the accumulation of expertise and experience the Arabs had organized, and their training and stud resources, were professional in their scope. The Maktoum brothers from Dubai, Crown Prince Khalid Abdulla of Saudi Arabia, and Fahd Salman (who had been racing in Britain since he was twelve) comprised a new group of rich, clever and powerful families with the same purpose as the aristocratic owners of the eighteenth century: to win the Derby. The competition

Above: Willie Carson on Nashwan led in by Sheikh Hamdan al Maktoum, followed by Sheikh Mohammed al Maktoum, as Epsom chairman, Sir Evelyn de Rothschild, applauds.

at Epsom, like English racing itself, would have been much the poorer without them.

In 1989 Sheik Hamdan Al-Maktoum, Dubai's finance minister, was the first to succeed with Nashwan (5–4 favourite), a Blushing Groom colt ridden by Willie Carson and trained by Major Dick Hern. The team of Hern and Carson was highly experienced and had won twice before, with Troy and Henbit, in successive years. Carson had been champion in five years. But they had had their downs as well as their ups: Carson had had crashing falls (especially in 1981 and 1984), and in 1989 Hern was still recovering from a fall in which he had broken his neck while out hunting in Leicestershire five years before. And in 1989 the Queen's advisors decided that Hern's lease of the royal stables at West Ilsley should not be renewed. So Carson's jubilant return to the winner's enclosure with Nashwan a five-length winner, and the grin with which Hern welcomed them from his wheelchair, had more than just a Derby Day significance.

Nashwan had an exceptional season by almost all standards. He won the Derby, the Two Thousand Guineas, the Eclipse and the King George VI and Queen Elizabeth Stakes. But he failed in a preparatory race for the Arc de Triomphe and was retired. Sheik Hamdan had declared that winning the Derby had been a lifetime's ambition; he had also wanted to go for the Arc instead of the easier St Leger (which Hern had hankered after) to establish Nashwan's reputation beyond any question. But the horse's pluck was not enough to beat the lesson of hard experience: after four big races at home English three-year-olds seldom manage to keep their best form, or even usual luck, by Arc time.

The next year, 1990, was Crown Prince Khalid Abdulla's turn with his Quest for Fame (7–1), ridden by Pat Eddery and trained by the youthful Roger Charlton. Mr Abdulla (as he likes to be called), a man as rich as he is modest, had a comfortable win with Quest for Fame, a Rainbow Quest colt, by a good three lengths. Racing's balance of power now seemed to have been decisively tipped in an Arab direction at the start of a new decade. And this seemed to be confirmed by the trouncing that Mr Fahd Salman's Generous (9–1) gave everything else in the 1991 Derby. Generous, ridden by the new hero Alan Munro and trained by Peter Cole at Whatcombe, beat the second and third by five

1989. A worms-eye view of Nashwan, achieving his owner's, Sheikh Hamdan al Maktoum, life-time ambition – winning The Derby – and giving trainer Dick Hern his third success.

1990. Mr K. Abdulla's Quest for Fame, ridden by Pat Eddery, wins the most valuable Derby yet – £355,000 first prize.

lengths and seven lengths in a conclusive performance. He was the second grandson of the great Nijinsky (Kahyasi was the first) to win the Derby. Marju, the second horse, was owned by Hamdan Al-Maktoum with the perky Carson riding. But not even Generous managed to take the Arc.

And in 1992 there were new and singular challengers to the Arabs, just as it seemed they were settling in. Dr Devious, an Ahonoora colt, had been sold twice (the first time by Robert Sangster), an unprepossessing distinction for a Derby winner, and had been given to Sidney H. Craig by his wife as a sixtieth birthday present. She had spent $2½ million on the colt to win the Kentucky Derby for him ('You must be mad,' her husband had said); Dr Devious was duly flown to Louisville, where he was unhappy with the dirt and failed, and then back to Peter Chapple-Hyam's stables at Marlborough. It was not an ideal preparation for Epsom, but Dr Devious was none the worse for it – and all future international champions will doubtless have to be bred to like flying, just as Victorians got used to trains.

Dr Devious's owner was unusual: he ran one of the biggest slimming companies in the United States. So was his trainer: Chapple-Hyam had trained for just two years. And so was his jockey: John Reid was sufficiently unfashionable to have ridden his only classic winner ten years before. But Dr Devious stayed in the race, the 8–1 second favourite, to win as a good colt should. Behind him he had a very considerable colt indeed. St Jovite, trained by Jim Bolger, the coming trainer in Ireland, went on to beat him by a dozen lengths in the Curragh Derby and to win the King George at Ascot by six. He was owned by Mrs Virginia Kraft Payson, an American sports publicist, who was sure the spirit of her dead husband helped St Jovite over the winning line.

Dr Devious and St Jovite fought out a ding-dong finish at Leopardstown, Dublin, in September, their warm-up race for the Arc de Triomphe. Dr Devious won by a nose but it was sufficiently tough a run to take the edge off both of them at Longchamp on 4 October. Derby winners, English and Irish, find the Arc a bit too late in the season for them.

Royal Runners

There was a royal runner in the first Derby in 1780 – a quickly forgotten one. George III's youngest brother, Prince Henry, Duke of Cumberland, ran an unnamed colt by Eclipse which did not distinguish itself. Cumberland was the black sheep of the family, readily attracted to married women, and his own marriage to a young widow, Ann Horton, though a successful one, was considered improper for a royal duke and prompted the passage of the Royal Marriage Act of 1772 which is still in force today. George III himself did not keep a racing stable but he liked racing (Queen Charlotte thought it 'a vulgar business') and he went to watch at Epsom from time to time.

None of Cumberland's four attempts at the Derby succeeded. Even so, his raffish influence was felt, chiefly because his nephew, the young Prince of Wales (later George IV), learned to drink, wench and gamble at Cumberland House and soon set up his own racing establishment. Cumberland had a colt, Fencer, in the first international Derby in 1784, when the Duc de Chartres entered a rival, Cantator. Both were beaten by Colonel O'Kelly's Sergeant. The Duc de Chartres came to a sticky end in the French Revolution: although he even changed his name to Philippe Egalité and voted for the execution of Louis XVI, his cousin, he himself went the way of all aristocrats.

Both the Prince of Wales and his brother, the Duke of York, took to racing in a big way. The Prince ran two colts in the 1786 Derby, and in 1788 his Sir Thomas (the middle-aged jockey William South wearing the royal colours, crimson with purple sleeves) came in first. Sir Thomas was the first odds-on winner and stayed in training for two more seasons without much success. But his name was safely in the record books.

The Prince gave up racing in a huff in 1791 when his jockey, Sam Chifney, was accused of pulling a royal horse at Newmarket to get better odds in its next race. He chose to stand by Chifney and was promptly told by the senior Jockey Club steward, Sir Charles Bunbury, that, if he did so, no gentleman would race against him again. Prinny returned to racing in 1805 when he was back at Epsom with Mrs Fitzherbert; but he never succeeded in the Derby again, though he tried right up to his death. His last effort was with Young Orion in

Eclipse, by George Stubbs, 1770. Foaled in 1764, the year of the great eclipse, he first won at Epsom in 1769 – 11 years before the first Derby Stakes. Unbeaten in 18 races, Eclipse became the sire of three Derby winners – Young Eclipse, Saltram and Sergeant, as well as the curiously named Pot-8-os, from whom are descended over 100 Derby winners

LE DERBY DE 1821 À EPSOM *by Theodore Géricault, who came to London in 1820 and was a source of inspiration to Dégas*

Previous page: The first Grand Stand on Epsom Downs, an engraving by Charles Hunt, after a painting by James Pollard, showing Mundig winning the 1835 Derby
Above: The 1835 winner, Mundig, the first of John Bowes's Derby winners, in a painting by J.F. Herring

Left: Cotherstone, John Bowes's second Derby winner, 1843, ridden by W. Scott. Painting by J.F. Herring

Above: The New Entrance to Epsom Grand Stand, 1846, after an original by Smyth

West Australian, Mr Bowes's fourth Derby winner, 1853, with trainer John Scott and jockey Frank Butler who rode him in all his races. Painting by Harry Hall

Andover, winner of the 1854 Derby, owned by ex-prize-fighter John Gully, trained by John Day and ridden by his son, Alfred. Engraving, from a painting by Harry Hall

Detail from DERBY DAY *by William Frith, 1857. The dejected Eton schoolboy is said to have been inspired by Harry Hastings. The game on the table is thimblerig; behind the Scotsman a sharper operates the three-card trick . . . 'the whole world is here'.*

THE COMING IN: *Smyth's engraving of the finish of the 1860 Derby, which was won by H. Custance on Thormanby*

DERBY DAY AT EPSOM DOWNS, *1863. Watercolour by T.C. Dibdin*

'THE DEMON'. *A cartoon by Spy, dated September 1882, depicts George Fordham in the Rothschild colours carried by the centenary Derby winner Sir Bevys, in 1879*

Overleaf: THE WEIGHING ROOM AT EPSOM, 1883, *by Isaac Cullin, also known as 'Pantaloon'*

Isaac Cullin

DERBY HEROES OF THE LAST TEN YEARS *by John Sturgess, 1889.*
The horses and jockeys are, above from left: F. Archer on Bend Or (1880), S. Loates on Harvester (1884), F. Archer on Melton (1885),
C. Wood on St Gatien (1884), G. Fordham on Sir Bevys (1879), F. Archer on Ormonde (1886). The 1884 race was a dead heat

Above, continuing from left: F. Archer on Iroquois (1881), T. Cannon on Shotover (1882), J. Watts on Merry Hampton (1887), F. Barrett on Ayrshire (1888), C. Wood on St Blaise (1883)

Lord Rosebery's three Derby winners,
painted by Emil Adam. Opposite above:
Ladas (1894); opposite below: Sir Visto
(1895); above: Cicero (1905)

Right: Hyperion, Lord Derby's 1933
winner. Sir Alfred Munnings described this
as 'my one really good portrait of a horse'

Derby Day on Epsom Downs, as seen by Raoul Dufy, 1930
(opposite above), A.E. Cooper, 1933 (opposite below) and
John Gilroy, 1968 (above)

Right: The Prince's Stand, built c. 1784 for the use of the Prince
of Wales, later George IV. Watercolour by Frank Ashley

Lester Piggott is the Derby's most successful
jockey, having won the race nine times between
1954 and 1983. His three most recent wins are
shown here: on Empery in 1976 (opposite above
left); on The Minstrel in 1977 (opposite, above
right and below); and on Teenoso in 1983 (above
and right)

Today Derby Day is one of the highlights of the fashionable social calendar

Above: The royal party inspecting the pre-race parade, 1992, showing Dr Devious, the eventual winner

Left: Queen Elizabeth The Queen Mother escorted in the Paddock by Sir Evelyn de Rothschild and Mr Tim Holland-Martin

Above: Queen's Stand, Epsom Downs, opened by Her Majesty The Queen on 3 June 1992
Left: Dr Devious and jockey John Reid victorious in 1992
Below: Dr Devious in Epsom's unique winner's circle, 1992

1830, when Priam won – Priam being owned and trained by Bill Chifney, the son of his old, disgraced jockey.

Prinny, now King George IV, was less than enamoured of Epsom in 1821 when his estranged and unappetising wife, Princess Caroline of Brunswick-Wolfenbüttel, took it into her head to go to the Derby to drum up support for her to be recognised and crowned with him at Westminster Abbey. She had ceased her gallivanting around Europe and wanted her rights. So she turned up at Epsom in her carriage with six horses in scarlet liveries, accompanied by Lord and Lady Hood. (He was with her when, eventually, George had her turned away weeping at the Abbey door.) To charm the customers on the downs she wore a Leghorn bonnet, 'with a few flowers gracefully inserted,' and a blue scarf across her shoulders. She 'returned the warm applause of the people by a graceful inclination of her head.'

She watched the race from the top of the hill, but when the grey Gustavus had won, she had the carriage top opened and drove past the royal party (Duke of Clarence, Duchesses of Clarence and Kent) by the winning post, followed by loud cheers and 'a great number of gentlemen on horseback' as she departed. The reporter from *The Times* was so delighted by this demonstration by 'Her Majesty' that he even forgot to mention the winning jockey's name (the elegant Sam Day, the elder). Such was the first, if brief, visit of a Queen of England to the Derby.

Prinny's brother, the Duke of York, had been hopeless as a field commander against the French (he was the general who marched 10,000 men up and down the hill) but he did better after 1795 at a desk job as commander-in-chief; this allowed him to resume his interest in racing. (He had even more time between 1809 and 1811 when he had to resign for a while because his mistress had been caught selling army promotions.) The Duke had his first Derby victory with his colt, Prince Leopold, in 1816, the year after Waterloo. The colt, which had not raced before, ran in the deceptive name of the Duke's racing manager, Warwick Lake, so no offence could be taken. Prince Leopold won by half a length. Later he became savage and died while being gelded. (The real Prince Leopold had married the Prince Regent's daughter – and so the Duke's niece – Charlotte, and, after her death, was made the King of Belgium.)

The Duke of York's second Derby winner, which he ran in his own name, was Moses in 1822. Moses won by a head, giving his jockey, Tom Goodison, his fourth Derby success. Moses was retired to the royal stud at Hampton Court.

William IV, called the Sailor King, knew little about horse racing but was determined to keep up kingly appearances. It was his habit, however, to stand at the front of the royal box, invariably with his back turned on what was happening below when his conversation grew animated. Once, asked which of the royal horses should run at Goodwood, he replied: 'Why, the whole squad, first-raters and gunboats; some of them, I suppose, must win.' Queen Victoria went to the Derby once, in 1840, but did not like it, and the Epsom crowd was not enthusiastic about her either. She did not even bother to return for the Oaks, much to the chagrin of the Epsom directors who had tried to spruce the Jockey Club box up. Albert did go again, by himself.

Victoria was increasingly worried by the bad company, chiefly of racing men, which attracted her eldest son, Albert Edward. Among his close friends at Oxford had been Henry Chaplin and Sir Frederick Johnstone, both later owners of Derby winners and both habitual gamblers. Although the Prince of Wales had joined the Jockey Club in 1864, his mother's displeasure stopped him from racing under his own colours until 1877. He liked going to Epsom and he made sure his wife and his cronies went with him. But when he tried for the Derby as an owner the early efforts were depressing, and he moved his horses from John Porter's yard at Kingsclere to Richard Marsh's at Egerton House, Newmarket, in 1893.

Two years later the Prince's racing manager, Lord Marcus Beresford, went down to Newmarket specially to see Persimmon, an unraced two-year-old colt by St Simon, tried out against a four-year-old filly. Instead of getting 37lb from the filly, as he should have done on the weight-for-age scale, Persimmon gave her 28lb and still won easily. Beresford declared: 'Well, this is the first time, and it may be the only time, we shall ever have a chance of having a Derby horse. All I can say is he must be a high-class horse to have done what he has done this morning.'

That was prescient; even so, Persimmon was a big horse whose legs were always at risk on firm going, and he was so slow to lose his winter coat in the spring of

1896. The second Royal Derby winner, HRH The Prince of Wales' Persimmon; the first was Sir Thomas in 1788.

1896 that he was not sent out to run in the Two Thousand Guineas. Still, the Prince of Wales was pleased with him before he went off to Epsom: 'I'm very delighted, Marsh. Everybody wants to win the Derby, and with a horse of one's own breeding too; I am looking forward to it very much.'

It was a close finish with St Frusquin, but Persimmon just got in front with less than 100 yards to go and won by a neck. Riding into the winner's enclosure the jockey, Jack Watts, was impassive until Marsh slapped him on the thigh and said: 'Do you not know you've just won the Derby for the Prince of Wales?' Only then did Watts relax and smile. *The Times* leader writer, like the crowd, was ecstatic: 'When the result was made known everybody seems to have cheered and shouted himself hoarse, while the reported destruction of headgear was on so extensive a

scale that a considerable stimulus must accrue to the hat-making industry.'

The Prince had waited twenty years for the success. He had only to wait four more for his second.

Diamond Jubilee, named for Queen Victoria's sixty years on the throne, had been pampered as a foal at Sandringham and when he went into training proved wilful and difficult – and he got worse with time. He bit off a stable lad's thumb and kicked a stableman in the hand. He took a dislike to his first two jockeys, Jack Watts and Mornington Cannon, throwing the first off and savaging the second. Cannon tactfully declined the honour of riding the royal horse and the trainer had to fall back on suggesting Diamond Jubilee's own lad, Herbert Jones. The Prince agreed. Jones had the colt's trust, too, and rode him to success not only in the Derby (by a length and a half) but in the Eclipse and by securing the triple crown. The Prince and Princess (Alexandra was wearing mauve) were at Epsom to watch the triumph:

The cheering was continued long after the formal declaration that all was right had been made and the Prince of Wales, evidently much touched by the imposing demonstration of loyal delight, had to run the gauntlet of the Jockey Club enclosure before he rejoined the Princess of Wales, at whose suggestion the name which Diamond Jubilee so suggestively bears was given.

The Prince headed the list of winning owners with a total of £29,585.

In 1909 King Edward was judged to have won his third Derby with Minoru, again ridden by Bertie Jones, by a short head. The crowd cheered loyally and long and sang 'God Save the King'. It was the zenith of royal racing success. Within a year Edward was dead, and the Derby was no longer quite what it had been in his heyday. Try as all his royal successors might, none of them has had anything like his luck.

1909. Minoru carried the colours of King Edward VII to a short-head victory amidst tumultuous excitement. From left: Mr Richard Marsh (trainer), The King, Lord Marcus Beresford and the future King George V.

Her Persistent Majesty

The Queen's enthusiasm for racing has been tested time and again by her lack of luck over the years. She is regularly at Epsom for the Derby but has yet to win it after thirty-nine years of trying. It needs more than commitment. After all, no sovereign has done it since her great-grandfather, Edward VII, with Minoru in 1909 – and that was considered by some (those who were not singing 'God Save the King') to be because the judge had remarkably loyal eyesight. Neither her grandfather nor her father managed it.

It was the Queen's luck, or misfortune, to have come closest to winning in 1953, the year of her coronation, when she had Aureole, probably the best of all her horses over the years. Aureole was a gifted chestnut, but highly strung, and, as often, there was a better colt, Pinza; although Aureole finished second it was by a clear four lengths and no luck about it. As Pinza was ridden by Sir Gordon Richards, who was winning his first Derby after twenty-eight attempts, the crowd was just as pleased as it would have been by a royal win. Pinza went on to beat Aureole again by three lengths in the King George VI and Queen Elizabeth Stakes.

Aureole was increasingly difficult and stubborn to train and was readily beaten in the St Leger, but he turned out to be a first-class four-year-old, winning the Coronation Cup, the Hardwicke Stakes and the 1954 King George VI and Queen Elizabeth Stakes. Chiefly as a result of his successes the Queen was the leading owner of the 1954 season, winning £40,944. Aureole sired the 1960 Derby winner, St Paddy, and was the top sire that year and the next.

Twice since Aureole in 1953 the Queen and her patriotic followers have had their hopes raised, if only momentarily. First, in the 1954 Derby her Landau headed the field (a trifle surprisingly) with just three furlongs to go, but the colt did not stay and faded out shortly afterwards. Landau had impeccable royal credentials: his sire was Big Game, George VI's winner of the wartime Two Thousand Guineas in 1942, and his dam was the incomparable Sun Chariot, also running in the royal colours that year; she had won the wartime One Thousand Guineas, Oaks and St Leger. But Big Game, like the unfortunate Landau, was a disappointment in his Derby, failing to stay the distance.

The second time regal hopes were lifted at Epsom in the new reign was in 1959 when Above Suspicion, sent off at 100–6, had a bad run down the hill to Tattenham Corner but, once in the straight, made up ground quickly. Again, it was too good to last; the colt finished fifth. The Queen regularly sent out Derby runners in the 1950s, but the less said about most of them, the better. The same goes for her later efforts.

It is not that she has given up. She eagerly attends the early races of those of her horses that show any promise; she has taken up breeding opportunities in Kentucky and in France; but the Derby magic hasn't happened. It appears to be the fate of the House of Windsor to be faithful in their attendance on Epsom Downs, without much reward. George V, after the suffragette brought his horse Anmer down in 1913, tried again the next year; his Brakespeare played up for twenty minutes before the start, ruining his own chances and wasting the crowd's patience. The King was a better judge of horseflesh than his father, but his runners in the 1920s were not of much quality.

George VI, besides his disappointment with Big Game, had just as poor a record. It would have been highly popular, after the Abdication crisis, if his Licence had won in 1938, but the colt revealed no such ability. The two royal entrants in 1944 and 1945 showed a desire to entertain a war-weary public but not by tipping them the way to a winner. Compared with those let-downs, the Queen has been a successful owner in the classics, winning the Two Thousand Guineas (Pall Mall, 1958), the One Thousand (Highclere, 1974, who went on to win the French Oaks – the Prix de Diane – and £93,000), the Oaks (Carrozza, 1957, and Dunfermline, 1977) and the St Leger (Dunfermline, 1977).

By any standards, Dunfermline was an impressive filly. She may have been lucky in the Oaks when Durtal, the favourite, took fright on the way to the Epsom start, dumping Piggott in the process, and was withdrawn. It was the week of Dunfermline's owner's Silver Jubilee. In the St Leger she beat the highly gifted Alleged, which proceeded to win the Arc de Triomphe two years running. The Arc, too, is a race that has eluded the Queen.

MAY — Settling for the Derby – Long odds and long faces

All at Hazard

Luck, sheer luck – from good to appalling – is a great river that flows through the Derby story, in turn buoyantly carrying and washing away individuals who tempted it. By its force and surprise it occasionally sustained or swamped innumerable fortunes and racing itself. Few trainers, owners and jockeys (let alone punters) have no stories to tell of how it all came right, or simply fell from their hands, when they least expected it at Epsom.

That unregenerate gambling cost the fourth Marquis of Hastings his fortune, estates and, finally, his life in 1868. Hermit's unexpected victory in the 1867 Derby cost him over £120,000 – and, as he said, broke his heart. Young men who plunged tended to take matters seriously. In 1813 Smolensko's victory cost Roger Brograve £10,000; Brograve did the decent thing and shot himself. In 1836 the Hon. Berkeley Craven groaned as Bay Middleton passed the winning post; he returned to London and also shot himself rather than show his face at Tattersalls as a defaulter. He had laid his fortune against the winner. Charles Greville noted: 'It is the first instance of a man of rank and station in society making such an exit.'

Hermit's win set off an exodus of impoverished young aristocrats from the smart life. The young Earl of Jersey retreated to the continent until his debts

had been paid. The Duke of Hamilton, another reckless plunger, had to sell up, and the Duke of Newcastle was taken to court. They followed Francis Villiers, successively manager of Lord Clifden's racing affairs and a steward of the Jockey Club, who had to flee the country in 1855 owing £100,000. They did not put pistols to their heads.

Others thought about it but were wise not to act too impetuously. In 1837 Lord Berners found his colt, Phosphorus, too lame to run. He had stood to win £30,000 on Phosphorus but sat down and wrote a note to have him scratched. The servant who took it had £100 on the horse at 25–1 and refused to pander to his master's scruples about the horse's leg. He tore the note up. Berners did not go to Epsom or buy a newspaper but, on entering his club in the evening, was startled by the servants rushing up to congratulate him. Phosphorus had been really lame in the last furlong, but had struggled home. He never raced again, but Berners forgave his now wealthy man.

Fitness itself needs luck – and determination. In 1911 Charles Morton, the trainer of Sunstar, told his

Above: George Cruikshank's caricature encapsulates the fortunes and misfortunes enjoyed and endured by gamblers on the Derby throughout the ages.

Sunstar, ridden by George Stern in the famous Joel colours (black, red cap) to Derby victory in 1911.

owner, J.B. Joel, that the horse was lame; it could run this time but would never run again. Joel insisted Sunstar should run. The horse did win – and could hardly walk back to the Epsom paddock.

After Running Rein's Derby in 1844, a dejected Captain Osborn who had backed the second, Orlando, returned to London where he was about to enter his chambers, write a farewell note and blow out his brains. A lad rushed up to him at the door and pushed a note into his hands; it said Running Rein was an imposter. Osborn took the hint and immediately began buying up all the Orlando bets he could. He won £30,000 when Running Rein was eventually disqualified.

When Ellington won in 1856 his trainer, Tom Dawson, was reckoned to have won £25,000. The next Monday was settling day at Tattersalls where Dawson duly collected from the losers. He put the banknotes in an old leather hat-box, fastened by a piece of string, and went off to catch the train home to Middleham in North Yorkshire. He was asleep when the train reached Northallerton, where he had to change, but the guard woke him. The hat-box, forgotten, stayed on the train all the way to Aberdeen. When Dawson realized his loss, telegrams were sent to stations all along the line. The box was sent on to Middleham a week later. It was unopened.

There were, of course, other big winners from gambling. Henry Chaplin won over £100,000 with his Hermit. John Gully, the old prizefighter, won his way into near-respectability and the House of Commons by his coups. William Crockford, Gully's enemy in many gambling enterprises, ran his own, palatial rooms and died worth £350,000, downcast that he had never owned a Derby winner. Many owners, like Lord George Bentinck, could not have run their large stables without using their brains and knowledge in the betting ring. Sir Joseph Hawley, who won the Derby four times, was known as the 'lucky baronet'; he picked up £43,000 on his Beadsman in 1858 and £80,000 on his Musjid the next year. Nine years later he gave his jockey the full £6000 Derby prize money for winning on Blue Gown. Towards the end of his life he decried all gambling.

Jockeys, in the days before 1884 when they were officially allowed to bet, insisted they needed the money. Fred Archer, who left £60,000 in his will and lived on a handsome scale, complained that his owners cut what they paid him, saying he knew enough to take care of himself by betting. But few were as knowledgeable or as sensible as he. Admiral Rous always maintained that 'any man who follows the advice of his jockey is sure to be ruined'.

Bill Scott was a rider who won the Derby four times before succumbing to drink. He believed in altering the odds his way, but it did not always work. While actually racing in 1840, on Launcelot II, he offered the young W.Macdonald on Little Wonder £1000 to pull the horse. 'Too late, Mr Scott, too late,' replied Macdonald, sweeping past.

Those jockeys who did not bet and were known to ride honestly throughout their careers were seldom fortunate. Jem Robinson, rider of six Derby winners, had to be saved from the workhouse; he and his wife set off for London at the end of every season to spend everything he had earned. George Fordham, a successful rider by any generation's standards, won the Derby only once and had to withstand recrimination about his unlucky failures. In 1863 Macaroni, the winner, had a close verdict over Fordham's mount. When Fordham heard he was being accused of pulling his horse, he thrashed his accuser and then spent the evening in tears on the stairs of his home, refusing to go to the party being held below.

If a rider could be trusted, it did not mean that fate was reliable. Stable lads could be bought. In 1825 Middleton started with a bucketful of water and a sponge in his stomach, but the people who bribed the lad were unlucky: Middleton still won. Nor could horses be trusted to stay part of a team. Diamond Jubilee, the Prince of Wales's winner in 1900, took a violent dislike to the jockey Mornington Cannon. It turned out that Cannon had ridden him when he was in pain with his teeth, and he never forgave Cannon for it. So Herbert Jones, an unknown lad from the royal stables who knew Diamond Jubilee's ways, got the Epsom ride which was the making of him. Jones had another royal winner with Minoru in 1909, but it was as the royal jockey that he had the bad luck to be brought down with his mount, Anmer, by the militant suffragette, Emily Davison, in 1913.

Starters could be bought. There was even a practice of winning owners giving them a present, presumably for not doing them down. Even when the starters were honest they could be incompetent. Tom McGeorge started most of the horses ahead of the post in the 1862 Derby, leaving some behind; he was threatened with dismissal. Next year he was so nervous there were thirty-four false starts, all in the teeming rain, not an experience to get the best out of horses tensed-up with

excitement. And for trainers beset by all the worries of health, injury, bribery, temperament and weather there were the simple problems of just getting their charges to the course and the start itself. Winners had several near-misses.

In 1855 the box to take Wild Dayrell to Epsom was sabotaged; the stable discovered this by testing it with a bullock inside. It collapsed, breaking the bullock's leg. In 1896 Persimmon refused to get into his box at the station and Richard Marsh, his trainer, had to pay the crowd watching the train to lift him in bodily. In 1922 Captain Cuttle got loose when being boxed to go to Epsom and trotted off. Everyone feared he would do himself an injury. But the Captain was very attached to his trainer, Fred Darling, and when he heard Darling's voice calling he turned round obediently and trotted back. He became an even bigger favourite in the yard.

In 1928 the crowd got out of control as the horses came on the course. It surrounded the favourite, Lord Derby's Fairway, picking hairs out of his tail, so that, not surprisingly, he was sweating and shaking with fright. In 1932 the horsebox taking April the Fifth, owned and trained by the actor, Tom Walls, was caught

1932. The actor Tom Walls was the owner and trainer of April the Fifth, the first Epsom-trained Derby winner since 1838.

in an impossible traffic jam. April had to be taken out and walked to the course which he reached in time and won. The times when luck destroyed other good horses' chances at Epsom cannot be calculated.

But there was one Derby winner who apparently never worried about anything, suited himself and always found bad luck passing him by. He was Cremorne (1872). He had one rule in life: he ate everything that came his way, usually his straw bedding. Before being saddled for his Derby he was found lying fast asleep in his box, his stable lad singing him a ditty from a penny song-book. In the race it was his jockey,

Maidment, who was almost caught napping, but Cremorne came home unworried.

He then won the Grand Prix de Paris and faced, equably as was his way, a hostile anti-English demonstration on his way back to the paddock. His apprehensive handlers decided to take him across the Channel on the Boulogne steamer that night. He was unperturbed by the storm, although it meant he got to his stable two and a half hours late. The next evening he was boxed to Ascot where he had a win and a walkover at the Royal meeting. At stud he ate himself to death in 1883. It was thought to be quite a way to go.

Back at Epsom, after six wartime years at Newmarket, the Derby is won by the grey Airborne, who started at odds of 50–1.

Winning Greys

Grey horses are easily recognised on the racecourse but they seldom win the Derby. Only four of them have, although the fastest time, 2min 33.8sec, recorded (by hand) for the race was set up by one of them, Mahmoud, in 1936.

Gustavus, said to be 'a shabby little grey,' was the first to win, in 1821. Bought for just 25 gns by a big gambler and Jockey Club member, J. Hunter, he started the 2–1 favourite and ran, it was said, neck and neck with Reginald almost all the way until 'within a short distance from the winning post, the jockey who rode Gustavus stood up in his stirrups, and laying on the whip . . . won the race' – by half a length. Gustavus failed in the St Leger and was eventually sold to Prussia. His jockey, Sam Day, enjoyed a high reputation for style and unusual probity, and went on to win two more Derbys.

It was not until 1912 that the filly Tagalie was the next grey to win, ridden by the American Johnny Reiff. She is the only grey filly to have won the Derby, and she was lucky even to have been given her chance. She won the One Thousand Guineas at 20–1, leading from the start, but then ran badly and her owner, Walter Raphael, a London financier, said he would take her out of the Derby. He changed his mind, and Tagalie, cleverly ridden in front by Reiff from start to finish, won by four lengths at 100–8 from an undistinguished field. The American-bred Tracery, bred and owned by August Belmont and thought to be the best horse in the race, was having only his first outing in England and finished third.

In the Oaks, Tagalie started the 2–1 on favourite but Reiff had been replaced by George Stern, who decided for some reason not to let her stride out as she liked, and she finished unplaced. She was also unplaced in the Eclipse and in the St Leger (which Tracery won).

The Aga Khan's Mahmoud (1936) was the third grey winner. A small colt with a skimming action over the ground, he was suited by the dry summer and the hard going on the downs, so this supposed non-stayer both won and lowered the record. He had been second in the Two Thousand Guineas, but he won nothing else after Epsom and the Aga had no doubts about promptly retiring him.

Airborne, the fourth grey, was the first post-war winner in 1946. Bred in Ireland by Col. Harold Boyd-Rochfort (brother of the royal trainer, Sir Cecil), the colt was backward as a two-year-old and started at Epsom an unnoticed 50–1 chance. He was ridden by Tommy Lowrey, the stable jockey for the initially lucky trainer Richard Perryman (no more classic winners), and won by a length from the Earl of Derby's Gulf Stream. Airborne may have been unfashionable, but he did pick up the St Leger. That was his last success. He was impossible to train the next year, and he failed as a sire. He has had no grey successor at Epsom.

Flying Fillies

The Derby has never been a sexist race. Fillies have taken their chances (with a 5lb weight allowance) and five of them have won at Epsom – a sixth, Fifinella, winning the wartime substitute race held at Newmarket in 1916.

Sir Charles Bunbury's Eleanor was the first, as early as 1801. She was very much an Epsom horse, her sire being Whiskey, a grandson of the great Eclipse, and her dam Young Giantess, a daughter of the first Derby winner, Diomed. Her trainer, Cox, died shortly before the race, gasping out to a surprised parson at his bedside: 'Depend on it, that Eleanor is a hell of a mare.' She duly won, the favourite in a field of nine.

The race was said to be 'very closely contested and afforded excellent sport' for 'a great number of the nobility, among whom were the Prince of Wales and Duke of Clarence.' (Nelson had just destroyed the Danish fleet at Copenhagen and the Guards had been ordered out to Egypt, but the future George IV and William IV had their own priorities.) Eleanor then

The filly Blink Bonny, winner of the 1857 Derby, who forty-eight hours later won The Oaks. She became the dam of Blair Athol, the Derby winner in 1864.

started 2–1 on in the Oaks and won that too, the first of only three fillies to do the Epsom double.

Blink Bonny, who did it in 1857, was a formidable competitor, said to have immense ribs and powerful quarters, who won eight of her 11 races as a two-year-old, including the Gimcrack at York. She was owned by William I'Anson, a Scot who trained at Malton, and had been the Derby favourite through the winter. However, she ran badly in the One Thousand Guineas – possibly because she suffered repeatedly from toothache – and started the Derby at 20–1. There were 35 runners, who contributed to twelve false starts, and the finish was a 'most exciting set-to', the result being 'Blink Bonny by a neck, the second beating the third by a head only, and a neck separating the third from the fourth.'

After that the Oaks was no trouble, and she 'came away by herself and won in a canter by eight lengths' at

5–4 on. Unsurprisingly, the crowd saw it as a foregone conclusion, 'regarded with a kind of listless indifference.' Blink Bonny then won four more races and started odds-on in the St Leger, but her jockey, John Charlton, was in the clutches of a leading Northern bookie of the day, John Jackson, and he pulled the filly too openly for the Doncaster crowd, who promptly blamed I'Anson himself. He was guiltless but was in serious danger of a lynching until the prize-fighter Tom Sayers intervened.

In 1882 Shotover, a big chestnut filly, won the Derby – but then all five classics were won by fillies that year. Shotover was bred by Henry Chaplin by his Derby winner Hermit, but she was almost given up as a yearling by her owner, the Duke of Westminster, and she did nothing as a two-year-old. However, the trainer, John Porter, thought she had wintered well and, as the colts were a poor lot, ran her in the Two Thousand

Guineas which she won easily from Quicklime at 10–1. She was made the 5–4 favourite in the One Thousand but was beaten by a head.

She started the Derby at 10–1 and again beat Quicklime after the favourite, Bruce, shied at a paper blowing across the course and ran wide at Tattenham Corner. Shotover's jockey, Tom Cannon (great-grandfather of Lester Piggott), had wasted severely to make full use of the 5lb advantage. Shotover was not allowed to run in the Oaks, Porter remembering how much the Two Thousand had taken out of her. He preferred a stable companion, Geheimniss, who duly won. When Shotover was sent out for the St Leger both she and Geheimniss were beaten by another filly, Dutch Oven. It was certainly not a year for the colts.

The Fenian murders in Phoenix Park, Dublin, meant MPs were not allowed their usual Derby holiday that year; Gladstone wished to pass an anti-terrorist act.

The winner in 1908 was the offspring of an equine love affair. Signorinetta was bred, owned and trained by the Italian enthusiast, Chevalier Odorado Ginistrelli, based at Newmarket. He had a mare, Signorina, who had been second in the Oaks and had won all her nine races as a two-year-old. But for ten years she had been barren at stud, although she did produce a son, Signorino, who was placed in both the Derby and the Two Thousand Guineas. Every day in Newmarket Signorina was grazing in her paddock when Chaleureux, a fair handicapper (he won the Cesarewitch), was led out for his morning's exercise, and their trainer suspected they had developed a fondness for each other. So, trusting to, as he put it, 'the boundless laws of sympathy and love,' he mated them. He was lucky. Signorinetta was the outcome.

She was said to be 'very nice' and 'sweet-tempered', but on the Derby's eve a winner she had not been, apart from a nursery victory at bottom weight. But the Chevalier was undaunted and he told his friends to follow his example and back her at 100–1. The miracle happened. 'Two furlongs from the judge's box Chev. Ginistrelli's filly took up the running . . . and won easily by two lengths.' The crowd was momentarily stunned but the reception the winner and owner got was warm. The French favourite, the unfortunately-named colt Sea Sick II, was unplaced. On the Saturday Signorinetta took the Oaks at 3–1, the favourite, Boss

Croker's Rhodora, being brought down at the mile post.

That was the filly's crowded hour. She won nothing else and greatly disappointed Rosebery, who had bought her, at stud. One of her daughters did breed a winner of the Scottish Grand National. Signorinetta's rider, William Bullock, thought himself unlucky too. It was said that the Chev. Ginistrelli did not favour presents for jockeys, even for those who had won both the Derby and the Oaks.

Tagalie's success in 1912 is recounted among those of the greys who won the Derby, she being the only winner with the double distinction.

Fifinella, owned by the newspaper magnate Sir Edward Hulton and the first Derby winner trained by Richard Dawson, won the wartime race (called the 'New Derby') at Newmarket in 1916. She was a difficult filly. Her jockey, Joe Childs, gave her a crack when she played up at the start of the One Thousand Guineas and she sulked and refused to try. She was in a bad mood before and during the New Derby, but 'after being baulked several times, eventually forced her way between the two colts and got the better of a remarkably keen and exciting finish by a neck from Kwang Su, who was a head in front of Nassovian.' She was the 11–2 joint second favourite. In the Oaks she was on her best behaviour, started the favourite at 2–1, and won in a canter by five lengths.

Had that Derby been run at Epsom, Fifinella would not have achieved her great success. She had not originally been entered for the Derby at all. The war and its disruption gave her the chance.

Fifinella, who beat the colts in the wartime 'New Derby' held at Newmarket in 1916.

07.35 hours on the day before the 1992 Derby: Lester Piggott and trainer Peter Chapple-Hyam enter the security stables area.

DERBY DAY 1992

by
Geoffrey Wansell

The damp air over the chalk downs on the southern outskirts of London is still heavy with the rain of the evening before. Silence seems to creep out of the lush green grass underfoot like fog, as three racehorses gently stand stock still, wet breath flaring from their nostrils. It is just before seven o'clock in the morning of Tuesday, 2 June, the day before the Epsom Derby of 1992.

At the stables tucked beyond Epsom's grandstand, a small knot of people is standing quietly talking to one another; some sit on the low walls that edge the stable lads' canteen, while others sip from styrofoam cups of tea and read British horseracing's daily bible, the *Sporting Life*. There are a spattering of photographers, camera bags heavy over their shoulders with the long lenses for photographing horses; a smaller group of television men stand with their larger video cameras. Everyone is waiting for just one jockey to make his appearance on the Epsom racecourse.

The Derby is more than a horserace; it is, and always has been, news. The most famous race in the world – ancestor to more than 300 other Derbies named after it all over the world – has never failed to attract attention. 1992 is no exception.

Brough Scott, presenter of television's Channel Four Racing arrives, sporting sleek riding boots and snappy green jacket, all boyish smiles and bonhomie for the assembled crowd. 'Not here yet, then, is he?' he says cheerfully, putting everyone's thoughts into words. For this small group are waiting for one of the English Derby's legends, the veteran jockey Lester Piggott, a winner of a record nine Derbies in a career which stretches nearly forty years in the saddle. As the tall, careful Mike Dillon of Ladbroke's, the mighty bookmaking concern, puts it, 'Lester is the Derby for most people.'

On this particular damp grey June morning, Piggott, a fifty-six-year-old grandfather, who rode his first winner in the Epsom Derby as an eighteen-year-old, is due to ride out the 1992 race favourite, Rodrigo de Triano, in the horse's last exercise before the race itself. Piggott alone is said by the experts to 'be worth ten lengths' in the Derby. That's why a crowd is gathered, waiting for this small slight man with a twinkling eye but a slight speech impediment which makes him a little difficult to understand for those who don't know him well.

A moment or two after seven Lester Piggott walks quickly round the corner of the stable block, wearing silks, racing helmet – complete with bobble and a magnificent pair of tassled riding boots. Though the lines are more deeply etched into his cheeks now than when he rode Never Say Die to victory in 1954, he looks as he has always looked, almost ageless, impassive and stonefaced, yet still amused by the interest he and this extraordinary race can arouse around the world.

With a polite wave of his whip Lester nods amiably, if a little distantly, to the crowd of reporters and photographers waiting for him and walks briskly out of the stables towards the course. Waiting for him are three horses trained by Peter Chapple-Hyam, the new twenty-nine-year-old star among British trainers, who has already won both the English and the Irish Two Thousand Guineas with Lester's mount that morning, Rodrigo de Triano. With barely a word, Chapple-Hyam gives Piggott a leg up into the saddle and he sets off at a steady walk towards the Derby start.

The pursuing cameramen are quickly left behind because it hasn't failed to catch Lester's attention that their attentions are making his horse nervous. The big chestnut is pulling and prancing under him, and he wants to settle him in private away from the attentions of the press.

Only four horses will be on the course on this last morning before the Derby. 'In the old days all of them used to come out,' says Tim Neligan, managing director of the racecourse and the man who – more

Alone with his thoughts, Derby maestro Lester Piggott on Epsom's hallowed turf in front of Prince's Stand.

it's being at Epsom that makes the Derby what it is – unique.'

Clearly, Lester Piggott agrees. Why else would one of racing's most famous practitioners drag himself to Epsom – 100 miles or more from his home in Newmarket – at seven in the morning to ride a horse that he is by no means sure has a chance to win the race? 'It's because he loves it as much as I do,' Neligan says.

He is by no means alone. Not all the crowd gathered to watch Piggott on board the favourite this morning are professionals. Wendy Meaby, for example, who used to live down the hill in Epsom before she retired to Bournemouth, has come to these stables before the race each and every year for more than thirty years. Wearing a mac and carrying her own little automatic camera, she stands on the edge of the crowd, pleased to be part of the event she loves. 'It's the excitement,' she confesses. 'I've never experienced anything like it.'

Wendy, like millions of others, adores the Derby and treasures its tradition. 'I had to stand on a bookmaker's box to see Lester win on Sir Ivor in 1968,' she remembers happily, 'so I decided to become a member of the course to get a better view.' She has been a loyal member ever since, but still comes out to watch the preliminaries to the race. 'My mother's father had race-horses and I used to work with polo ponies. I love racing, but there's nothing that compares with the Derby.'

Wendy Meaby walks back towards the winning post at the end of Epsom's five-furlong straight to wait for Lester to come back, perfectly happy in the certain knowledge that, as long as there's breath left in her body, she'll be doing exactly the same thing on the first Tuesday and Wednesday of every June. No one could more perfectly embody the affection in which the Derby is held among Londoners and locals.

This English carnival on 600 acres of downland captures the imagination of millions who would never otherwise go to a horse race. 'I reckon 90 per cent of the people who come to Epsom don't know anything about the racing,' Seamus Buckley explains, 'but that doesn't mean they don't enjoy it. They do.' Everyone involved in the race is touched by it. Wendy Meaby is no exception.

While Lester Piggott is walking his horse across the centre of the course, in Derby Stables across the road

than anyone else – keeps the Derby alive as a great English event. It clearly makes Neligan a little sad that this part of the race's tradition has faded slightly. 'Now the Newmarket trainers like to keep their horses at home until the day of the race, and even the French don't send theirs over until the day itself because they can use these special new private planes.'

A short, wispy-haired man with a lilting voice, Neligan knows that the Derby is always changing. It has to, for otherwise it could never remain the premier horse race in the world. 'If you looked at it sensibly, and the Derby hadn't always been here, you'd probably never run the race at Epsom at all,' he confides. 'But two men are quietly marking out the carparking spaces for the day to come. Lionel Burns and his cousin, Gerald Barnard, have family connections with the Derby stretching back more than 137 years. Five generations of Barnards have kept the stables behind the grandstand where the owners and trainers left their carriages and footmen when they came from London. Now the owners park their limousines and chauffeurs there instead.

'Never been a racing man myself,' Lionel Burns, a former chemistry teacher, admits ruefully, 'but I love the Derby, always have. The service bands, the gypsies, the characters, the fair, they were all part of the flavour of the race, the things that made it what it was, a great English day out.' Now retired, Lionel Burns still administers the parking in Derby Stables, together with his cousin, though neither of them ever see the race. 'Though I did used to have an odd bet,' Gerald Barnard admits.

It was one of their ancestors who first suggested a fair should be held in the centre of the Derby course. For more than a century the bearded ladies, and the snake charmers, the fortune tellers and the 'Guess your age' men mingled with the professional tipsters and the racing men like Prince Monolulu – with his cry of 'I've gotta horse.'

In 1971 that fair was removed, though another at Tattenham Corner remains to this day. Lionel and his cousin mourn its passing. 'Perhaps it was a more easy-going, happy-go-lucky atmosphere then because we were all freer of regulations. There was a kind of press-on-regardless atmosphere. But you can see why things have changed, we've got to be more safety conscious, more security conscious than we used to be.'

But that hasn't staunched the Derby's charm for Lionel and Gerald. 'You can still walk on to the centre of the course and watch the Derby, without paying a penny for admission, and have a wonderful day out. Maybe you were a little freer to swarm all over the place in my mother's day, but in those days the turf wasn't so well maintained.'

When Lionel's mother ran the Derby Stables, the horses were running on almost pure chalk by the end of the Derby. What rough grass there had been on the mile-and-a-half horseshoe across the downs had been destroyed by the hooves of its racing horses. 'Now it's watered and tended, there's no comparison.'

One man who knows that only too well is Lester Piggott. By now he is far across the downs from the Epsom grandstand and the Derby Stables behind it. Sitting calmly on Rodrigo de Triano, he pulls the big chestnut's reins through his hands and walks him steadily towards the start of the mile-and-a-half course, which will capture the world's attention for just two-and-a-half minutes the following afternoon. Though it doesn't show on his face, he knows only too well that he bears a huge responsibility. If the horse wins, an estimated £100 million will be won by housewives and workers up and down the country on the strength of his name alone; and, if he loses, a fifth of that sum will go into the pockets of the bookmakers – the bets of ordinary men and women in pubs and clubs, factories and offices, shops and farms up and down the land.

Alongside Piggott is walking Dr Devious, ridden by John Reid, the jockey who will partner him the following afternoon. (Dr Devious is the second of Peter Chapple-Hyam's two entries in the race.) Reid and Piggott, accompanied by Spanish Grandee from the Chapple-Hyam stable at Manton in Wiltshire to give them a lead, begin to trot in the grey morning light. Neither man says anything to the other: there is nothing to say. Each knows exactly what he has to do to make his journey worthwhile – help his horse win the Derby tomorrow.

As Piggott and Reid begin the first two furlongs of the Derby course, they canter past the motley gaggle of gypsy caravans that have gathered for Derby Day on these downs for the 200 years or more since the race began. Not horse-drawn and painted red and yellow as they would have been in days gone by, but all cream and silver chrome now, they are parked silently in the space specially allotted to them for generations. More than 200 Romany gypsies regularly inhabit the downs for Derby Day. The mothers and the grandmothers of those here this year were selling lucky charms, nosegays, sprigs of heather and bouquets to racegoers before the battle of Waterloo.

For Rodrigo de Triano and Dr Devious, it is their first sight of a unique course. For Epsom is the least likely racecourse in the world. More than one expert, such as the BBC's racing correspondent Julian Wilson, has insisted that the Derby should be held somewhere else, but that would be unthinkable. For it is the sheer eccentricity of Epsom that makes the English Derby a unique test of a racehorse. The Epsom course climbs and falls precipitously throughout its mile-and-a-half-long horseshoe, the camber first tilting the horses right, then left, then right again, then left again, before forcing them to run along a straight which is like the side of a small hill.

Lester Piggott once put it memorably, 'Epsom is like no other course in the world, no matter what you do it will always surprise you.' It is impossible to imagine the effect it has on a young racehorse who has never seen anything like it. From the start at the end of the horseshoe away from the grandstand, Piggott and Reid and their young horses climb steadily upwards and slightly to the right as the course rises towards the top of Tattenham Hill. In just over half a mile they climb about 130 feet, until they reach the farthest part of the course, about a mile from the finish.

At the top of Tattenham Hill, Piggott and Reid ask their horses to canter more quickly, then gallop down the steep, sharp, left-turning hill that distinguishes Epsom from every other racecourse in the world. As if released for the first time, the two horses stretch willingly as if they are in slow motion across the horizon from the watching crowd of pressmen now gathered at the finish. The speed and balance is overwhelming, unlike anything else in the racing world.

As Piggott and Reid come down to the sharp left turn of Tattenham Corner, at the beginning of the last leg of the horseshoe, their horses are running at almost racing pace, approaching thirty-five miles an hour, on a steep camber sloping towards the inner rails of the course that would not be out of place at the BMW test track or the Indianapolis 500. Undeterred they sweep into the straight, then cross the camber of the straight – where the inside rail of the course is some five and a

---

The racecourse on Epsom Downs. The chart represents a detailed survey conducted in 1978. The slight rise in the last 100 yards is accentuated after the finish.

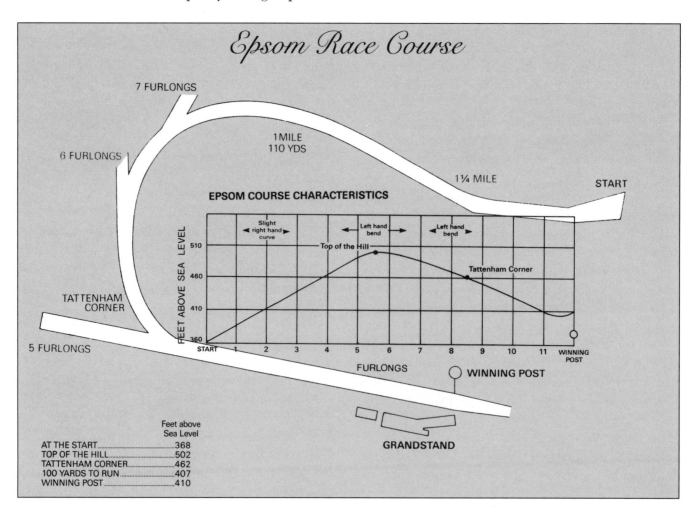

half feet below the other rail – and accelerate towards the finish. They hit the dip about 150 yards from the winning post at full speed, and then let the slight incline over the next 100 yards slow their horses as they come to the post. Looking neither right nor left both jockeys quicken again past the post, with Dr Devious slightly in front of Rodrigo de Triano; but both jockeys gradually pull their horses up as they ride back down towards the stables where they began.

About an hour later, in the subterranean Press Room beneath the new £9 million Queen's Stand, the members of the press are dissecting the day's events so far. Was Lester confident? Was Rodrigo de Triano (a horse named after one of Columbus' sailors to commemorate the 500th anniversary of the discovery of America) good enough to win? What should be the favourite?

No one talks much about Lester's riding companion, John Reid and Dr Devious; or the only other two horses that have worked on the downs that morning, the elegant Silver Wisp, trained in Epsom; or of muscular St Jovite from Jim Bolger's yard in Ireland, ridden out by Christy Roche, his rider in the race itself. Few had stayed to watch the big horse swing lazily around the course, watched admiringly by his owner and breeder, Mrs Virginia Kraft Payson from Kentucky. No other owner had taken the trouble to be there. No, the talk was of Lester and his trainer, Peter Chapple-Hyam, who appeared in the Press Room as enthusiastic and as uninhibited as only a young trainer embarking on his career can be.

The six-foot tall, Warwickshire-born Chapple-Hyam is confident, very confident, and everyone in the Press Room can see it. But the experts are still sceptical. 'Lester may start as favourite,' Richard Evans, racing correspondent of *The Times*, mutters darkly, 'but I very much doubt that he will win.'

Meanwhile, in the racecourse office itself, tucked away in the older 1914 building alongside the new Stand, pandemonium – as is usual every year – is breaking out again.

The phone rings incessantly. 'The price of admission is £20 for the grandstand, and £4 for the paddock,' the Club's secretary Joanne Dillon is saying patiently for the fifth time in as many minutes.

Dawn on Derby Day-minus-one. A solitary spectator sees Dr Devious (John Reid) and a stable companion followed by Lester Piggott on Rodrigo de Triano, all trained at Manton by Peter Chapple-Hyam.

'No, I'm not sure I can tell you exactly how to get here from Slough . . . Yes, there are certainly a number of hotels in Epsom, but I'm afraid I couldn't recommend one and I should warn you that they're very likely to be full . . . Yes, you will be able to park your car but I can't tell you exactly which car park will fill up first. It really is awfully difficult to say. It changes from year to year.'

In a momentary lull a young couple from Holland, who can hardly speak English, appear to ask if they can sleep in the grandstand overnight. 'I'm afraid security doesn't allow that, but the turnstiles do open at 8 o'clock in the morning,' Joanne says helpfully, 'and there are certainly some people who sleep out overnight on the downs.' Though she doesn't say it, there aren't quite as many doing that as there used to be a century ago, when all London seemed to take the night off before the Derby to pitch its tents or park its carts to be sure of a good spot for the race the following day.

The phone rings again. 'Can someone get into Queen's Stand without a top hat on? He says he's got morning dress, but he's lost his top hat.' There's a pause. 'Tell him we're afraid not, the rules are very clear – full morning dress or service uniform must be worn, and that includes hat or top hat.' The receptionist returns to the caller. 'He says, "What if he got a friend to throw his top hat over the railings to him so

that he could wear it passing through the entrance.'"
There is a long sigh from Joanne. 'Tell him no; but
there'll be plenty of top hats left over at the end of the
Derby if he wants to collect one for next year.' Another
brief lull – then the phone rings again. 'It's the man
who rings every year on the day before and demands to
book a table for two for lunch on Derby Day. What
shall I tell him?' Another pause. 'The same as last year.
We're fully booked. Why doesn't he contact us in
February for next year?'

Out on the course itself, the final touches are being
put to the military marquees and the beer tents, to the
helicopter landing tower and to the sponsor's grand
marquee. The sponsors of the race, the Ever Ready
battery company, previously part of the Hanson
empire, has its marquee set up right beside the winning post and directly beside Queen's Stand. Ever
Ready and Hanson, under the leadership of the irre-
pressible Lord White of Hull (or 'Gordy' to his
friends), have been enthusiastic supporters of the race
for nine years. The marquee's yellow and red flags and
bunting – the company's colours – flutter in the cool
breeze, but at least – as one rigger says loudly – '. . . at
least it's not bloody raining'.

The weather is the only imponderable. Snow fell
during the race in 1867 and, in the 1920s, there were
torrential downpours for three years in succession,
delaying the race on one occasion but never stopping
it. 'The odd storm has found a hole or two in the grandstand, but nothing we can't take care of,' says Tim
Neligan. 'They also usually block the drains, though
we've no idea how or why. It doesn't matter, we're used
to it.'

The 150-strong television team from Channel Four
Racing has laid out nearly eighteen miles of cable to
twenty camera positions around the course in preparation for its biggest event of the year – likely to be
watched by five million viewers in Britain and 450
million more around the world. The television men
disappear to the pub as the day draws to its close.

By the time dusk begins to fall, the great racecourse
seems almost to sigh in the cool evening air, hoping
that tomorrow the sun will grace it and its race.
Everything is as ready as it can be. The windows of the
Tote offices have been cleaned; the bookies' pitches
marked out in front of the grandstand; and the
Mahmoud and the Shergar bars have been stocked

with champagne and beer. The 800 catering staff know
exactly what's expected of them. There will be 7000
bottles of champagne consumed on Derby Day, along
with 1800 sides of smoked salmon and 5000 pounds of
strawberries, not to mention 48,000 cans of beer – and
six tons of ice to keep it all cool.

Now, in the gathering twilight, only the faint sound
of laughter can be heard in the Rubbing House pub in
the centre of the course as the Epsom grandstand waits
silently for dawn and the 213th Derby Day.

The damp grey clouds of the day before have disappeared. The sun shines benevolently as dawn breaks
over Derby Day on the morning of Wednesday, 3 June
1992. The Gods have smiled on what has been the
'English Carnival' for more than two centuries.

It is just before five o'clock in the morning. The air is
sharp and clear as the first tents are erected inside the
rails that lead down from Tattenham Corner towards
the straight and the grandstand. In the crisp light they
look like great white ocean liners waiting for their
gangplanks to be lowered. Beside them, the first cars
are backing up towards the parking spaces and the first
barrels of beer are rolling out. The 'Cockney's Day
Out', as Derby Day has always been called, may not
boast quite as many Pearly Kings and Queens as once
it did, but this is still London – and especially East
London – at play in the fields of their Lord: the
common land of Epsom Downs.

All along the edges of the racecourse families are
unpacking the boots of their cars. One is erecting a
specially designed canvas convenience, complete with
suitable sanitary loo; another is unpacking a barbecue
that would grace an Australian beach; another a set of
sun loungers that wouldn't be out of place at
Torremolinos; still another a battalion of flasks full of
warm liquids from soup to cocoa, to supplement the
regiment of more alcoholic beverages. 'We're here to
enjoy ourselves, and that's exactly what we intend to
do,' shouts one Londoner cheerfully, 'so don't you go
saying it's going to rain, 'Cos it isn't.' Somehow the
Gods wouldn't dare let it.

By 8 o'clock, bookmaker Jack Simpson of Stockport
is beginning to pitch his board. He left home – more
than 200 miles away – just before four, as he's done
every year for the past forty-six years. Jack has been at
Epsom every year since 1946, the year Airborne

became the only grey to win the race for fifty years – and he's always been lucky.

'The day I lose on Derby Day,' he says, 'is the day I stop coming to the Derby.' A grey-haired man, with a wide-open smile, his pitch is on the rails about five furlongs from the finish. On any other racecourse, he'd be miles away from the punters – and the action. Not at Epsom. All around him the cars and families are assembling; their tables and chairs being steadily set up, their copies of the *Sporting Life* open in front of them.

'Mind you, it's not cheap. It's £20 to park your car and £60 for a bookmaker's badge out here,' Simpson says ruefully. 'But I still reckon it's worth it. I don't come to Epsom on any other day, it wouldn't be worth while, but the Derby's something special – always has been.'

On the front page of the *Sporting Life* the headline reads 'Six Favourite Derby! Bookies are left baffled,' Its reporter, Gary Nutting, tells the thousands scouring the paper on Epsom Downs, that this is 'The most open Derby in living memory – that's what the bookmakers are saying.' Not Jack Simpson, he knows only too well that most of the mothers and fathers, sons and daughters, grandfathers and grandmothers, nieces and nephews parked around him will put their 50p pieces or their fivers on Lester Piggott.

'Always have done in the last thirty-odd years, and they always will while he's still riding.' Simpson takes it into account as he makes his book. It's as much part of the Derby tradition as jellied eels and fortune tellers; Piggott – the common man's champion – symbolizes the race for millions who never watch another race throughout the year.

About 200 yards below Simpson on the rails, one of the 200 or more carpark men manning the downs is telling an irate driver that it'll cost him £20 to park his car beside Tattenham Corner. 'You should be grateful, mate, it's the only time of the year you're even allowed to park on these downs.' The driver gives in and pays up phlegmatically.

'Listen mate, people want to forget that times are bad,' the carpark man confides, 'and pretend – just for a bit – that life's OK really. That's what the Derby's always been about. Forget your troubles, have a drink, have a good day out and go home to the grind again.' All around are families out to prove him right.

As the sun brightens to illuminate the view back towards London, the centre of the course is filling up. The market traders, with their T-shirts and running shoes, their mementoes and knick-knacks, their furry animals and funny hats, are lining their stalls up beside the cars and the caravans. 'Any three for £5 – pick the ones you like', is the shout. The T-shirt slogans are everything from 'World Cup 90' and 'Summer is Coming' to the rather less flattering 'I got pissed at Epsom'; trade is steady – just as it is for the mobile hot-dog and Coca-Cola wagons providing breakfast for the early arrivals.

By nine o'clock, the first buses and coaches begin to stream on to the course. Big red double-deckers from Romford and East Ham jostle beside the sleek, dark-windowed Range Rovers from Westminster. In the Walton and Lonsdale Enclosures opposite the grandstand, the first corporate hospitality tents are being unfurled to provide lunch beside the track.

Down at the paddock the bigger, more permanent, hospitality tents – for American Express Gold Card members or BP – have been up for a week. But now the finishing touches are being added: geraniums and daisies in pots beside the tents in the sponsor's colours, slogan signs pinned to the canvas. Inside, white table-cloths are being spread across the tables, the bottles of Pimms and Martini set out beside the champagne.

Each of these grander tents boasts its own television and its own Tote office, so that guests need hardly set foot on the racecourse. 'Most of them don't bother,' remarks one waitress, as she smooths the linen napkins for a table of twelve. 'They come for a good time, and to say they've been here, but they don't usually bother much with the racing – except for the Derby itself. Then they have a bet.' She returns happily to polishing the spoons that will help the guests regain their composure over the coffee after the big race.

Four hundred yards away, by the winning post, they're also laying for lunch in the Members Restaurant of Queen's Stand. 'It's £68 a head each for the day,' one young waitress confides, 'but that means you can keep the table all day, which most people like to do; but you have to buy your own drinks for that.' The lunch menu features smoked salmon and Dover sole, the details printed on an elegant folded card with a fine etching of a Victorian Derby on its cover. Time is moving on. It's as if the call-boy is about to call,

'Beginners, please,' in the last five minutes before a show. Moments before ten the first cars begin to park in the specially reserved spaces in the Derby Stables; they are manoeuvred into place by twelve members of the Corps of Commissionaires. 'People bring their picnic tables here, too, you know,' Commissionaire Jack Wade of Dagenham explains, 'even though it is £130 for three spaces.' Jack has had to leave his home in Essex at 5.30 that morning just to get to Epsom. 'But it's worth it. It's a nice day – special somehow – better than sitting behind four walls watching it on television.'

Behind him in the Derby Stables, like stage hands at the opera, ladies working for Ever Ready are banging and hammering at the new trailer from which the Derby's prizes will be presented just before four o'clock that afternoon. It's the first time the float has been tried, 'and to be honest, we're a bit nervous about it', one admits. 'I hope the blessed thing doesn't get stuck.' The ladies smile at one another and pile on the £2500 worth of flowers it takes to decorate the float. Those flowers have been imported specially, but the ones standing proudly in front of Queen's Stand have been grown at Epsom's own greenhouse, hidden behind the paddock. In these last minutes they, too, are being unloaded from a flat-bed truck and carried to their official places.

The curtain is about to go up on the 213th Epsom Derby, and a subtle air of anticipation spreads across the sunlit course as the staff know that it's barely moments before the first Members and their guests, sporting the top hats and tails that the Dress Regulations demand, arrive for Derby Day 1992.

*P*recisely at 10 o'clock, the first chauffeurs open the doors to their large black limousines, and the first ladies in spring dresses with unexpectedly large straw hats, accompanied by slightly selfconscious companions in unaccustomed top hats, are deposited in the road in front of the grandstands. They are greeted by an army of gypsies.

'Buy a nice spray, darling – bring you luck it will, got to.' Like a defending infantry battalion they are positioned around the stands to repel all those who do not succumb to their incantations. 'You're going to have great good fortune, young man. I can always tell. No doubt about it. Here, take this.' She presses a small, mock-ivory elephant into the uncertain Member's hand as he fishes for the pound she is expecting. 'Thank you darling. Be lucky.'

It was once estimated that a quarter of Britain's gypsy population came to the Derby every year; but the numbers have dwindled. 'It's different now than it was once', Harriet Lee, one of the gypsy fortune tellers explains outside her caravan, parked opposite the Tattenham Enclosure. 'Used to be more of us, but now we educate our children so that they're in the grandstand instead of being out here on the course with us.'

Harriet Lee and her sister Margaret have been coming to Epsom for more than twenty years, 'Our mother was the famous Nancy Lee who'd been to every Derby since the First World War – she was an institution.' Harriet and her sister are still telling young women that a tall dark stranger is about to enter their lives, and young men that they are likely to meet 'someone who is going to make a big difference', as they've always done. Only now the price is £10 rather than the half-a-crown it was in their mother's day.

'Used to be a lot better for us before those great big steel fences went up across the road,' Margaret Lee confesses. 'In those days people would just walk across from the side of the course and talk to us. Now they've got to have their hand stamped so they can go back in again. It's made it all a bit more difficult.' But the fortune tellers, and their cousins the charm sellers, haven't stopped coming. They are every bit as much part of the particular charm of the event – this mixture of peep show and pageant – as the horses themselves.

No matter what the future holds, back in the grandstand office the club secretary, Joanne Dillon, is still grappling with the day's problems. 'Listen, I've no idea where Major Webster is, I haven't seen him for hours, perhaps he's out on the course,' she spits into one of the hundred or more mobile phones that are spewing out fractured messages faster than almost anyone can understand them. 'They've asked if they can bring in three more helicopter loads at 10.45, is that all right? . . . I've no idea where the carpark signs have gone . . . The close-circuit television in the Stewards' Room isn't working, and they're beginning to arrive . . . There doesn't seem to be anyone looking after the A2

Opposite: The crowd builds up on Derby Day. Compare the architectural styles of Prince's Stand 1879 (left) Queen's Stand 1992 (centre) and the 1927 grandstand.

Carpark . . . Where's the Head of Security? . . . I don't know why there are so many of them.' The phones are ringing incessantly. Anxious racegoers want to know whether they can park their cars, what they have to wear in the grandstand, whether it's going to rain, whether there's still room for lunch. Throughout the office staff are resolutely cheerful. 'I've been saying for months it's going to be a great Derby and it is.'

In the Walton Enclosure a red open-top bus, carrying twenty-seven members of the Garrick Club from London, together with the Club's secretary and staff, has just pulled in. The bar is being set up and members are considering their racecards, fortified by a glass or two of champagne.

The Garrick has been coming to the Derby for longer than anyone can remember. In 1968 it was forever immortalized in a painting by John Gilroy, showing the staff dancing a jig at the end of the race. This year's members are no different. 'We've come to have a marvellous time,' one explains, 'and so we shall.'

By eleven a crowd is beginning to spill into the road in front of the Tattenham Corner pub, towards the fairground which is about to spring into life. There are fewer jellied eel and whelk stalls than once there were – they've been replaced by hamburgers and the ubiquitous hot-dog – but there's still a magnificent carousel, as well as the modern version of the big wheel, and the customary dodgems and rifle ranges, darts and hoopla amidst the roundabouts and racket. Just for the moment, however, as the morning draws to its close, the fair remains still, waiting for its patrons to get themselves into the mood before offering its extra delights for the day. 'It's a shame they moved the other fair out of the dip in the middle of the course twenty years ago,' the man cleaning his dodgem cars explains. 'There's a lot of people who'd like to see it back.' He's not alone. There are a good many senior officials of the racecourse who believe it added something special to Derby Day, even if the police saw it as a haven for pickpockets and assorted scoundrels.

At the turn of the century more than a few racegoers were convinced that horseracing was conducted 'for the delight and profit of fools, ruffians and thieves', as George Gissing memorably remarked in 1903. Derby Day in 1992 hardly bears this out. Notices at every corner may scream, 'Beware of Pickpockets', but the Metropolitan Police, who are monitoring the event, are extremely relaxed. The days of footpads in their hundreds rampaging across the downs in the dusk after the Derby is no more than a memory to today's constables. Now their concerns are drinking and driving, though with a clear eye on protecting the Sovereign and her party who are about to leave Victoria Station on the Royal Train bound for Tattenham Corner station.

Racegoers and traffic are now kept strictly under control in a way the present monarch's great-grandfather, King Edward VII, would not have imagined possible in 1909 when his horse, Minoru, won the Derby and he was mobbed on his way to welcome it back to the winners' enclosure. The threat of terrorism and the car bomb have made policemen everywhere especially watchful wherever there is a Royal presence. 'But no Irishman would dream of interrupting a great horse race now, would he?' one constable remarks. 'Be more than his life's worth, wouldn't it?'

On the downs themselves hardly anyone is paying the slightest attention to the activities of the Metropolitan Police – they are too busy enjoying themselves. For, by now, Derby Day 1992 has developed a momentum of its own. Nothing and no one can stop it now. Not even if the heavens opened and soaked every single spectator from head to foot would the good spirits leave.

By noon the traders' stalls are thronged with potential purchasers: mothers pushing babies, fathers carrying their youngest sons on their shoulders, grandmothers looking for a bargain amidst the denim jeans and the 'Derby Day Special Mirrors – Only £7'. Their husbands sit studying the form, the first beer of the day in their hands. There may be hubbub everywhere, but there is still the serious matter of paying for the day out with a sensible bet on the Derby.

Above their heads the steady throb of helicopter engines has been growing in volume for the past hour as the flights come in from London's Battersea heliport and Sandown Park racecourse a few miles away. The race's sponsor, Lord White of Hull, arrives with his twenty-nine-year-old fiancée, Victoria, and their party; they are whisked across the course to the Ever Ready marquee by a fleet of hire cars. Joan Collins arrives with her escort, the American actor George Hamilton. Hers is one of more than 300 helicopter movements

Mounted officers of the Metropolitan Police, who escort the Derby runners to the start and the winner back to unsaddle.

during the day, each one of them controlled from the temporary tower erected in scaffolding at the top of Tattenham Hill just a few yards from the one-mile post on the Derby course. But Robert Sangster, owner of Lester Piggott's mount, Rodrigo de Triano, makes his way by car.

Throughout the morning there has hardly been a sign of a horse, except for the police horses gently shuffling the cars and pedestrians out of the way – as if the last thing on anyone's mind is a horserace. But that is the Derby's special illusion. At the stables the horse-boxes have been arriving since shortly after dawn, to give their occupants time to recover from the 100-mile trip from Newmarket or Lambourn.

Alnasr Alwasheek, the winner of the Craven Stakes at Newmarket and the famous Dante Stakes at York the previous month, has arrived from Michael Stoute's victorious yard at Newmarket which has sent out Shahrastani and Shergar to win the race in the past decade. Ninja Dancer and Paradise Navy have also made their way from Newmarket, as have Twist and

Turn and Young Senor, while Guy Harwood's Young Freeman and Thourios have both come from Pulborough in Sussex. Great Palm has travelled from Paul Cole's stable, near Lambourn, which sent out Generous to win the race last year. Indeed, well before Her Majesty the Queen sets foot upon the racecourse, the equine participants in the race have quietly settled into their stables; though hardly a member of the gathering crowd has noticed it.

On the lawn in front of Queen's Stand, one of Epsom's annual members, jeweller David Kozak, who is now seventy and has been coming to the race for forty years – 'couldn't miss it, it's like Christmas' – is surveying the sunshine and the gathering crowd with intense satisfaction. 'I know things are bad for some people, but there's still the Derby to cheer them up. It's a tradition. You can't take it away from England, it would be a loss to the country.'

Across the lawn towards him comes the slight figure of Alan Munro, the winning jockey last year. The old racegoer and the new rising star among jockeys nod warmly to each other. 'You think you have a chance?' Munro smiles cautiously, 'Great Palm is a great horse, and he's been working well; we must have.' Munro looks every inch a schoolboy, hair brushed to one side away from the parting, face as open as if it had never faced the reality of a hard race for a prize of more than £350,000. There's just undimmed enthusiasm for the race. 'Winning the Derby last year was something no one will ever take away from me,' he says quickly. 'It's very, very special, ask any jockey.'

A yard or two in front of him on the lawn a group of uncertain young men are looking distinctly uncomfortable in their grey top hats. One is wearing it at the angle normally reserved for stetsons in John Wayne westerns, while another is wearing his jammed above two magnificently jewelled earrings. They are engrossed in that morning's copy of the *Sporting Life*, and earnestly discussing form. 'It'll never get the trip. No chance. Never. Even Lester couldn't do it.' Virtually unnoticed in front of them, the band of the Welsh Guards has quietly taken its seats opposite the winning post. Though the young men don't notice it, Her Majesty Queen Elizabeth II is travelling down the five-furlong straight towards them in the Royal car.

The Royal family has come to the Derby ever since Her Majesty watched the legendary Sir Gordon Richards win the race for the only time on Pinza in her Coronation Year of 1953. But the Derby doesn't hold its breath for the Royal party, as Ascot does just two weeks later. 'The Derby's always been more about racing and ordinary folk,' one Metropolitan Police constable standing at the edge of the course, waiting for Her Majesty, remarks. 'It's not about pomp and circumstance; never has been – that's Ascot.'

Nevertheless, Her Majesty duly climbs out of the limousine, which has conveyed her from Tattenham Corner station, at precisely 12.20 p.m. to announce to the world, and to those members of the crowd who are taking any interest, that Derby Day 1992 has officially begun. The band of the Welsh Guards strikes up the National Anthem and the four young men suddenly realize that something unexpected is happening. For a moment they stop discussing the form and look up, only to see Her Majesty smile warmly at them. As the strains of 'God Save the Queen' echo across the lawn, a slight fluster overtakes them. None of the four seems sure whether or not to take off his top hat. The

earringed one does so, but his three friends don't. No one seems unduly perturbed. As the music ends, the young man with the two earrings puts his top hat gratefully back on the back of his head.

Pausing briefly to unveil a plaque announcing that she has opened this new stand which bears her name, the Queen, together with the Duke of Edinburgh, is ushered into the new cinema to see a specially prepared five-minute video of the history of the race, before being allowed to retire to the Royal Box and the lunch she traditionally holds for those members of her family who choose to accompany her. The only price they have to pay is to buy a ticket in her sweepstake on the Derby itself. 'It gives Her Majesty the greatest pleasure,' one member of her party explains. 'She's always loved the Derby – and her sweepstake.' Last year she won it herself – rather than the race – but she's never made any secret that one of her most cherished ambitions is to emulate the feat of her great-grandfather, Edward VII, by owning a Derby winner. So far the dream may have eluded her, but she shows no sign of giving up her passion for the race.

Neither do the crowds. In the centre of the course the first gin and bitter lemon is being poured out on the folding picnic table, 'which we usually take down to Hayling Island'; a young mother with her twin daughters in a pushchair is struggling to get them an icecream; 'They don't mind where they are really, so long as there's icecream,' she murmurs, rummaging in her purse for change. A man sporting the distinctive bacon-and-egg-coloured tie of the Marylebone Cricket Club strolls past and confides to his friend, 'It's almost like one gigantic car-boot sale.' A queen's ransom of ready cash is changing hands.

The mobile National Westminster Bank, parked outside the grandstand, bears witness to that. The two young men behind the cramped counter have been turning cheques and credit cards into cash all morning, and there is still almost three hours to go before the race itself. 'We give plenty out,' one says cheerily, 'but in the six years I've been coming here on Derby Day we've never, ever, seen anyone pay any money back in again.'

In the grandstand itself, the box holders are also preparing to sit down for lunch. The waitresses in the International Racing Bureau box have had to leave their homes in South Wales shortly after 4.30 that morning to be transported to Epsom by coach, but they're in good heart. 'We enjoy it, always enjoy it. Mind you, hospitality boxes like this have changed racing, just as they've changed the other big sporting events like Wimbledon. Means there's more emphasis on the commercial side of things.' Neither waitress minds in the least. Meanwhile, the guests are comparing Epsom with other Derbies they've witnessed around the world.

The genial Ed Bowen, senior editor of *The Bloodhorse*, who lives not far from Churchill Downs in Louisville, home of the American Kentucky Derby, is reflecting that 'the two races are really very much the same. Even given the difference that Churchill Downs is really in the middle of an industrial estate, while Epsom is downland, the atmosphere at the two races is strikingly similar.' This is not Bowen's first Derby; he comes as often as he can, 'But I tell you one thing that's different. Her Majesty couldn't set foot on Churchill Downs, the courtesy of the crowd just couldn't be relied upon.'

Outside the plate-glass window of the box the crowd is settling down to enjoy its lunch. The members of the Garrick on their open-topped bus are also tucking into their appetisers, while the Romford double-decker is hosting the prawn cocktails. The threat of rain, forecast

for the afternoon, has ebbed away and the downs are bathed in warm June sunshine: just as the Derby should be.

*B*y the time the strawberries are served, the first handful of racehorses has begun to pick its path carefully through the crowd on its way back from exercise on the gallops that are part of Epsom Downs. These horses are the harbingers of the business which is about to occupy the 150,000 people assembled on these 600 acres of chalk downs south of London.

The first two races of the afternoon, traditionally the Woodcote Stakes and the Diomed Stakes (named after the winner of the first Epsom Derby in 1780), pass in a flash. The coffee is barely served in the grandstand, the port passed on the open-topped buses, or the brandy broken out on the downs, before the first of the Derby horses is led into the newly painted and flowered paddock. The horses look like a Stubbs painting, the nap of their coats glossed to a sheen, their manes plaited and groomed, tails flicking in the gentle afternoon breeze. More than £25 million of horseflesh walks steadily around the green lawn. Holidaymaking, rather than horseracing, may seem to fill the air, but that is the Derby's illusion. Gaiety there may be, but now there is a seriousness amidst the laughter, especially for the

An essential feature of Derby Day – picnicing on Epsom Downs alongside the open-top buses which line the course.

owners and trainers who flood into the paddock behind their horses.

Her Majesty the Queen arrives to a sprinkling of gentle applause, as does Her Majesty Queen Elizabeth, the Queen Mother, but the horses themselves are the true stars. For though Derby Day itself may have changed over the years, the race itself has steadily improved in quality so that it is still acknowledged as the finest and most testing race for three-year-old thoroughbreds held anywhere in the world. 'There's still only one Derby,' Tim Neligan says proudly, '. . . only one supreme test of a racehorse: the Derby on Epsom Downs.'

Though thousands of the crowd may never take any further interest in the sport of kings, they will forever be able to tell their grandchildren that they were there when one of the nineteen horses being led round the paddock in front of them wins the 1992 Derby. 'I can still remember Snow Knight's Derby as if it were yesterday,' says the bowler-hatted gateman barring the way to outsiders trying to join the throng in the paddock. 'You never forget a Derby winner, never.'

Like figures from a Spy cartoon the trainers solemnly arrive from the saddling boxes, looking much as they must have done a hundred years before – serious about their purpose, their black top hats standing out against the grey ones of the owners. The weathered leather of their binocular cases bangs gently against their sides as they walk across the well-mown grass. Former pools tycoon, Robert Sangster, greets his trainer and son-in-law, Peter Chapple-Hyam; Mr Khaled Abdulla welcomes André Fabre from France; Mrs Virginia Kraft Payson from America is joined by her trainer, Jim Bolger from Ireland; while Mrs Shirley Robins shakes hands warmly with the redoubtable former jockey, turned trainer, Geoff Lewis from nearby Headley.

Suddenly, like circus acrobats emerging into the big top, the jockeys themselves stream into the paddock. There is the odd subdued cry of 'Come on Lester' to greet the nine-time winner of the race, but conversations in the paddock are conducted in whispers rather than shouts. Sentences are short. Instructions from trainer to his jockey are brief.

'Give him every chance, but don't force the colt . . . He may not handle the course . . . Make sure you are two off the rails as you come round Tattenham Corner . . . Don't watch Lester . . . Don't panic.'

To win the race is every jockey's dream, but they remain studiously calm in the final moments before they parade the horses in front of the grandstands and set off across the downs to the furthest corner of the horseshoe that makes up the Derby course. On their tiny racing saddles the nineteen jockeys look, for all the world, like the 'monkey on a stick' as Tod Sloan, the innovative American, was once described. They perch precariously, legs gripped along the sides of the thoroughbreds beneath them, while the mounts strain and pull at the reins, anxious now to put the preliminaries behind them and get on with the race.

Indeed, as they walk through the milling crowd towards the course, the horses look more excited, more keyed up than their riders. 'You can't afford to be,' Alan Munro puts it. 'The race is too important. You've just got to keep your animal as calm and balanced as you can.' His mount, Great Palm, shows every sign of being a little more nervous than his jockey might prefer, 'but you've got to do everything you can.' It is no easy task.

These pampered and cossetted beasts, as delicately bred and prepared as any prize-winning greenhouse orchid, watch the world through their large liquid eyes as they walk past the gypsies and the T-shirt sellers towards the starting stalls. As Simon Barnes of *The Times* puts it later, 'They live in a different world of awareness, and have a different system of responses. They are creatures of extraordinary sensibility . . . animals that love to express themselves by running.' As they circle at the Derby start shortly before 3.45 in the afternoon, waiting to be loaded into the stalls, this group of nineteen three-year-old thoroughbred colts knows precisely what is expected of them. Now they want nothing more than to be left to accomplish it.

*B*ack in Queen's Stand, Mr Roy Wright, the owner of Well Saddled, is struggling through the crowd on his way back from the paddock. 'Excuse me,' he says patiently. 'I'm awfully sorry, but I do have a runner.' The crowd parts happily, delighted to let anyone who is contributing to the race see the result. 'He's a nice horse,' Mr Wright mutters almost to himself, as he focuses his binoculars on the stalls half a mile away. 'I just hope he gets through it all right.'

Opposite: Looking over Epsom Downs, a section of the 100,000 crowd watch the Parade of Derby runners begin.

In the commentary box above Mr Wright, the Australian race reader, J.A. McGrath, is telling the crowd that everything is going smoothly. 'There are just one or two more to go in now . . .' There is a slight, but significant, pause: '. . . the handlers seem to be having a little difficulty with Young Senor'. The mount of jockey Ray Cochrane is refusing to go into the stalls in spite of gallant efforts by the handlers and the assistant starters. Though he has done it on a racecourse six times before, and countless times during his days in training, at this precise moment the three-year-old colt cannot accept the need to be pushed into a small steel cage – Derby or no Derby. Even having a grey flannel blindfold pulled over his head, and being led round in circles, doesn't do the trick. Young Senor is withdrawn. The downs seem to hold their breath as the starter raises his white flag.

A great stillness drapes itself across Epsom like a blanket. For a moment, even the bookies stop shouting the odds. Every eye is concentrated on the grass horse-shoe all around them. 'They're under starters orders,' McGrath bellows. 'They're off!' As St Jovite and Pollen Count make their way to the front of the runners streaming up the first furlongs right-handed towards the top of the hill, Young Senor is left behind at the stalls. His owner and trainer are inconsolable, but it is the horse himself who decides whether, and if, he is going to run.

'At the top of the hill, it's Twist and Turn from Pollen Count and St Jovite in second, with Great Palm and Alflora close behind,' McGrath says calmly. 'They're turning down the hill towards Tattenham Corner, and it's still Twist and Turn from St Jovite and Pollen Count, with Rodrigo de Triano making some progress through the field, followed by Rainbow Corner and Silver Wisp.'

The eighteen remaining runners in the 1992 Derby have been racing for a little over a minute, covering half the twelve furlongs of the race. As they come down Tattenham Hill at a speed of more than thirty-five miles per hour they turn sharply to the left. It's here the race is won or lost. There are restraining rails here, but it is still the place on the course which is most dangerous for horse and jockey. They are on a camber sloping to their left, and every rider knows that he must gather his horse now for the race up the straight towards the finish.

No one knows that better than Lester Piggott, but his mount, Rodrigo de Triano, the horse that galloped this course just thirty-six hours earlier, isn't in the best position. He is on the inside with a wall of horses in front of him. By contrast, Dr Devious, the horse that joined Rodrigo on these downs at seven the previous morning and ridden by thirty-six-year-old John Reid, is in the perfect position.

'As they come round Tattenham Corner it's still Twist and Turn from Great Palm and Pollen Count,' McGrath says from the commentary box, 'with Dr Devious coming up smoothly on the outside.' The horses turn into the straight and, with little less than half a mile to run, the long-time leader Twist and Turn, ridden by Michael Kinane from Ireland and trained by Henry Cecil at Newmarket, is still in front. But behind him the race is on in earnest. St Jovite, ridden by his fellow Irishman Christy Roche, ranges up alongside, while Dr Devious is increasing his speed with every stride. 'At the two-furlong marker, it is St Jovite just the leader from Dr Devious and Twist and Turn, with Silver Wisp making his way through the field, chased by Muhtarram.'

For a second the crowd again holds its breath and then – just as suddenly – breaks its self-imposed silence. A great roar grows steadily as the horses race towards the dip in the course less than 150 yards from the finish. 'It's Dr Devious with St Jovite and Silver Wisp.' The screams melt into a single deafening chorus as Dr Devious streaks past the winning post two lengths clear of St Jovite and Silver Wisp. 'With Muhtarram fourth and Twist and Turn fifth.' The relief and joy in McGrath's voice is matched by every man and woman on the downs.

The winning jockey, John Reid, who has ridden in the race seven times before, but never won, shakes his fist with pleasure as he pulls his horse up slowly after the winning post to let a beaming stable lad run out and greet him. 'Today I realized a dream,' he explodes, moments after he climbs down from the horse and collects the saddle and girths for the trip back to the scales to weigh in. 'There'll never be another day like it in my life.' This gentle, popular jockey, who won Europe's richest race, the Prix de l'Arc de Triomphe, in 1985, says simply, 'I always hoped that one day it would come true – and it has.' His smile is large enough to light up a small town, and warm enough to heat it too.

Dr Devious, on the rails, gives jockey John Reid his greatest moment, as he wins the 1992 Derby by two lengths.

The smile on the face of Peter Chapple-Hyam, trainer of Dr Devious, is even larger. In just his second season as a professional he has saddled the winner of three classic races; the English Two Thousand Guineas, the Irish Two Thousand Guineas and now the Epsom Derby. No trainer has matched that performance in recent years, and it's a gilded start to his career. 'Everyone has tried to run this horse down,' the greengrocer's son tells the press crowded around him. 'Most of you gentlemen laughed at him. But this is a very good horse. This is a serious horse.' And to underline his own special delight he repeatedly kisses Dr Devious on the nose.

On the new Presentation Float, which has been wheeled effortlessly out in front of the grandstand, Lord White of Hull is beaming every bit as enthusiastically as he presents the Derby trophy to the winning owner, Mr Sidney Craig of the United States.

For his part Mr Craig looks not a little dazed. He has only recently been given the horse as a sixtieth birthday

Triumphant expressions in Epsom's Winner's Circle. Dr Devious was a birthday present to Mr Sidney Craig (centre) from his wife Jenny.

[109]

present by his wife, Jenny, because she couldn't think of anything that would delight him more. A stunned, rather than beaming, Mr Craig simply manages to tell the cheering grandstand, 'It is a great, great privilege to win this race – of all races. I never dreamed I would.'

But the Epsom Derby has always been the race that dreams are made of.

*M*r Craig has hardly had time to pick up his gold trophy, together with a prize of more than £350,000, before the celebrations and the postmortems begin. In the Owners and Trainers bar the talk is all of the winning. 'Do you realize the horse has been sold three times in the past year . . . Robert Sangster sold it for $600,000 to Lucianno Gaucci, then it was sold for $2.5 million to Mrs Craig after it had failed in the Kentucky Derby . . . Doesn't matter a jot, it's worth four times that now . . . It's just Epsom . . . It spent two days in a container on its flight back from America because they hadn't got the quarantine papers right . . . Do you think Lester knew it was the other Chapple-Hyam horse that would win . . . you know, concentrate all the attention on Rodrigo and then win with Devious?'

The champagne and the gossip flow across the tall silver stools in the glass-fronted bar with its view of the next race. But no one is paying attention to the Night Rider Stakes – all that matters is the Derby. Out on the course, among the spare ribs and the baked potatoes, the conversation is only a little different. On the rails of the Walton Enclosure couples are standing by the running rail in the sunshine, drinking tea from thermos flasks. 'Lost the lot on Lester, should have known better . . . That John Reid did well though, didn't he? Never looked in any trouble at all . . . Minnie had it – the winner – at 8 to 1. Not bad . . . Well, at least we got something. Silver Wisp did us nicely. Couldn't ask for better . . . No, Cauthen couldn't do anything, horse was all over the place as it passed us. Nothing he could do about it . . . Never been a grey winner, not since 1946 anyway, so I couldn't see Great Palm making it today . . . Made twenty quid. Mind you, I lost more on the race before. Still . . .'

As the Queen's party prepares to leave, this time taking the road outside the stand rather than the racecourse itself, the young people on the grass opposite the grandstand are paying even less attention than they were five hours earlier. They are more intent on getting

to know each other better. Mrs Patrick Campbell would probably have approved; though they may be warming up to make love, they clearly aren't frightening the horses. Certainly, in front of the Garrick bus, three couples are amorously ignoring the sixth and final race of the day. But no one is in the least perturbed. Every member has enjoyed it. 'Well worth getting up early for . . . wouldn't have missed it for the world . . . and we've made a profit'. The Club's secretary is clearly relieved everything has gone so well. 'We'll be off before too long, take it easy going back to London, perhaps stop just once on the way. It's been a beautiful day. Great fun. Always is.'

Thankfully, it's been the same for almost everyone. No dangerous injuries, no awful accidents, just the usual crop of minor complaints and medical emergencies. But in front of the unsaddling enclosure the senior medical officer, Dr Richard Glover, and the St John's Ambulance team are preparing for their busiest time. 'It's been a very relaxed day so far, thank goodness,' Dr Glover remarks calmly. The fourteen ambulances on duty haven't been unduly overworked. 'A few collapses in the sun. One or two cardiac calls. Nothing serious. It's more often people forgetting their pills, although one chap did have a suspected broken ankle.'

The medical team is not too relaxed, however. It knows from experience that the greatest danger lies as the crowd begins gradually to disperse. 'The fights; they usually give us the biggest headache . . . They can get quite nasty . . . People have a bit too much to drink and don't know when to stop,' says Bob Hutton, the Assistant Commissioner of the St John Ambulance Service on duty on the downs. 'Mind you, we've not had anything really nasty at the Derby for years. The worst thing we have to deal with is radio interference on our portable radios – ever since the tick-tack men changed from hand signals to their own walkie-talkies we've had nothing but trouble;' but he smiles as he says it.

Not everyone is intent on getting inebriated, however. The High Wycombe Evangelistical Christian Group, who've been regulars at the Derby for more than twenty-five years, are spreading their message of goodwill, even if Shirley from Dagenham and Andrew from New Cross have just lost £20 to a gentleman demonstrating the intricacies of the three-card trick.

'Part of the tapestry of life, my friends . . . Didn't stand a blooming chance, did we? . . . I'm going back to the beer tent . . . Plenty of time before we need to leave.'

In the Mahmoud Bar beneath the grandstand the singing is getting louder. Taking their cue from the Welsh Guards, who played the song as the prizes were presented to Mr Craig and his wife, two groups of young men are treating the remaining punters to a healthy rendition of the old Cliff Richard hit, 'Congratulations'. The remaining racegoers are determined to go home happy. Her Majesty has departed but things aren't all that different in Queen's Stand, only there isn't any singing – just distinctly loud voices. Tea is being served, along with Dundee cake and small cucumber sandwiches, though there's the odd celebratory bottle of champagne thrown in for good measure in both places.

The queue of buses and cars crossing the course on its way back to London signals the beginning of the end of the Day. There was a time when the carriages and carts could take six hours to make their way back to Stepney and Bethnal Green, but the double-deckers and Sierras will do it comfortably in half the time, leaving a good hour for a stop at a friendly pub on the way. The fair is in full swing, but that's more for the revellers who are going to risk the last train from Tattenham Corner than the families with their tents and tables, cool boxes and barbecues.

If any final sign were needed to mark the end of Derby Day, it comes just before six o'clock. A lone figure walks sedately across the now deserted bookies' pitch in front of the grandstand and quietly enters the Mahmoud Bar. But he doesn't want a drink, he just wants to feel the atmosphere, remember the feeling of the Derby in 1992. Mr Mario, as the badge on his hat declares, has been coming to the Derby since Prince Monolulu became the race's most famous tipster in the 1930s. Wearing a Union Jack hat, a picture of the Prince and Princess of Wales stuck to a clock hanging on his chest, and covered in small badges of every kind, declaring everything from 'Have a Nice Time' to 'Remember to be Happy', Mr Mario has tipped the winner – as he does every year, or so he says. 'I told everyone who asked me . . . and I had £100 each way myself . . . I'll show you the ticket if you don't believe me.'

At the end of Derby Day no one could possibly doubt him. How could they? One of the Derby's

Mr Mario, part of the Derby scene for more than fifty years.

characters, like Lee Bennett who still practises the famous Derby pastime of 'Guess Your Age' near Tattenham Corner, Mr Mario loves the Derby. 'For the day as much as the race. It's the people. That's what makes it for me. Couldn't be anything else, couldn't be anywhere nicer.'

The best part of 150,000 people would agree with him. The Epsom Derby, which costs £500,000 to stage and a little over £1,250,000 to administer during the year, and which attracts more than £40 million of bets and seventy-five tons of litter, not to mention the attention of more than 450 million people around the world on television, retains the affection of millions of people who hardly know a hoof from a hock.

As Mr Mario walks sadly out of the grandstand, like Chaplin at the end of an old two-reeler, the spirit of the Derby seems to leave with him, for this is more than a great race for thoroughbreds. The Derby is a bulwark of England and its individuality.

PIGGOTT AND THE DERBY

by

Richard Onslow

For more than forty years Lester Piggott has been making history in the Derby. Having become one of the youngest jockeys to be mounted in the race in 1951, he was the youngest to win it during the present century just three years later. In 1972 he equalled the record for the number of riding successes at Epsom (that had stood for 136 years), and in 1976 broke that record; then, in 1983, he set a record that probably will never be broken – by anybody but himself – by winning the most famous race in the world for the ninth time.

In June 1954, while no more than eighteen years of age, Lester created one of the sensations of the postwar decade by winning the Derby on the 33–1

Opposite: Eighteen-year-old Lester Piggott after winning the 1954 Derby on Never Say Die.
Above: Sir Ivor gives Lester Piggott his fourth Derby winner in 1968, comfortably beating Connaught.

outsider, Never Say Die. Possibly he was the youngest rider ever to win the race. The stable lad Parsons, successful on Caractacus in 1862, was reputed to have been sixteen, but there is no proof on that point.

Rounding Tattenham Corner the joint favourite, Rowston Manor, ridden by Doug Smith, disputed the lead with The Queen's Landau on whom Willie Snaith deputized for the injured Gordon Richards. Never Say Die, the chestnut conspicuous for his long white blaze, was handily on the outside. Shortly afterwards, with two furlongs to run, Lester sent Never Say Die to the front and, staying on strongly, the colt won by a decisive two lengths from Arabian Night.

Asked by the press for his reaction to having won the Derby, the teenage jockey replied impassively, 'It's just another race.' He meant it. One of his most important assets is total imperturbability and refusal to become emotionally involved in professional commitment.

Although his acute brain will be brought to bear upon the problems posed by a race, his heart will never miss a beat. While many another jockey finds the tension in the hours before the Derby all but unbearable, Lester remains perfectly cool and in a frame of mind to exercise tactical judgement quite dispassionately.

Never Say Die was trained by Joe Lawson at Newmarket and owned by the seventy-eight-year-old American millionaire, Robert Sterling Clark, whose horses Lester had agreed to ride when he was available that season. He was not necessarily pleased to ride Never Say Die who had not run up to expectation on the two previous occasions he had ridden him. Consequently, he had not accepted the mount when Never Say Die had been beaten into third place at Newmarket in his race immediately prior to the Derby.

Robert Sterling Clark did not think it worth coming over from America to see Never Say Die run in the Derby and, knowing that Lester had been disappointed by him at Liverpool and then at Newmarket, Joe Lawson, who never lost faith in the colt, offered the mount to Charlie Smirke and then Manny Mercer. Having found neither available, Lawson reluctantly reverted to Lester, despite the young rider's lack of confidence. Only when he saw Never Say Die in the parade ring at Epsom, and immediately recognized the enormous physical improvement the handsome chestnut had made in a matter of weeks, did Lester Piggott realize that there was a real chance of winning the Derby.

With the retirement of Sir Gordon Richards later in 1954, Lester became stable jockey to Noel (later Sir Noel) Murless for whom he won the Derby on Sir Victor Sassoon's Crepello, a heavy-topped chestnut colt by Donatello II, in 1957. By way of contrast to Never Say Die, Crepello was hot favourite for the Derby as he had already proved his class by winning the Two Thousand Guineas and was bred to be a great deal more effective over the mile and a half. The only real doubt about Crepello, so far as the winning of the Derby was concerned, lay in misgivings as to whether his conformation would enable him to act on the switchback Epsom course.

Riding with the consummate skill of an experienced jockey, Lester, still only twenty-one, kept Crepello beautifully balanced on a track that was certainly not ideal for him. Having had him just behind the leaders from the start, Lester set the big chestnut alight with a little more than a furlong to run, and Crepello produced the instant acceleration (characteristic of the high-class racehorse) to go away to beat the Irish challenger Ballymoss, hard ridden by Scobie Breasley, by a length and a half.

Three years after the success of Crepello, Lester won his third Derby on St Paddy, also trained by Noel Murless for Sir Victor Sassoon. A handsome and powerful bay colt by the Queen's stallion Aureole, St Paddy had an obvious chance in the Derby as he had been a promising sixth in the Two Thousand Guineas and then won the Dante Stakes over a mile and two-and-a-half furlongs at York in May. On the strength of those performances, St Paddy figured third in the betting at 7–1, the French colt Angers being favourite at 2–1.

Through nobody's fault, this was a thoroughly unsatisfactory Derby. Coming round Tattenham Corner, three and a half furlongs from home, Die Hard led from Auroy and Tulyartos, with St Paddy just behind them in much the same position as Crepello had been at that stage of the race. Neither Lester, nor the riders of the three leaders, could know that no challenge from the favourite would materialize – Angers had shattered the cannon bone of his near fore halfway down the hill. Auroy, ridden by Geoff Lewis, took the lead off Die Hard, two furlongs out, only to be immediately challenged by Lester on St Paddy who secured a clear advantage after another furlong and went away to win by a commanding three lengths from Alcaeus, another Irish colt ridden by Scobie Breasley, Lester's great rival of that era.

The following year, 1961, the stage was set for Lester to win another Derby for Sir Victor Sassoon and Noel Murless on Pinturischio, a massive bay colt of great strength by Pinza. Although he had been unable to run as a two-year-old on account of a coughing epidemic just before he was to have made his first appearance in public, Pinturischio was favourite for the Two Thousand Guineas and the Derby on the strength of his obvious superiority over stablemates on the gallops at Newmarket. He was to have a belated first outing in the Wood Ditton Stakes on Thursday, April 13, the third day of Newmarket's Craven meeting. As Aurelius, to whom Pinturischio was demonstrably far superior, won the Craven Stakes on the first day of the fixture, the Wood Ditton looked a formality, and so it proved, with Pinturischio winning comfortably.

Although Pinturischio was no more than a respectable fourth in the Two Thousand Guineas, he remained firm favourite for the Derby with the Dante Stakes his intermediate objective. A week before the Dante, a gang broke into Murless's Warren Place stable and nobbled Pinturischio with a powerful drug used for treating elephants. The Dante Stakes was out of the question, but there seemed a fair chance of Pinturischio running in the Derby after all, as Murless gently brought him back into work; but he was nobbled for a second time by the gang in the employment of bookmakers who had laid heavily against the colt. Pinturischio never ran again and, having declined to ride Psidium for Harry Wragg's stable, Lester was left without a mount in the race for the first time in eleven years. Watching the race on television in the sitting-room of his Newmarket home, he saw Psidium, ridden by the Frenchman Roger Poincelet, win at 66–1.

In the middle of 1966 Lester shook the racing world by announcing that he was no longer stable jockey to Noel Murless, from whom he was receiving no retainer by that time, and was becoming a freelance so that he would be able to ride strongly fancied runners from the yards of Vincent O'Brien and other leading trainers in the big races.

In the Derby of 1967, his first full year as a free-lance, he rode Mr Charles Englehard's Ribocco, trained by Fulke Johnson Houghton, a friend from boyhood. After being brilliant as a two-year, Ribocco was beaten in each of his first three races in his second season, thereby giving rise to suspicion as to whether he was genuine. Bearing in mind the doubts as to his temperament, Lester gave Ribocco plenty of time to settle, and he was still nearer last than first of the twenty-two runners as he rounded Tattenham Corner on the wide outside, according to plan, so there was no chance of his being discouraged, or sulking, as a result of being jostled in the scrum of a big field going round a tight bend. Soon after straightening up for home, Lester asked Ribocco, still racing on the far outside, for an effort. The colt responded well, making up ground on the leaders, but could not quite go through with his effort and was beaten two-and-a-half lengths into second place by Royal Palace – trained by Noel Murless.

While Lester had no formal agreement with Vincent O'Brien, there was an understanding between them that Lester would ride any top-class horse that the Tipperary trainer ran outside Ireland. Thus Lester came to ride Mr Raymond Guest's Sir Ivor in the Derby of 1968. As the combination had already triumphed thoroughly convincingly in the Two Thousand Guineas Sir Ivor went to the post an odds-on favourite at Epsom.

When winning the Derby on Crepello in very early manhood Lester's leathers were pulled up so that he gripped the withers with his knees, his legs beneath the knee perpendicular in the style of Charlie Elliott, Charlie Smirke and the rest of the previous generation of English jockeys. Eleven years later, he rode Sir Ivor in a very different manner. As a result of having pulled up his stirrup leathers his knees were well above the withers if he stood up in his irons and, when he sat down, his heels all but touched the saddle. In action he crouched with his long thighs and backside high in the air, and his shoulders so low that they were just above his knees. In consequence the minimum demand was made on the strength of his mount for the bearing of his bodily weight as almost all of it was concentrated directly above the shoulder, that part of the anatomy of the horse best calculated to bear it, so that strength and energy that would have been used for weight bearing was released for galloping. With such short leathers, Lester appeared to many people so precariously perched on the back of a horse that he would be faced with an impossible task keeping it balanced around the turns and gradients of a course like Epsom – but, ever a law unto himself, he readily gave the lie to such misgivings.

The confidence with which Lester rode Sir Ivor, a beautifully moulded bay colt, in that Derby of 1968, was almost incredible. Settling him towards the rear of the field, although there were no doubts about his temperament, Lester did not begin to make up ground until moving into sixth place on the run down to Tattenham Corner where the massive Connaught went to the front. Once in line for home, Connaught length-ened his stride to set such a terrific gallop that, two furlongs from home, he had set up a lead that seemed to assure him success. Sir Ivor, though, was still on the bit and, coming through with a long steady run on the outside, drew upsides Connaught a furlong out;

Piggott mastery at Tattenham Corner in the 1970 Derby: Nijinsky, poised three off the rails, has a clear run up the finishing straight.

but it was not until inside the last 100 yards that Lester played his ace. On asking for the blinding turn of speed he knew would be forthcoming, Sir Ivor simply sprinted away to win by a length and a half without being extended.

The Derby of 1970 was generally seen as a match between Charles Engelhard's Nijinsky, whom Lester rode for Vincent O'Brien, and the French-trained Gyr, the mount of the Australian Bill Williamson. The cards were clearly stacked in favour of Nijinsky who started favourite on the strength of his fluent success in the Two Thousand Guineas. A really magnificent bay by Northern Dancer, Nijinsky was a colt of enormous presence, and still unbeaten. At 11–8, he was starting at odds against for the only time in his career.

In some ways the race that Lester rode on Nijinsky against Gyr was very like the one he had ridden on Sir Ivor against Connaught, though it was sheer class, rather than an almost miraculous turn of foot, that won the race. Once again making headway on the run down to Tattenham Corner, he took Nijinsky into fifth place, on the rails, with Gyr on his outside, behind Long Till, Meadowville and Mon Plaisir. Just as he had done with Connaught, Lester allowed Gyr first run and, at more than two furlongs from home, the French horse held a clear lead. Lester then shook up his mount and, as Nijinsky raced with the improving Stintino just behind Gyr at the two-furlong marker, the issue looked a great deal more open than backers of the favourite could have relished. It was, however, no more than a momentary impression. Nijinsky quickly shook off Stintino and, taking the measure of Gyr a furlong from the post, strode away to win by two-and-a-half lengths without being extended.

Lester had to ride what was probably the most powerful finish of his whole career to win his sixth Derby, on Roberto in 1972, thereby equalling the record set up by Jem Robinson on Bay Middleton in 1836. Steve Donoghue also rode six Derby winners, but two of them were wartime substitute races at Newmarket. Unfortunately, the circumstances that led to Lester riding Roberto were surrounded by a great deal of controversy, not to say unpleasantness.

Roberto was a rangy, well-made brown colt by Hail to Reason, owned by the American John Galbreath and trained by Vincent O'Brien. Lester was offered the mount in the Two Thousand Guineas and in the Derby, but declined as he wanted to ride the unbeaten Crowned Prince for Bernard van Cutsem in both races. Consequently, Bill Williamson was engaged to ride Roberto in the English classics.

As Crowned Prince was found to have a soft palate after being beaten in the Craven Stakes in early April, and never ran again, Lester rode Mirage in the Two Thousand Guineas, but was unplaced to High Top who held a strong challenge from Roberto by half a length. That performance suggested that Roberto would be still more effective over a mile and a half at Epsom – and he soon became favourite for the Derby. Meanwhile, Lester's name was associated with a number of possible runners such as Hard to Beat, who went for the French Derby, Boucher, who ran disappointingly at Chester, Martinmas and Manitoulin, O'Brien's second string, and Pentland Firth. Finally, matters were resolved by the announcement that he would ride Manitoulin who belonged to John Galbreath's wife.

Ten days before the Derby, Williamson injured a shoulder in a fall at Kempton Park and, although passed fit to ride by the doctors on the Monday before the Derby, John Galbreath decided to replace him by Lester (Williamson receiving the same present in the event of success). The supplanting of Williamson was badly received by the public and a large section of the press who felt that Galbreath and O'Brien were being unsporting as well as disloyal; Lester was widely regarded as having usurped a ride for which another jockey had been booked since the outset of the season.

Pentland Firth led into the straight with Roberto in the middle of a bunch of horses, some three lengths behind him. A little under two-and-a-half furlongs out Roberto, with Rheingold on his outside, began to close on the leader. After another half furlong the three were line abreast, as Pentland Firth began to come away from the rails. At the same time, Rheingold was hanging left, so that Roberto was in the uncomfortable position of being the meat in the sandwich. Soon, Pentland Firth dropped out of the race, leaving Rheingold, ridden by Ernie Johnson, with a slight advantage over Roberto at the outset of their desperate duel over the final furlong. First one, then the other, of two very tired horses had an edge, Rheingold continuing to hang left towards his rival so that they bumped several times. Standing up in his short leathers, Lester towered over Roberto as he tried to swing his whip in his right hand (despite the proximity of Rheingold), driving as only he knows how. As they came up to the post his titanic efforts seemed to have been all in vain as Rheingold's head showed in front but, in the dying stages of the race, Lester made a last frantic effort to retrieve the situation and in the final twenty yards contrived to give Roberto four more cracks of the whip. On the line Roberto won by a short head.

The inevitable Stewards' enquiry as to whether there had been interference followed but, not surprisingly, the places remained unaltered. With Rheingold hanging towards him, Roberto had been far more sinned against than sinning. The announcement confirming that the favourite was the winner was greeted by a silence unprecedented on Derby Day; the result had not diminished by an iota the unpopularity of the decision to replace Bill Williamson by Lester Piggott. Yet there were two things that nobody could deny. The first was that the owner had an inalienable right to decide who should ride his horse in the absence of a formal contract. The second was that the wiles of Williamson would never have carried the day, whereas the power of Piggott prevailed.

Ironically, Lester's feat of equalling Jem Robinson's record of riding six winners of the Derby could so easily have been acclaimed, on a very much hotter favourite, had Crowned Prince remained sound. On two-year-old form Crowned Prince was demonstrably far superior to Roberto and Rheingold as he had beaten Rheingold by five lengths in the Dewhurst Stakes.

Contrary to his own expectations, Lester set up a new record in 1976 by winning his seventh Derby on

Vincent O'Brien's beaming head lad, Jerry Gallagher, greets Lester Piggott after The Minstrel's 1977 Derby victory.

Empery, a colt of singularly cosmopolitan connections: he was ridden by an Englishman, owned by the American, Nelson Bunker Hunt, and trained in France by Egyptian-born Maurice Zilber. That year the Derby was dominated by Two Thousand Guineas winner, Wollow, trained at Newmarket by Lester's friend, Henry Cecil. Wollow was to start hot favourite at 11–10, with Empery one of three joint-second favourites being laid at 10–1. Had any other rider been in the saddle, Empery would almost certainly have been at twice that price.

A sturdy bay, with an attractive action, by Vaguely Noble, Empery had won a race over a mile for unraced two-year-olds at Longchamp in September 1975, then finished unplaced in the Grand Criterium before being third in the Prix Thomas Bryon. As a three-year-old he had had three more races before going for the Derby, being fourth, ridden by Lester in the French Two Thousand Guineas, fifth in the Prix Daphnis over a mile and a furlong at Evry and third to his stablemate Youth in the Prix Lupin over a mile and two and a half furlongs at Longchamp. The form was distinctly useful, while some way below top class. But, as had been the case with Never Say Die twenty-two years earlier, Empery had a trainer with implicit faith in his potential.

Lester may have had his misgivings about his mount's ability to take the measure of the unbeaten Wollow, but he could be confident about a son of the Prix de l'Arc de Triomphe winner, Vaguely Noble, getting every yard of the mile and a half. Empery was up with the leaders from the start. As they made the turn round Tattenham Corner, Vitiges led from Radetzky and Relkino, with Empery on their heels. Two furlongs from home, Lester moved Empery into third place and, exerting heavy pressure on entering the final furlong, obtained the burst of speed that took the lead off Relkino. Staying on strongly, Empery won by three lengths, with Wollow, who had enjoyed anything but a clear run, fifth. Once again Lester had prudently raced towards the centre of the course up the straight, thereby avoiding the possibility of being shut into a pocket on the rails or otherwise being left without room in which to manoeuvre.

An eighth Derby winner followed immediately when Lester rode The Minstrel, owned by Robert Sangster and trained by Vincent O'Brien in 1977. The Minstrel was a medium-sized chestnut colt of considerable quality by Northern Dancer out of a half-sister to Nijinsky, with a large white blaze and four socks. Unlike Never Say Die and Empery, he had obviously discernible claims to winning the Derby, having won the Dewhurst Stakes and both his other races as a two-year-old before establishing himself as being of classic calibre by finishing third in the Two Thousand Guineas and second in the Irish Two Thousand Guineas, beaten by a short head.

Seeing Willie Carson on the Chester Vase winner, Hot Grove (an obvious danger), improving just before the top of the Hill at Epsom, Lester went with him so that he was in his usual, though not absolutely invariable, position just behind the leaders as they came round Tattenham Corner into the straight behind the pacemaking Milliondollarman. Shortly afterwards, with three furlongs still to run, Hot Grove looked the probable winner as he went on from Milliondollarman, but, at the same time, Lester set The Minstrel alight as the French-trained favourite Blushing Groom entered upon the reckoning. The Minstrel was not long in getting the upper hand of Blushing Groom and, taking the colt through with a smooth, unspectacular run – on the outside again – Lester had him almost upsides of Hot Grove two furlongs out. From thereon in, it was a duel between the two of them. For most of that quarter of a mile Hot Grove retained the advantage and, although Lester did not have recourse to exerting the same tremendous pressure that he had done on Roberto in that unforgettable Derby of five years earlier, he had to ride very hard indeed to force The Minstrel up in the dying strides to win by a neck.

Seeing that the record of riding six Derby winners at Epsom had stood for more than a century, it seems almost incredible that Lester should not only have broken it but also gone on to ride half as many winners again as Jem Robinson.

Lester's ninth Derby triumph materialized in 1983 when he rode Teenoso, a tall, rangy bay colt by Youth, owned and bred by E.B.Moller, and trained by Geoff Wragg who had taken over Newmarket's Abington Place stables from his father at the end of the previous season.

While trained very patiently by Harry Wragg as a two-year-old, Teenoso had been unplaced in the first two of his three races; he then revealed distinct

The number board on Epsom Downs, 1983. International jockeyship is demonstrated by the presence of the world's winning-most jockey, the American Willie Shoemaker (8,833 winners at his retirement in 1990) who flew across the Atlantic to ride Mr Sangster's Lomond. Steve Cauthen and Cash Asmussen, from USA but now based in Europe, rode The Noble Player and Gordian. Italian champion Gianfranco Dettori rode Tolomeo; the French ace Yves St Martin partnered Slewpy, an American colt flown over for the race, whilst the Irish champion Michael Kinane finished second on Carlingford Castle. The winner was number 25, Teenoso – Lester Piggott's unparalleled ninth Derby winner.

promise by finishing fourth of seventeen over a mile at Newmarket in the middle of October 1982. During the early part of his three-year-old days, Teenoso revelled in the heavy ground that persisted throughout the inordinately wet spring of 1983. Reappearing at Haydock Park in early April he was second over a mile and a quarter. A little under a fortnight later his stamina was given far greater play in another maiden race over a mile and a half at Newmarket; he won by eight lengths without having been challenged. Stepping up in class to contest the Derby Trial Stakes, on heavy going, at Lingfield in May, Teenoso came further to the forefront of the Derby picture by beating Shearwalk by three lengths.

As spring became summer, with the ground showing no signs of drying out, the Epsom course was still riding heavy on Derby Day when the greatly improved Teenoso started favourite at 9–2 in a field of twenty-one. Once again, having complete confidence in the stamina of his mount, Lester had Teenoso with the leaders from the start and turned into the straight in third place behind the outsiders Mitilini and Neorion. Three furlongs out, rather earlier than usual, Lester hit the front and Teenoso galloped on to give his rider that amazing ninth success in the Derby by beating Carlingford Castle by three lengths, without being extended.

When he won the ninth Derby on Teenoso, Lester was forty-seven years of age. He had been just fifteen when he had his first mount, Zucchero, in the Derby in 1951, less than three years after he had ridden his first winner on The Chase at Haydock Park in August 1948. Owned by the bookmaker, George Rolls, and trained by Ken Cundell at Compton in Berkshire, Zucchero was a dark bay colt of great ability; this was allied with the exasperatingly wayward temperament of his sire, Nasrullah, that accounted for his unpredictability at the starting gate. Ken Cundell, resplendent in morning coat, accompanied Zucchero to the start of the Derby and, taking hold of him by the bridle, tried to throw him into the race, almost literally, as the tapes rose. But Zucchero was in no mood to cooperate and, jumping off in his own time, was never in the race with a chance. In the circumstances he did well to finish thirteenth of thirty-three to Arctic Prince.

Twelve months later, in 1952, Lester became involved in a Derby drama for the first time, riding Mrs Pat Rank's Gay Time, trained by his first cousin (three times removed), Noel Cannon, at Druid's Lodge. Gay Time, an earlier winner at Salisbury, could not go the early pace and inevitably met with a good deal of interference in that huge field of thirty-three runners. Once in the straight, Lester found a clear run up the outside, the first of many times he would beat that particular path, and, at the distance, Gay Time had only Tulyar ahead of him. As he tired, Tulyar hung away from the rails to his right, though retaining the advantage to beat Gay Time by three parts of a length.

Convinced that he would have won, had he not been hampered as Tulyar came over to him, Lester would have objected had not Gay Time stumbled and thrown him on pulling up. As it took twenty minutes to catch him there was a long delay before Lester could weigh in. By that time it was too late to object.

The third mount to be taken by Lester in the Derby was Prince Charlemagne, trained on the spot at Epsom by Tommy Carey, in 1953. Not surprisingly, Prince Charlemagne started at 66–1 as he had only been third in a maiden at Hurst Park on his previous appearance; he finished fifteenth of twenty-seven to Pinza, ridden by Gordon Richards in what proved to be his last Derby. Prince Charlemagne may not have taken Lester to victory in the Derby, but he did provide him with the most important of his twenty successes over the sticks in the Triumph Hurdle, run at Hurst Park in March 1954.

After his splendid success on Never Say Die in 1954, Lester came down to earth again on the 33–1 chance, Windsor Sun, in 1955. In 1956 he rode another 33–1 shot in Doris Thelwall's Affiliation Order, fresh from winning a maiden race at Hurst Park for the Blewbury stable of Helen Johnson Houghton, mother of Fulke. Neither Windsor Sun nor Affiliation Order ran any better, or any worse, than they should have done. Windsor Sun, trained by Seamus McGrath in Ireland, was thirteenth of thirty-three to Phil Drake, while Affiliation Order was not in the first ten of twenty-six behind Lavandin. The rides on those two unplaced outsiders came between two winners as Lester landed his second Derby on his seventh mount in the race, Crepello, in 1957.

Like Crepello, Lester's mounts in the next three Derbies, Boccaccio, Carnoustie and St Paddy, were trained by Noel Murless. Having run disappointingly in his only previous races as a three-year-old, Sir Victor Sassoon's Boccaccio wore a hood when he started at 20–1 in 1958 but, after being prominent at Tattenham Corner, dropped back to be unplaced to Sir Victor's other runner, Hard Ridden, trained in Ireland. Colonel Giles Loder's Carnoustie was a well-backed 10–1 chance in 1959 but, although he made up ground well in the last furlong, he could do no better than finish sixth to Parthia. Lester was riding in the Derby for the tenth consecutive year when he won on St Paddy in 1960.

However, he had no ride following the defection of Pinturischio in 1961, nor in 1962 when he had been suspended two days before the race as a result of an

1965 was a year Lester Piggott did not win the Derby: riding the fancied Irish colt, Meadow Court, he pursued the French champion, Sea Bird II, at a respectful distance. The Epsom-trained I Say finished third.

incident that had taken place at Lincoln towards the end of May.

Resuming riding in the Derby in 1963, Lester favoured the blinkered Corpora, trained by Ernie Fellows in France. As Corpora had been third in the Two Thousand Guineas, he was more than mildly fancied and ran a good race to be fifth to the favourite, Relko, another French colt, after being third at Tattenham Corner. In 1964 Lester was riding again for Noel Murless in the Derby, as he wore the colours of Lady Sassoon, widow of Sir Victor, on Sweetmoss. Although he had won the Dante Stakes at York the previous month, Sweetmoss, never a factor in the Derby, was unplaced to the hot favourite Santa Claus. Following Relko and Santa Claus, the Derby went to the favourite for the third year running in 1965 when Sea Bird II, widely regarded as the best winner of the race in living memory, was successful. Lester's mount was G.M. Bell's Meadow Court, trained by Paddy

Prendergast in Ireland and second favourite at 10–1. After improving from the halfway stage, Lester brought Meadow Court through with a strong run in the final furlong; this never looked like making the slightest impression on Sea Bird II who won by two lengths.

Lester rode for Vincent O'Brien in the Derby for the first time in 1966, when he partnered Charles Engelhard's dark-brown colt, Right Noble, joint favourite at 5–1 on the strength of an easy win of the White Rose Stakes over a mile and a half at Ascot in April. In an attempt to exploit his stamina to the full, Lester sent him to the front after only two and a half furlongs, but he weakened rapidly after the turn into the straight and finished only ninth to Charlottown. Twelve months later he rode Ribocco for Fulke Johnson Houghton, and finished second to Royal Palace; in 1968 Sir Ivor became the first of the four Derby winners he has ridden for Vincent O'Brien.

Whereas Sir Ivor had started favourite for the Two Thousand Guineas and won, Ribofilio, whom Lester rode for Johnson Houghton in the Derby of 1969, was favourite for the Two Thousand and yet ran so atrociously that he had to be pulled up. Although no proof could be adduced, Ribofilio was almost certainly doped and, despite his having to miss work subsequently, he ran a satisfactory race in the Derby to be fifth to Blakeney, staying on strongly in the last furlong and a half. In 1970 came the magnificent triumph of Nijinsky, and in the Derby of 1971 Lester renewed the association with Noel Murless to ride The Parson, a maiden, who ran on over the final quarter of a mile to finish sixth to Mill Reef.

Lester very nearly won a second Derby in succession, riding Cavo Doro in 1973, the season after the hard-fought success of Roberto. Trained by Vincent O'Brien, Cavo Doro had just won the Royal Whip Stakes at the Curragh; in the Derby he finished fast to run Morston to half a length. In 1974 Lester rode Mrs J. Hanes's Arthurian for Henry Cecil, and in 1975 Charles St George's Bruni for the late Captain Ryan Price, before winning on Empery in 1976 and The Minstrel in 1977. Arthurian, fresh from success in a maiden at Newbury, was a 28–1 outsider and unplaced to Snow Knight, while the grey Bruni was down the field behind Grundy after being prominent for seven furlongs.

After his successes on Empery and The Minstrel, Lester rode the apparently fast-improving Inkermann for O'Brien in 1978. Favourite at 4–1 on the strength of his having won a maiden at the Curragh and the Gallinule Stakes, Inkermann was prominent until half-way, then dropped back to be twenty-first of twenty-five to Shirley Heights. In the two hundredth Derby in 1979, Lester rode the Queen's Milford for Major Dick Hern whose slightly better backed Troy was the mount of stable jockey Willie Carson. Troy won and Milford, who had been second to Lyphard's Wish into the straight, weakened two furlongs out to be tenth.

In the Derby of 1980 Lester rode Robert Sangster's Monteverdi who had been the top-rated two-year-old after winning the Dewhurst Stakes and his other three races for O'Brien's stable. At Epsom, Monteverdi, for a fourth time, completely failed to show normal improvement on juvenile form and was unplaced to Henbit. The next season, 1981, Lester had his first

mount in the Derby for a northern stable, riding Guy Reed's Shotgun, trained by Chris Thornton at Middleham. Having won the Heathorn Stakes at Newmarket in the spring, Shotgun was second in the betting which was completely dominated by Shergar; he ran respectably to be fourth to the hot favourite who won by ten lengths. Lester did not ride in the 1982 Derby but triumphed on Teenoso in 1983. He rode Mr Khalid Abdullah's Lingfield Derby Trial winner, Alphabatim, for Guy Harwood in 1984; having made his effort in the straight, Alphabatim finished fifth to Secreto. Ireland provided Lester with another Derby mount in 1985 when he rode Bertram Firestone's Theatrical, trained by Dermot Weld, a four lengths' winner of the Derrinstown Stud Derby Trial at Leopardstown in May. Although well enough placed at Tattenham Corner, Theatrical was unable to make any significant headway in the straight, and finished fifth to Slip Anchor.

With the close of the 1985 season Lester came to the end of thirty-eight years of continuous race riding – and retired from the saddle. After a spell of training and a short custodial sentence (arising from prosecution for tax offences), he dumbfounded millions of people, well beyond the perimeter of the racing world, by coming out of retirement to resume riding at the age of fifty-four in October 1990. He was, therefore, fifty-five years of age when he had his thirty-third ride in the Derby on Hokusai, trained for Charles St George by Henry Cecil in 1991. Prominent at Tattenham Corner as usual, Lester asked the question two furlongs out, but though Hokusai did his best he could not find the pace to go through with Generous, and finished seventh.

The Derby has been a showcase for all the diverse talents of Lester Piggott in a way that no other race could have been. The coolness of his handling of Never Say Die as a boy of eighteen, his balancing of the heavy-topped Crepello, the use of the incredible speed of Sir Ivor like a precision tool, the confidence displayed on Nijinsky, the sheer power that drove Roberto past the post, the judgement that exploited the stamina of Empery and that memorable ninth success on Teenoso, together with other masterly displays on St Paddy and The Minstrel can never be forgotten. Nobody has ever understood the mystique of the Derby as comprehensively as Lester Piggott.

22 May 1844. All roads from London lead to Epsom Downs – and all sorts and conditions of Londoners are about to witness the sensational Derby, after which Running Rein was disqualified.

A LONDON HOLIDAY

by

Alastair Burnet

The London that took it in mind to have a holiday going racing on Epsom Downs once a year knew it was the biggest, fastest growing, richest, most boisterous, roisterous, lusty and earthy city in the world – and its holiday, naturally, was just like itself. Derby Day started because gentlemen had raced their horses for years on the downs, and they gambled, as gentlemen do, and others heard of it. Racing was always the sport closest to gambling; the ring, the prize-fight, followed on its heels. Wherever men raced, other men fought, and the sharks and hustlers, the jugglers, tumblers, musicians, beggars, cripples, gypsies and vagabonds swarmed and luxuriated in their wake. It was a robust England and it lived chiefly as it liked.

Epsom, the little town on which London descended as the eighteenth century gave way to the nineteenth, had been used to the horsemen 100 years before. Indeed, genteel Londoners, like Samuel Pepys, had driven out to drink the spa waters (Pepys found he 'had some very good stools by it' in 1667), lunch off wine and fowl and inhale the country air. Epsom's fate was settled because it was only sixteen miles from the city, close enough to go and return in an early summer's daylight, without a change of horses. The stylish fours-in-hand and the costermongers' ponies, once watered and rested, could alike get their gambling, drinking, revelling owners back to town. Ascot, eighteen miles further west, was just too far away; its races were for the toffs, and remained so.

To the sportsmen of England, from its prime ministers down to what the aristos called the *canaille*, the superiority of the English thoroughbred was a matter of unchallenged English pride. The thoroughbred epitomized both the values and the triumphs of a rural society which, as an increasingly urbanized country grew in the smoke of industrialization, all classes still professed as their ideal. Even as the railways spread in the 1840s, and carried horses and people to race meetings, the Englishman's heart remained with the

stagecoach and the turnpike; in the age of the train Charles Dickens deliberately planted the adventures of Mr Pickwick and his friends on the high roads of an engaging, slowly disappearing country.

The expectations of the men, women and children who took the Epsom road each Derby Day fitted comfortably into the rough English ideal of sport. The Derby crowd, pouring out of London, took their pleasures and asserted their individuality as the English took their politics. Europeans who were appalled at the venality of English politics and politicians still averred that the great mass were richer, happier and even more respectable than they had expected. The English had adroitly turned their politics into sport – in the unreformed parliaments, as in the Eatanswill by-election – so that the French historian, Elie Halèvy, assessing the country that had won the Napoleonic wars, concluded that early nineteenth-century elections were explicable only 'if we regard the electoral contests in the light of a national sport, as popular as, indeed more popular than, horse racing'.

This was not democracy: the word would not have been voiced, in admiration or loathing, by anyone on the Epsom road. What they did know was that it was a day on which, however they got there and whatever they did there, they were all equal in opinion, in expectation, in the very exchange of abuse at the crossroads, and simply in being out together on a special day, that rarity in pre-Victorian England – a holiday. That Parliament itself would come to regard it as a holiday in 1847, and allow itself a holiday on Derby Day for forty-five years, would not have troubled those on the Epsom road. They had declared it for themselves, and they meant to keep it London's holiday whatever might be legislated. It was patriotic; that mattered more than it being constitutional. It was in no sense royal: Queen Victoria only went to it once, in 1840, and was disappointed at her reception. *The Times* admitted: 'There certainly was not that general enthusiasm which we have sometimes seen on similar visits of Royal person-ages to similar scenes.'

In 1865, the very year when the French overturned the superiority of the English thoroughbred with Gladiateur, the paper took a careful assessment of why Derby Day did matter to the people who mattered:

Parties for the Derby are formed among the operative class as much as two or three months before the race: every expense, including even turnpikes, is calculated, and the proportion which each should bear adjusted to a nicety; so that by a steady payment to the common fund of a couple of shillings weekly, or such other sum proportioned to their means as may be determined upon, the committee are in a position to make all necessary preparations before the Derby-day, and nothing remains for the party but to put on their best clothes and enjoy themselves.

The great day had thus added to it the high Victorian virtues of thrift and cooperation, two proprieties which only enhanced the entertainment. Once people were at Epsom, the moralist could say, they could indulge in

any rascality that their conscience allowed, but the basis of the day was proper – and popularly established:

When men for months together, unite for a common object, entailing considerable self-denial, the institution in connexion with which these qualities are exhibited deserves the name of one of the permanent institutions of the country.

So the Derby became, in its heyday, as secure and even as sacred as Christmas itself. Perhaps even more so. It was not until 1871 that Sir John Lubbock got his Bank Holiday Act through Parliament, and Londoners could turn, if they wished, to other attractions, to Easter and Whit Mondays and to the jolly August Monday on 'Appy 'Ampstead. But the lure of Epsom, of all its pleasures and hopes, did not go away.

The railway, and its excursion fares, made the Derby a national, not just a Londoners', day. By 1850 all England had ready access to London, and it and its habits, tastes and preoccupations came to dominate the country, as the crowds swarming to the Great Exhibition of 1851 demonstrated. The train, the tele-

1847. A 'Rocket' type locomotive draws the first race-train direct to Epsom, discharging a motley crowd to see thirty-two horses compete in the Derby. Cossack won at 5–1.

graph, the aeroplane, the popular papers, the radio and television were to turn it into a British occasion, independent of statute, and an international one, still obedient to its roots and self-confident in its traditions and its resilience.

*T*he road to Epsom was busy almost from the beginning. Neither war nor rumours of war got in the way of the gentry, the fancy and the punters. In 1793, when Pitt's England went to war with revolutionary France, the Derby and its myriad hangers-on went on with their business. *The Times* reported with gusto:

The road to Epsom . . . was crowded with all descriptions of people hurrying to the races, some to plunder and some to be plundered. Horses, gigs, curricles, coaches, chaises, carts, and pedestrians, covered with dust, crowded the Downs, the people running down, and jostling each other as they made contact. Hazard, cock fighting, E.O. and Faro assisted in plucking the pigeons, and the rooks feathered their nests with the plunder.

E.O. was a form of roulette, one of many devices to separate customers from their money. In 1795, with the French already thinking of invasion, life still had to go on: 'The blacklegs had a good harvest . . . at Epsom Downs, where many went to do, and many more to be undone.'

In May 1805, when Nelson had last been seen pursuing and losing the French fleet in the West Indies, the Prince of Wales, Mrs Fitzherbert, the Duke of Grafton, thirteen assorted lords and Sir Charles Bunbury (he who might once have given his name to the race) were all there with 'a number of city bloods'. It was a pugnacious crowd, in a bellicose country:

The spectators on horseback cut away the ropes which form a part of the fence for keeping the equestrians out of the course. Those persons whose business it was to keep the ground clear endeavoured, notwithstanding, to oppose the riders from passing their boundaries; the consequence was that a battle-royal ensued. The infantry arming themselves with sticks from the hedges, and large stones, attacked the cavalry with the greatest ferocity, and when obliged to fall back by the plunging of the horses, took shelter behind the carriages . . . The horsemen having nothing to defend themselves with but such small sticks as are generally used on horseback, were worsted in the engagement.

There were distinguished casualties: 'Mr Idle, of the Strand, an eminent Wine merchant . . . received a dreadful cut from the enemy, over his eye, and was obliged to be carried off the ground; another unfortunate Gentleman actually had his thigh broken in the affray.'

In 1814 the allies were occupying Paris and the race 'excited unusual interest'. Blücher, appropriately named, won by a neck. In 1815 Napoleon was back on the loose, Wellington was short of troops (much of the army was across the Atlantic dealing with the Americans), and Waterloo was still unfought:

Epsom Race-course was thronged . . . by an immense concourse of people of all descriptions, who were much disappointed, as the Derby stakes were won in one heat, by the Duke of Grafton's Whiskerandos. It proved a very true race, as there were 11 horses nearly neck and neck, till within 100 yards of the winning post.

Not a lot ever got in the way of the people's entertainment.

London was proud of its quick wit and sense of equality: any man could ask a lord, or even a prime minister, who he thought was going to win. But it was a holiday for the hard-bitten. In 1819, at the end of the meeting, *The Times*, rather squeamishly, followed the sporting gentry:

When the races were concluded, they endeavoured to amuse themselves by a view of a ruffianly sort of fight between Oliver and a black of the name of Kenrick, in which the former obtained the victory, without suffering the slightest injury. We should not have thought this circumstance worthy of mentioning, had we not had the sorrow of perceiving among the spectators of this brutal exhibition several well-dressed females, who, though they have almost forfeited their claim to the name of woman, by appearing at such a spectacle, will no doubt arrogate to themselves the name of ladies.

Another prize-fight started an affray on the course in 1824 when 'upwards of 500 horsemen, besides carts, waggons, etc., galloped indiscriminately down to the spot':

Many persons were knocked down and trampled on by the horses; one lady had her jaw broke by a horse treading on her, a countryman received a severe fracture of his arm, and a boy was so dreadfully kicked by a horse that he was completely stove in. He was conveyed instantly to the Magpie, in Epsom, where he died in about an hour afterwards.

Still, there was no day out like it. There were crowds along the side of the Epsom road just to see the London crowds going down it, one unbroken line of vehicles as far as the eye could reach. And they were there again to see the tipsy rout going home. The next year brought out the greatest agglomeration of the coachbuilder's craft:

The dashing four-in-hand, the coronetted landau, the four-posters, glass coaches, stage-coaches in prime style, post-chaises, gigs, tandems, cabriolets, caravans, post-waggons, slow waggons, hay-carts, dung-carts, and costermongers' barrowchettes, all were mingled in the promiscuous group, each striving for precedence.

For many of the travellers, betting was the main business of the day. It was the attraction for Disraeli at the start of *Sybil* (Phosphorus's Derby, 1837). Thackeray, in *Pendennis*, has Sir Francis Clavering facing ruin after the race. Henry Kingsley in *Ravenshoe* turns it into full melodrama when Lord Ascot, betting madly against his own horse, 'fell headlong down in a fit, like a dead man' when it wins, so that 'forty years' rents of his estates wouldn't set my lord on his legs again'.

The swells rode over to the starting post as soon as they arrived, to get their betting books up to date.

Hemmed in by a dense, sweating mass, they returned to lobster salad and champagne:

There were speculators of every class, from the swell Corinthian, who risks his thousands, to the humble Leg, who ventures his crowns. Nothing could be more animated or amusing than the intense anxiety manifested in every countenance, and the Babel-like confusion which prevailed throughout the morning till all doubts were at rest. It was a matter of astonishment to us how, in the midst of such noise, they could understand each other, or make correct memoranda of their engagements.

For those who wanted elegance, the arrival of the new Grand Stand, with its saloon, in 1830 was an encouragement to superior manners:

Whatever might be lost in point of numbers was fully compensated by a comparative increase in splendour. There was less of the canaille than usual; the company was more select and exhibited a greater uniformity of magnificence . . . We should think there were between 3,000 and 5,000 in the Grand Stand.

They enjoyed a ball and supper in the saloon after racing. Up on the hill, in the fairground, the singers, dancers, freaks, boxers, cheats and hucksters settled down to a night's profitable endeavour.

'How much did it cost full many a belle and beau that struggled, strove and fought and fainted to pay for their railway tickets?'

The new railway station was opened at Tattenham Corner in 1865. The Royal Party arrives here on Derby Day every year.

The railways made it easier for the horseless to get to Epsom and increased the crowd so that even the most improbable mid-century estimates had the ring of truth. The first trains ran from Nine Elms to Surbiton in 1838, leaving a mere walk of five miles, nothing in those days. The first direct journey from London Bridge station to Epsom itself was in 1847. The horde of passengers was so vast and the trains were so few that the company could not cope:

A delay of an hour kept those who had contrived to enter in anxious expectation for the arrival of the carriages in which they were to embark. On their arrival a fearful rush to obtain places took place. People who had paid for first-class places were glad to clamber up the sides of the cattle vans and get into them as well as they could. The mob which had waited from 1 o'clock began to move along the rails at ten minutes to 2, and reached the Epsom terminus by half-past 3, where they learnt that the Derby was over, and met a crowd of persons returning towards London.

But the trains proved both cheap and quick; even fashionable parties soon found that they could arrive at the course in the nick of time for lunch or for the race itself.

A second station was built for Epsom Downs and was favoured by the swells; eventually, a third at Tattenham Corner provided for the picnicking families. The rival companies advertised widely; every season the trains became longer and more frequent. It was the traditionalists who insisted on going the whole way by road; but there were many of them, rejoicing in the antiquity of the stagecoaches with names reminiscent of the old days: the Excelsior, the Perseverance, the Defiance, the Venture and even, a recognition of the iron enemy, the Rocket.

These were the great Derby days, epitomized by Frith's greatest success at the Royal Academy in 1858; this took him fifteen months to complete. It was the English carnival, the day for larks. It adhered to a folk instinct which brought seriously inclined gentlemen, like Dickens, Ruskin and the Frenchman, Hippolyte Taine, to the downs simply to observe the people, not the horses. Taine, in the 1850s, was struck by the sheer animal vigour of both men and women, normally so proper in their everyday lives:

Twenty-four gentlemen triumphantly range on their omnibus seventy-five bottles which they have emptied. Groups pelt each other with chicken bones, lobster-shells, pieces of turf. Two parties of gentlemen have descended from their omnibuses and engaged in a fight, ten against ten; one of them gets two teeth broken. There are humorous incidents: three men and a lady are standing erect in their carriage; the horses move on, they all tumble, the lady with her legs in the air; peals of laughter follow.

Henry James, when he went in the 1870s, chose to go by road, and saw as little of the race as anyone:

A dozen furiously revolving arms – pink, green, orange, scarlet, white – whacking the flanks of as many straining steeds; a glimpse of this, and the spectacle is over. The spectacle, however, is of course an infinitesimally small part of the purpose of Epsom and the interest of the Derby.

He marvelled rather at 'the British female of the lower orders' out to enjoy herself in her tens of thousands, 'too stout, too hot, too red, too thirsty, too boisterous'. In George Moore's *Esther Waters* (1894) the heroine and her friend simply wander in the dust and heat through the booths, the sideshows, the carriages and stands in a square mile of downland, fluttering with flags, parasols and canvas, where 'the great mob swelled, and smoked, and drank, shied sticks at Aunt Sally and rode wooden horses'. They do not even know that the race has been run. As the evening comes over the downs strewn with waste paper and covered by tipsy men and women, they can see 'a screaming and disordered animality'.

It was commonplace to say by the 1880s that the race was not what it was, and no longer the most important or interesting race of the year. *Bell's Life in London* was offhand about it: 'The intense, far spread interest once excited by the race has departed. The great days of the Derby ended, I think, about the period when Hermit and Blue Gown made the grand hit.'

That had been twenty years before. But the crowds did not noticeably fall off except in wet years, and were

Then, as now, open-top coaches provide Londoners with vantage points to watch the Derby. Here in 1879 they cheer Favonius owned by Baron Meyer de Rothschild.

King Edward VII on Derby Day, with members of The Jockey Club. The King won the great race in 1909 with Minoru. The Monarch traditionally leads the throng on Epsom Downs.

courage to make their way to the paddock and share their expertise. There was more expertise about, too. Races were now timed by means of Benson's marking chronograph, and even a 'photograph on a large scale is now considered indispensable' – supplied by a Mr Herbert Watkins. Derby Day was growing up.

The Derby's social apogee was reached, in a sense, in 1847, with its recognition by the House of Commons. Lord George Bentinck (who, a year before, had sold his entire stud, including the future Derby winner, Caprice) proposed that the House should take the day off. It had usually done so, unofficially. Now he wished to make it constitutional: 'Sir, for more than half a century the Derby-day [*cheers*] has been a recognised holyday. [*Renewed cheers.*]'

It could not fail to be popular, even if it were not holy in any way, with the two leading politicians, Derby and Palmerston; both had horses always in training and intent on the prize. Neither, in fact, was anything like as successful as John Gully, the MP for Pontefract and former prizefighter, who won the Derby twice. The Derby spirit was widespread, however, among Members of Parliament.

When Palmerston became Prime Minister he made the adjournment resolution Government business, 'as part of the unwritten law of Parliament', and moved it himself. He had his priorities. When his trainer, John Day, went to the House with an urgent question about the horses, Palmerston left an Irish debate and met him in the Lobby. Day congratulated him on getting to No. 10. 'Oh, thanks, John,' Palmerston said. 'I have won my Derby.'

None of this was to the liking of John Bright and the Radicals, but Palmerston ignored them. In 1860 he rode from Piccadilly to Epsom to see his horse Mainstone, third favourite, lose to Thormanby. He epitomized the sporting Englishman's idea of himself; he had already spoken up for prize fighting, to admiring applause.

Gladstone, too, was content to adjourn for the Derby. When, in 1872, he was faced with criticism that the race encouraged drink, gambling and worse, his deflection was astute:

The House agreed with his Hon. friend in his denunciation of the foolish, vicious, and even ruinously vicious practices in many cases associated with what they nevertheless believed

said to be getting better behaved and sometimes even 'marvellously orderly'. The fashionable world was regularly reinforced by the presence of the Prince of Wales and his friends. He gave the Derby a respectability among loyalists and it gave him a new popularity, especially when he won in 1896 and 1900 – and once as king in 1909. *The Times* commended him: 'He is a typical Englishman, and that is a character which cannot be fully attained except by one who shows himself to be in sympathy with that love of sport which is almost a passion with all ranks and classes in this country.'

Diamond Jubilee's victory, almost coinciding with the relief of Mafeking and the defeat of the Boers, was a particular signal for patriotic demonstrations. Despite the war, there was no evident fall in the attendance, though there were fewer military marquees; there did seem to be many more women than usual. Ladies, usually confined to the seats in the grandstand or carriages on the hill, now found the

Merry maidens celebrate backing Cremorne at 3–1 in time-honoured champagne style; the beer brigade are not left out!

to be in itself a noble, a manly, distinguished, and he might almost say historically national sport. [*Hear, hear.*] The House would act on the principle that it was not . . . expedient to take cognisance in connexion with such a motion as this of abuses which after all were not essential to the sport itself.

He knew he could count on support among many Irish MPs, and also among the persevering who preferred to get on with quiet Committee business at Westminster while the big stars were away at Epsom. Disraeli had Tory loyalty at his back, even if not all of his MPs had read *Sybil*, and his own respect for the memory of Bentinck. He did not need to argue: 'I rise, Sir, to make a motion which, as I understand, will be in accordance with the general wish of the House.'

It was not entirely agreeable to all MPs. Sir Wilfrid Lawson, the Cumberland Liberal who was the Derby's perennial opponent, refused to accept that the day was a national occasion:

Not long ago a letter appeared in *The Times* from Admiral Rous, who said that, were it not against the law, he would go a hundred miles any day to see a cock fight, and who knew but that some day the House might be called upon to adjourn for that pastime. [*Laughter.*]

The House plainly preferred the advice of an old-fashioned racing MP:

He had three reasons for voting for the adjournment – first, he was fond of sport; second, he thought it was the duty of every good citizen to encourage a great and ancient national pastime; and third, he believed he would meet more of his constituents on the course than anywhere else. [*Laughter.*]

Still, when Disraeli went to the Lords in 1876, the Chancellor, Stafford Northcote (who was leading in the Commons), dropped the adjournment as Government business. There were willing backbenchers to take up the responsibility but the unquestioned authority of Derby Day had slipped. Gladstone, preoccupied with trying to pacify Ireland, did not allow it in 1882. In the Liberal Party Nonconformity, and its political conscience, had gained support both at Westminster and in the provinces. By 1890 the House's holiday could not be taken on the nod: it had begun to be a serious debate. The Tory defenders of precedent refused to believe that a popularly elected House would dare reject both time-honoured custom and a national festival. Lord Elcho put it robustly:

There was no body of men more respected in the country than the members of Her Majesty's Government, yet if tomorrow the country were to hear that all the occupants of the front bench were laid low with a severe attack of influenza the news would be received with feelings that would be resigned, calm, and philosophical as compared with the feelings of the people if they were to hear that the favourite for this year's Derby was affected by a mild attack of the same complaint.

The evils of drink and gambling and the damage they did were strenuously evoked by the Opposition, except by the maverick Henry Labouchère who thought it preferable 'to encourage the toiling thousands to go down to enjoy themselves on the Downs at Epsom instead of soddening themselves in the public houses in London'. And, anyway, it was the people who went to race meetings who did the work of the teetotalers by actually wrecking public houses.

But the new House of Commons was more serious, more selfconscious than that. Its ambition was to reform and change; to it, Derby Day was a demeaning relic of the past. The return of a Liberal government in 1892 meant the end of Parliament's holiday. It continued voluntarily, of course. That year the Commons was still so empty it could not transact any important business.

Naturally, the Derby's supporters did not give up. In 1894 they felt they had an advantage: the owner of the Derby favourite, Ladas II, was the Liberal Prime Minister, Rosebery. Their resolution for the day off was anodyne; 'to give a little rest to the members and officials who had been so constant in their attendance'. The Chancellor, Harcourt, would have none of it. After all, the House was debating his Finance Bill. An old Tory, John (later Sir John) Maclure (Manchester Stretford) got up:

To him it was a matter of perfect indifference whether the House adjourned or not: to the Derby he would go. [*Loud laughter and cheers.*] He had not missed that event for 30 years, and he was not going to miss it at his present advanced period of life. [*Laughter.*] He looked upon the Derby as an exact specimen of all the national sports. He had never had a bet on a race in his life; and as a churchwarden [*Great laughter*] and a member of the House of Laymen of the Province of York he saw no harm in his witnessing a national sport conducted on highly moral principles. [*Laughter.*]

On Epsom Downs, a gipsy girl with a racecard in Thormanby's year. A delightful study by E. Corbet, 1860.

The debate on the Finance Bill went ahead. Rosebery himself went to Epsom (as a member of the Lords, the debate was not his business) and Ladas II won. To his party this was a matter for some heart-searching. Had Rosebery encouraged the national sport or, rather, the most demoralizing among the national vices?

The Conservatives were back in power in 1896 and the backbenchers tried again for an adjournment on Derby Day. They said they wanted to adjourn the House because the business, the Benefices Bill, was too important to the Church of England to be assigned a day so liable to absenteeism. Mr (later Sir) G.C.T. Bartley (Islington North) was not a racing man, but he had a sense of occasion:

If they did adjourn for the Derby they ought to do so properly and bodily. They ought to request Mr Speaker to go to Epsom himself. [*A laugh.*] They ought to take the mace there and have a grandstand all to themselves, and really do the thing properly. [*Renewed laughter.*] If they did that he might possibly stretch a point and attend the race.

Sir Wilfrid Lawson, a member of the Liberal party, aware that he was on the winning side even with the Tories, had his say:

If they wanted a holiday, why should they not take it when the All England Eleven play the Australians? [*Hear, hear.*] He would vote for that [*Oh*] – well, he would not oppose it very strongly. [*Laughter.*] There would be a great deal to be said for that, because cricket was a noble and national game which had not yet, he believed, been corrupted by the canker and cancer of gambling.

Derby Day was beaten by 141 votes. The Parliamentary privilege, having been lost, was not to be rewon. The last, ineffectual attempt to restore it was made in the euphoria of victory in 1919. That particular clock was not to be turned back, though some MPs doggedly got the name of the winner into their interventions in the House – to let the sleeping ones know – up to 1939.

An even more conservative institution stuck to tradition. It was still the practice, often criticized in Parliament, for judges either not to sit on Derby Day or to arrange a hearing that lasted no more than an hour, leaving them plenty of time for a leisurely train journey to Epsom. This continued over the years. In the High Court it was never better put than by a judge in 1938, in a case in which the defendants were accused of sending winning bets by telegrams which, curiously, were always timed just before the off. Ladbrokes was among those taking exception. A Post Office clerk was one of those in the dock.

Tactfully, the judge let it be known 'that some members of the jury are interested in the sporting event which takes place on Wednesday, and that it might be a matter of great inconvenience and expense to them if they had made arrangements to attend that event but were compelled to come to the Court'.

He knew how to get the verdict he wanted – quickly.

The traditional Derby Day picnic on Epsom Downs. Only the mode of transport has changed since the Victorian era.

*A*fter the Great War, when the Derby returned to Epsom in 1919, there was a half-hearted attempt to call it the Victory Derby. It was not like that. There were still uniforms around, Americans among them, but the crowds knew they were in a sadder and wiser Britain, going through a ritual which belonged to more exuberant days. It was a sad, grey day anyway. The rain arrived in time for the first race; the pleasure was in having survived. *The Times* was sombreness itself:

The joy of it was rather that of a home-coming, of revisiting after long absence the scenes of youth (the war has aged us all), and of renewing the old associations every step amid which is like treading on an organ pedal, increasing the volume and dignity of the feeling . . . We do not think anyone who compares yesterday's Derby with those of fifty or even twenty years ago will doubt that, some appearances to the contrary, we are a more rational and a more sensible people than we were.

The twenties changed that, of course. There were high stakes and big players. Steve Donoghue rode four Derby winners in five years. The Aga Khan had his first three successes, starting with Blenheim in 1930. The grandstand was rebuilt hastily in 1928 and loomed, 'ostentatiously new', above the downs; the painters were still at work the day it opened; it even had lifts, an unheard-of luxury. For the first time the course itself got priority: the crowds were stopped from parading up and down it between Tattenham Corner station and the stands. The Tote arrived. There was still no racecourse commentary; that came as a surprise to the new King and Queen in 1939 when (missing the Derby) they went to Woodbine, outside Toronto, on their North American tour almost on the eve of the Second World War.

The car was coming into its own. A strike meant there were no special trains in 1921; nor were there any in 1926 because the miners stayed out after the collapse of the General Strike. To the worried, the Derby was even thought to have national therapeutic qualities:

By means of a great public holiday cheerfully enjoyed we can prove to ourselves and to the world that, in the familiar phrase, we are not downhearted. Since men of all sorts of opinions on politics and economics go to make up the Derby Day crowd, some temporary forgetfulness of the questions at issue may bring about some little fellow-feeling, to the possible alleviation of the difference.

In quieter years the Southern Railway's new electric trains decanted their tens of thousands, at 3s. (15p) return for those who set out before 9 a.m., and the toffs in the Pullman cars had luncheon on the down journey and tea on the way back. The tube, having got as far as Morden, half-an-hour from Charing Cross, ran at intervals of two minutes or less, and 180 omnibuses and coaches, at half-minute intervals, took the crowds to the course. Those going directly from town found that the modern motor-coach, starting from Westminster at 11 o'clock, got them there before lunch. The General Omnibus Company itself had 200 vehicles on the road, taking parties out and then doubling as small grandstands along the rails (and blocking other people's sight of the first three furlongs of the sprint course). But it was the car that ruled now, in rain or shine.

There were, as ever, huge jams along the way, not helped by negligent authorities: 'Contrary to expectations, it has now been decided not to employ wireless in the actual direction of traffic . . . So much had been learnt from control by the air and by wireless that it had now become possible to dispense with both.'

Three years running – 1924, 1925, and 1926 – when the weather was detestable, cold, windy and wet, and when the cars that got to Epsom sank into the mud, were actually welcomed for discouraging the crowds:

Wholly unimpeded by the dreaded Derby traffic, one drove to Epsom Downs in the heavy rain and one drove back again in the heavier rain, mildly cheerful at last because every mile was bringing one delightfully nearer to a hot bath and a complete change into good, stout, sensible winter clothes.

When the sun shone, of course, everyone sweltered inside the mass-produced Austins, Morrises and Fords. To an admiring eye they could look decorative:

From the outside of an omnibus or the roof of a motor-car the scene had the innocence and bright colours of a child's jigsaw puzzle spread rather disjointedly over the Downs . . . In the grassy concavity within the course a reverberant fair had been set, and on the rise beyond the roundabouts and swing boats the paintwork of hundreds of private cars flashed in the sun.

The crowds streaming away on foot in 1931 got a quick preview of what would come one day. A small plane had to make a forced landing on the railway track at Epsom Downs station, just as the special trains were about to leave for London after the last race. The pilot and two passengers were slightly hurt. The future had shown its face.

They were orderly Derby crowds most years between the wars, as they usually were at football grounds. In 1930, as the country and the world moved towards depression, protection and unemployment, they took their pleasures calmly – half a million people disciplined into order and even politeness by an inescapable fate:

The number of persons arrested on Epsom Downs yesterday was 12. Today seven of them will be charged with 'welshing', three with gaming at 'Crown and Anchor', one with larceny, and one with drunkenness. The number of Derby Day prisoners has considerably decreased in recent years. At the 1923 Derby 108 persons were arrested.

And now this well-behaved Derby was heard around the world. The radio, or the wireless, took in the Derby in the late twenties; *The Times's* racing correspondent, R.C. Lyle, did the commentary, to his own paper's evident satisfaction. In 1930 it patted him officially on the back: 'The delay at the start, caused chiefly by Silver Flare, was very well described, and the details of the race itself were given with great clearness.'

The audience was widespread, so widespread there was excitement at each and every novelty: 'Fifty-five miles from Paris, and at an altitude of 3,000 ft, 17 passengers in an Imperial air liner bound for Croydon heard every word of the broadcast through a portable wireless set.'

Passengers on both the up and down Flying Scotsmen expresses between London and Edinburgh also heard the result while the trains were doing 60 m.p.h.; the reception was said to be excellent. From New York it was reported that hundreds of thousands of Americans followed the Derby, the BBC's commentary being sent across the transatlantic phone line and re-broadcast by a chain of stations across the United States: 'Interference often drowned out the voice of the announcer. But it was possible to get what Americans call the "high spots" of the race, and at the finish there was no doubt which horse had won.'

It was a matter of great pride how the earth had shrunk so that it took only three seconds for the commentary to reach Australia. It gave reassurance that the Empire was living and thinking as one, not least for those who stood to win fortunes in the two

great sweepstakes, the Calcutta and the Stock Exchange. The Calcutta paid £250,000 to winners in the twenties, often from far-flung corners of the Empire. The big prize went to Cape Town in 1927, and seven Barnstaple workmen picked up £100,000 in 1930.

Much more was on the way. In 1931 the Baird Television Company set up at the racecourse to transmit the occasion live, 'including the parade of horses before the start and the scene at the winning post during the race'. There had been film coverage for years, the first rushes being seen in West End cinemas on the evening of Derby Day. But television promised to know no bounds. *The Times* was enthusiastic: 'The first attempt which has been made, in this or any other country, to secure a television transmission of a topical event held in the open air, where artificial lighting is impossible.'

It was felt that the problem of interference could be overcome – as it duly was, though not by Baird. By 1938 the BBC at Alexandra Palace gave the race a full forty minutes in the afternoon, followed suitably in the evening by *Derby Day*, a comic opera by A.P. Herbert. The race was seen not only by the scattered Home Counties audience but by 200 people in the Tatler News Theatre in town, on a screen 8ft 6in square. They all saw pictures of the crowd, the funfair, the bookmakers, the unsaddling enclosure and, finally, the King and Queen going back to their box from the paddock:

As the race began so did the rain, and the pictures were very much less clear. But from Tattenham Corner on, where the third camera came into play at much closer range, the pictures were excellent in spite of the rain, and the finish of the race was as thrilling as anyone could wish, so that the whole transmission must be judged a great success.

In 1939 the era ended. The war was coming and, besides Hitler's air force, there was another, even closer, enemy, as the *Daily Telegraph* discovered: 'In view of the possibility of an IRA outrage, plain clothes men were posted at various parts of the course, and the two outdoor totes are being watched. Detectives are reinforcing the usual guards on stables.' That threat was going to stay longer than Hitler.

*T*he Derby continues to flourish as a great horserace, the biggest and best test, worldwide, of the three-year-old thoroughbred. Its winners are still real win-

Saturday afternoon on Epsom Downs. The Derby was moved from its traditional Wednesday by a Post-War Government Edict from 1947 to 1950, and again in 1953 because of the Coronation.

ners, the stud fees speak for themselves, and its stage is international.

It is a great midweek holiday still, both for the well-heeled and the plain punters of London. It has gone marginally up-market; corporate entertainment has moved in. Helicopters fly in and out on shuttle services. Television, catching the Derby field at the top of the hill before the descent to the test of Tattenham Corner, reveals the most crowded heliport of south-east England.

Londoners from the City, the East End and the suburbs still respond to the urge to be there, rain or shine. A workers' holiday that the bosses can't quite cavil at isn't to be deprecated, even in the 1990s. The funfair is there; the gypsies, accused of making nuisances of themselves, signed a peace treaty in 1971 which allowed them an official caravan site. The traffic from town, still edging its way down the Epsom road, still sets an annual headache for the police. Any celebration still encourages people ·to knock a few ostentatious toppers off self-satisfied heads. It's not

exactly the old London, but it keeps up appearances.

In 1946, after the Second World War, the Derby was released from the artificiality of Newmarket back to its old home. This was a day that the devotees long remembered:

Men at the innumerable stands selling such minor refreshments as winkles wore perhaps half their battle-dress, others justified their war-time belief that an American pattern of waterproof jacket would be useful in peace-time, and the leather jacket of an airforce pilot helped one wandering musician to look the part with some hill-billy tunes.

The fortune-tellers were back as if the daughters of the original Gypsy Lee had never gone away. The traffic, helped by the constraints of petrol rationing, ran smoothly for once. But the coverage for everyone at home fell well behind that of 1938–9; television was not allowed at Epsom at all. It was only restored to the country three days later to cover the Victory Parade. After the General Election the Labour government, beset by strikes and desperate trade figures, ordered that midweek holidays were out. To help factory production, the Derby must be run on a Saturday.

Epsom itself was doubtful about how to handle the new media. In 1952 the clerk of the course declared that commentaries on the Derby and the Oaks should be sound only. This was to last until 1960; for many people, this was far too long. It was still a sprightly racing world. The French challenge after the war set off insistent questioning about the weaknesses of English training.

The Derby was changing as racing was changing. In 1949 Nimbus was adjudged the winner: the first time a photograph had been used. Nimbus was being passed but he still had enough of his head out in front. After that there came the patrol cameras, the starting stalls (for the 1967 Derby), and the rows over drug tests. It was still a national occasion. In 1969 Stanley Wootton, the former jockey and trainer, presented his 206 acres of the downs to the Horserace Betting Levy Board to ensure that the Derby could never be put in jeopardy – until at least 999 years later. It was the most notable of the quiet, unrecognized gestures that saved the Derby from the repeated uncertainty of the Grand National's future at Aintree. The very name, like the Grand National's, still attracted the housewife's bet, as no other races did or do.

Because of George VI's death in 1952 the Royal family did not go to Epsom that year, but the impresario, Herbert Wilcox, did put on his play, *Derby Day*, in which Anna Neagle starred. The plot was complicated, but what annoyed *The Times*'s reviewer was that 'she wears an Ascot dress at Epsom'. That was a solecism. As Britain struggled through the booms and bumps of its economy, there remained a political divide between the two meetings. Harold Macmillan, Prime Minister and actor-manager of the last staging of paternalist Conservatism, sat top-hatted on Epsom's lawn in 1972 and offered a populist distinction: 'I always preferred the Derby to Ascot.'

In 1953, because of the coronation, the Derby was put back to Saturday again. It went off well. Sir Gordon Richards was, for the first and only time, the winning jockey; the young Queen owned the second; and the crowds who had watched through periscopes outside Westminster Abbey brought them along to get their best view of the race. Epsom obediently accepted a blank day in the 1955 meeting to let the electorate vote in the General Election that returned Anthony Eden.

The Derby slowly came to terms with the most important medium of the declining years of the twentieth century. In 1960 Epsom reached an agreement with ITV that it should cover Derby Day as a meeting. Because the Derby had been singled out by Parliament as a national event, the BBC retained the right to broadcast it if it wished. It did so in 1960, but only as a single race, while ITV transmitted other races, gave more coverage to betting and began to build a reputation for its own distinctive style. The BBC was to go in and out of coverage in the years ahead, until it finally fell away.

Transmission became increasingly international; big, live crowds watched the monster screens in Hong Kong, and the race was beamed into the Gulf, Japan, and wherever betting men gathered. Sponsorship since 1984 by Ever Ready brought new resources to the Derby and to the racecourse, helping the rebuilding of the members' stand and the renovation of the 1928 grandstand. It became clear that the road to Epsom Downs was going to stay open for future generations who could endorse the Derby as the greatest fun, rain or shine, win or lose, for better or worse, that the turf has to offer.

The Ever Ready Sponsorship of The Derby

On 4 May 1780, the inaugural Derby Stakes on Epsom Downs carried a purse of 1075 guineas, being the total entry fees subscribed by the owners of the thirty-six entrants. On 2 June 1993, the corresponding purse will be some £750,000. In addition to the owners' entry fees and forfeits there are now contributions from Epsom Racecourse, from the Horserace Betting Levy Board (funded from off-course betting turnover) and from commercial sponsors Ever Ready.

Until 1983, The Derby was considered ineligible for sponsorship. Within days of the Jockey Club's change in attitude, Epsom's Tim Neligan met Sir Gordon White (now Lord) over tea and muffins at the London home of Bob Dean, co-director with White of Hanson Trust, parent company of Ever Ready. Within the hour, precise dynamics of a sponsorship arrangement were established and the fine print of a contract was drawn up over Christmas. It was signed on 13 January, just eighteen weeks before Secreto's 1984 triumph on Epsom Downs. As a consequence the purse leapt from £276,800 to £382,800, re-establishing the intrinsic value as well as the prestige of Derby Day.

Additionally, Ever Ready has made annual donations to a Heritage Fund, which helped to finance the urgent replacement of Epsom's ancient buildings by Queen's Stand, officially opened by Her Majesty Queen Elizabeth II in 1992.

In 1992, the Ever Ready Derby was seen live on television by many millions worldwide. In Hong Kong – a major market for Ever Ready – the simulcast at 10.45 p.m. local time generated HK$36,800,000 betting turnover in less than one hour.

This synergy between the world's premier battery brand and the world's premier horserace is an example of the value both parties derive from a properly structured sponsorship.

On behalf of the Derby sponsors, Ever Ready, Sir Gordon White (right) makes a presentation to the Aga Khan, owner of the 1986 winner, Shahrastani.

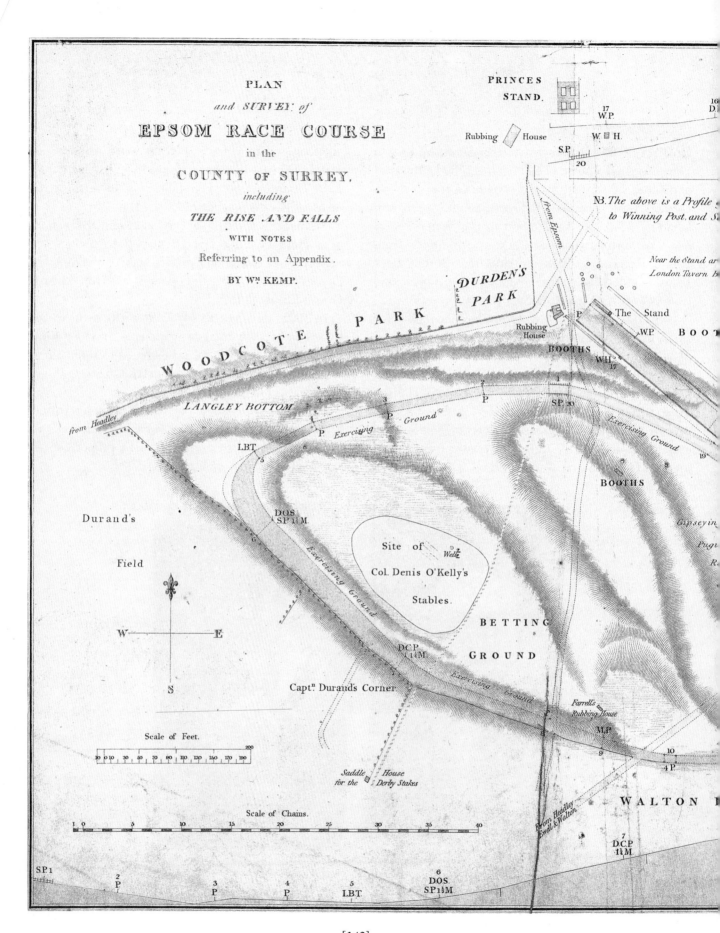

PLAN
and SURVEY of
EPSOM RACE COURSE
in the
COUNTY OF SURREY.
including
THE RISE AND FALLS
WITH NOTES
Referring to an Appendix.
BY Wᵐ. KEMP.

PRINCES STAND.

Rubbing House

NB. *The above is a Profile*
to Winning Post, and S

Near the Stand ar
London Tavern B

DURDEN'S PARK

WOODCOTE PARK

Rubbing House

The Stand

BOOTHS

BOO

W.P.

LANGLEY BOTTOM

from Headley

Exercising Ground

LBT

BOOTHS

Durand's

Field

DOS
SP 1½M

Site of
Col. Denis O'Kelly's
Stables.

Well

BETTING

GROUND

Gipseyin

Pug

R

DCP
1¼M

Exercising Ground

Capt. Durand's Corner

Farrell's
Rubbing House

M P

Scale of Feet.

10 0 10 30 50 70 90 110 130 150 170 190 200

From Headley
Ewell & Walton

Saddle House
for the Derby Stakes

WALTON

Scale of Chains.

1 0   5   10   15   20   25   30   35   40

SP 1

2
P

3
P

4
P

5
LBT.

6
DOS
SP 1½M

7
DCP
1¾M

[142]

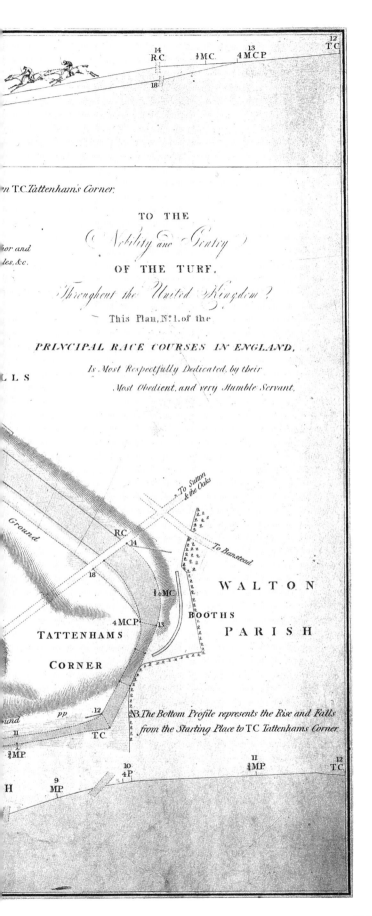

APPENDICES

The Derby Results

Year	Winner	Owner	Second	Third
1780	Diomed	Sir Charles Bunbury	Budrow	Spitfire
1781	Young Eclipse	Major O'Kelly	Crop	Prince of Orange
1782	Assassin	Lord Egremont	Sweet Robin	Fortunio
1783	Saltram	Mr Parker	Dungannon	Parlington
1784	Sergeant	Colonel O'Kelly	Carlo Khan	Dancer
1785	Aimwell	Lord Clermont	Grantham	Verjuice
1786	Noble	Mr Panton	Meteor	Clarter
1787	Sir Peter Teazle	Lord Derby	Gunpowder	Bustler
1788	Sir Thomas	H.R.H. The Prince of Wales	Aurelius	Feenow
1789	Skyscraper	Duke of Bedford	Sir George	Brother to Skylark
1790	Rhadamanthus	Lord Grosvenor	Asparagus	Lee Boo
1791	Eager	Duke of Bedford	Vermin	Proteus
1792	John Bull	Lord Grosvenor	Speculator	Bustard
1793	Waxy	Sir F. Poole	Gohanna	Triptolemus
1794	Daedalus	Lord Grosvenor	Colt by Highflyer	Leon
1795	Spread Eagle	Sir F. Standish	Caustic	Pelter
1796	Didelot	Sir F. Standish	Stickler	Leviathan
1797	Fidget colt	Duke of Bedford	Esculus	Plaistow
1798	Sir Harry	Mr J. Cookson	Telegraph	Young Spear
1799	Archduke	Sir F. Standish	Gislebert	Eagle
1800	Champion	Mr C. Wilson	Colt by Precipitate	Mystery
1801	Eleanor	Sir C. Bunbury	Colt by Fidget	Remnant
1802	Tyrant	Duke of Grafton	Colt by Young Eclipse	Orlando
1803	Ditto	Sir H. Williamson	Sir Oliver	Brother to Stamford
1804	Hannibal	Lord Egremont	Pavilion	Hippocampus
1805	Cardinal Beaufort	Lord Egremont	Plantagenet	Goth
1806	Paris	Lord Foley	Trafalgar	Hector
1807	Election	Lord Egremont	Giles Scroggins	Coriolanus
1808	Pan	Sir H. Williamson	Vandyke	Chester
1809	Pope	Duke of Grafton	Wizard	Salvator
1810	Whalebone	Duke of Grafton	The Dandy	Eccleston
1811	Phantom	Sir J. Shelley	Magic	No official place
1812	Octavius	Mr R. Ladbroke	Sweep	Comus
1813	Smolensko	Sir Charles Bunbury	Caterpillar	Illusion
1814	Blücher	Lord Stawell	Perchance	No official place
1815	Whisker	Duke of Grafton	Raphael	Busto
1816	Prince Leopold	Mr Lake	Nectar	Pandour
1817	Azor	Mr J. Payne	Young Wizard	No official place
1818	Sam	Mr T. Thornhill	Raby	Prince Paul
1819	Tiresias	Duke of Portland	Sultan	No official place
1820	Sailor	Mr T. Thornhill	Abjer	Tiger
1821	Gustavus	Mr J. Hunter	Reginald	Sir Huldibrand
1822	Moses	Duke of York	Figaro	Hampden
1823	Emilius	Mr J.R. Udney	Tancred	No official place
1824	Cedric	Sir J. Shelley	Osmond	No official place
1825	Middleton	Lord Jersey	Rufus	Hogarth
1826	Lapdog	Lord Egremont	Shakespeare	No official place
1827	Mameluke	Lord Jersey	Glenartney	Edmund

(1780–1992)

(Year)	Jockey	Trainer	Value to Winner	Runners	Time	Starting Price
(1780)	S. Arnull		£1065 15s	9	(Not recorded	6–4
(1781)	C. Hindley		£1312 10s	15	until 1846)	10–1
(1782)	S. Arnull		£1155	13		5–1
(1783)	C. Hindley		£945	6		5–2
(1784)	J. Arnull		£1076 5s	11		3–1
(1785)	C. Hindley		£1023 15s	10		7–1
(1786)	J. White		£1155	15		30–1
(1787)	S. Arnull		£1050	7		2–1
(1788)	W. South		£971 15s	11		5–6
(1789)	S. Chifney, sen.		£1076 5s	11		4–7
(1790)	J. Arnull		£1102 10s	10		5–4
(1791)	F. Stephenson		£1076 5s	9		5–2
(1792)	F. Buckle		£834 15s	7		4–6
(1793)	W. Clift	R. Robson	£1653 15s	13		12–1
(1794)	F. Buckle		£1391 5s	4		6–1
(1795)	A. Wheatley		£1470	11		3–1
(1796)	J. Arnull		£1470	11		Not recorded
(1797)	J. Singleton		£1155	7		10–1
(1798)	S. Arnull		£1233 15s	10		7–4
(1799)	J. Arnull		£1155	11		12–1
(1800)	W. Clift		£1207 10s	13		7–4
(1801)	Saunders		£1102 10s	12		5–4
(1802)	F. Buckle	R. Robson	£1024 16s	9		7–1
(1803)	W. Clift		£929 5s	6		7–2
(1804)	W. Arnull		£1076 5s	8		3–1
(1805)	D. Fitzpatrick		£1338 15s	15		20–1
(1806)	J. Shepherd		£1348 15s	12		5–1
(1807)	J. Arnull		£1333 10s	12		3–1
(1808)	F. Collinson		£1260	10		25–1
(1809)	T. Goodisson	R. Robson	£1443 15s	10		20–1
(1810)	W. Clift	R. Robson	£1365	11		2–1
(1811)	F. Buckle		£1680	16		5–1
(1812)	W. Arnull		£1601 5s	14		7–1
(1813)	T. Goodisson		£1653 15s	12		Evens
(1814)	W. Arnull		£1706 5s	14		5–2
(1815)	T. Goodisson	R. Robson	£1680	13		8–1
(1816)	W. Wheatley		£1653 15s	11		20–1
(1817)	J. Robinson	R. Robson	£1811 5s	13		50–1
(1818)	S. Chifney, jun.	W. Chifney	£1890	16		7–2
(1819)	W. Clift		£1837 10s	16		5–2
(1820)	S. Chifney, jun.	W. Chifney	£1758 15s	15		4–1
(1821)	S. Day		£1758 15s	13		2–1
(1822)	T. Goodisson		£1706 5s	12		6–1
(1823)	F. Buckle	R. Robson	£1863 15s	11		11–8
(1824)	J. Robinson		£1968 15s	16		9–2
(1825)	J. Robinson	Edwards	£1995	18		7–4
(1826)	G. Dockeray	Bird	£1800	19		50–1
(1827)	J. Robinson	Edwards	£2800	23		9–1

Year	Winner	Owner	Second	Third
1828	Cadland°	Duke of Rutland	The Colonel°	No official place
1829	Frederick	Mr Gratwicke	The Exquisite	No official place
1830	Priam	Mr W. Chifney	Little Red Rover	Mahmoud
1831	Spaniel	Lord Lowther	Riddlesworth	Incubus
1832	St Giles	Mr R. Ridsdale	Perion	Trustee
1833	Dangerous	Mr Sadler	Connoisseur	Revenge
1834	Plenipotentiary	Mr S. Batson	Shilelagh	Glencoe
1835	Mündig	Mr J. Bowes	Ascot	No official place
1836	Bay Middleton	Lord Jersey	Gladiator	No official place
1837	Phosphorus	Lord Berners	Caravan	No official place
1838	Amato	Sir G. Heathcote	Ion	Grey Momus
1839	Bloomsbury	Mr W. Ridsdale	Deception	No official place
1840	Little Wonder	Mr D. Robertson	Launcelot	Colt by Mulatto out of Melody
1841	Coronation	Mr A.T. Rawlinson	Van Amburgh	No official place
1842	Attila	Colonel Anson	Robert de Gorham	Belcoeur
1843	Cotherstone	Mr J. Bowes	Gorhambury	Sirikol
1844	Orlando	Colonel Peel	Ionian	Bay Momus
1845	The Merry Monarch	Mr Gratwicke	Annandale	Old England
1846	Pyrrhus the First	Mr J. Gully	Sir Tatton Sykes	Brocardo
1847	Cossack	Mr Pedley	War Eagle	Van Tromp
1848	Surplice	Lord Clifden	Springy Jack	Glendower
1849	The Flying Dutchman	Lord Eglinton	Hotspur	Tadmor
1850	Voltigeur	Lord Zetland	Pitsford	Clincher
1851	Teddington	Sir J. Hawley	Marlborough Buck	Neasham
1852	Daniel O'Rourke	Mr J. Bowes	Barbarian	Chief Baron Nicholson
1853	West Australian	Mr J. Bowes	Sittingbourne	Cineas
1854	Andover	Mr J. Gully	King Tom	Hermit
1855	Wild Dayrell	Mr F.L. Popham	Kingstown	Lord of the Isles
1856	Ellington	Admiral Harcourt	Yellow Jack	Cannobie
1857	Blink Bonny	Mr W. I'Anson	Black Tommy	Adamas
1858	Beadsman	Sir J. Hawley	Toxophilite	The Hadji
1859	Musjid	Sir J. Hawley	Marionette	Trumpeter
1860	Thormanby	Mr J. Merry	The Wizard	Horror
1861	Kettledrum	Colonel Towneley	Dundee	Diophantes
1862	Caractacus	Mr C. Snewing	The Marquis	Buckstone
1863	Macaroni	Mr R. C. Naylor	Lord Clifden	Rapid Rhone
1864	Blair Athol	Mr W. I'Anson	General Peel	Scottish Chief
1865	Gladiateur	Count F. de Lagrange	Christmas Carol	Eltham
1866	Lord Lyon	Mr Sutton	Savernake	Rustic
1867	Hermit	Mr H. Chaplin	Marksman	Vauban
1868	Blue Gown	Sir J. Hawley	King Alfred	Speculum
1869	Pretender	Mr J. Johnstone	Pero Gomez	The Drummer
1870	Kingcraft	Lord Falmouth	Palmerston	Muster
1871	Favonius	Baron Rothschild	Albert Victor King of the Forest	(Dead-heat for second place)
1872	Cremorne	Mr H. Savile	Pell Mell	Queens Messenger
1873	Doncaster	Mr J. Merry	Gang Forward Kaiser	(Dead-heat for second place)
1874	George Frederick	Mr Cartwright	Couronne de Fer	Atlantic
1875	Galopin	Prince Batthyany	Claremont	Repentance colt
1876	Kisber	Mr A. Baltazzi	Forerunner	Julius Caesar
1877	Silvio	Lord Falmouth	Glen Arthur	Rob Roy

° Cadland won the run-off after a dead-heat with The Colonel.

[146]

(Year)	Jockey	Trainer	Value to Winner	Runners	Time (mins. secs.)	Starting Price
(1828)	J. Robinson		£2600	15		4–1
(1829)	J. Forth	J. Forth	£2650	17		40–1
(1830)	S. Day	W. Chifney	£2800	22		4–1
(1831)	W. Wheatley		£3000	23		50–1
(1832)	W. Scott		£3075	22		3–1
(1833)	J. Chapple		£3725	25		30–1
(1834)	P. Conolly		£3625	22		9–4
(1835)	W. Scott	John Scott	£3550	14		6–1
(1836)	J. Robinson		£3725	21		7–4
(1837)	G. Edwards		£3700	17		40–1
(1838)	J. Chapple	R. Sherwood	£4005	23		30–1
(1839)	S. Templeman	W. Ridsdale	£4100	21		25–1
(1840)	W. Macdonald	W. Forth	£3775	17		50–1
(1841)	P. Conolly		£4275	29		5–2
(1842)	W. Scott	John Scott	£4900	24		5–1
(1843)	W. Scott	John Scott	£4225	23		13–8
(1844)	N. Flatman	Cooper	£4450	29		20–1
(1845)	F. Bell	J. Forth	£4225	31		15–1
(1846)	S. Day	John Day	£5500	27	2 55	8–1
(1847)	S. Templeman	John Day	£5500	32	2 52	5–1
(1848)	S. Templeman	J. Kent	£5800	17	2 48	Evens
(1849)	C. Marlow	Fobert	£6575	26	3	2–1
(1850)	J. Marson	R. Hill	£4975	24	2 50	16–1
(1851)	J. Marson	A. Taylor	£5325	33	2 51	3–1
(1852)	F. Butler	John Scott	£5200	27	3 2	25–1
(1853)	F. Butler	John Scott	£4450	28	2 55	6–4
(1854)	A. Day	John Day	£6100	27	2 52	7–2
(1855)	R. Sherwood	Rickaby	£5075	12	2 54	Evens
(1856)	T. Aldcroft	T. Dawson	£5875	24	3 4	20–1
(1857)	J. Charlton	W. I'Anson	£5700	30	2 45	20–1
(1858)	J. Wells	G. Manning	£5575	23	2 54	10–1
(1859)	J. Wells	G. Manning	£5400	30	2 59	9–4
(1860)	H. Custance	M. Dawson	£6350	30	2 55	4–1
(1861)	R. Bullock	Oates	£6350	18	2 45	12–1
(1862)	J. Parsons	Zachary	£6675	34	2 45	40–1
(1863)	T. Chaloner	J. K. Godding	£7100	31	2 50	10–1
(1864)	J. Snowden	W. I'Anson	£6450	30	2 43	14–1
(1865)	H. Grimshaw	T. Jennings	£6875	30	2 46	5–2
(1866)	H. Custance	J. Dover	£7350	26	2 50	5–6
(1867)	J. Daley	Bloss	£7000	30	2 52	1000–15
(1868)	J. Wells	J. Porter	£6800	18	2 43	7–2
(1869)	J. Osborne	T. Dawson	£6225	22	2 52	11–8
(1870)	T. French	M. Dawson	£6175	15	2 45	20–1
(1871)	T. French	J. Hayhoe	£5125	17	2 50	9–1
(1872)	C. Maidment	W. Gilbert	£4850	23	2 45	3–1
(1873)	F. Webb	R. Peck	£4825	12	2 50	45–1
(1874)	H. Custance	T. Leader	£5350	20	2 46	9–1
(1875)	J. Morris	J. Dawson	£4950	18	2 48	2–1
(1876)	C. Maidment	J. Hayhoe	£5575	15	2 44	4–1
(1877)	F. Archer	M. Dawson	£6050	17	2 50	100–9

Year	Winner	Owner	Second	Third
1878	Sefton	Mr W. S. Crawfurd	Insulaire	Childeric
1879	Sir Bevys	Mr Acton	Palmbearer	Visconti
1880	Bend Or	Duke of Westminster	Robert the Devil	Mask
1881	Iroquois	Mr P. Lorillard	Peregrine	Town Moor
1882	Shotover	Duke of Westminster	Quicklime	Sachem
1883	St Blaise	Sir F. Johnstone	Highland Chief	Galliard
1884	St Gatien	Mr J. Hammond	(Dead-heat for	Queen Adelaide
	Harvester	Sir J. Willoughby	first place)	
1885	Melton	Lord Hastings	Paradox	Royal Hampton
1886	Ormonde	Duke of Westminster	The Bard	St Mirin
1887	Merry Hampton	Mr Abington	The Baron	Martley
1888	Ayrshire	Duke of Portland	Crowberry	Van Dieman's Land
1889	Donovan	Duke of Portland	Miguel	El Dorado
1890	Sainfoin	Sir J. Miller	Le Nord	Orwell
1891	Common	Sir F. Johnstone	Gouverneur	Martenhurst
1892	Sir Hugo	Lord Bradford	La Flèche	Bucentaure
1893	Isinglass	Mr H. McCalmont	Ravensbury	Raeburn
1894	Ladas II	Lord Rosebery	Matchbox	Reminder
1895	Sir Visto	Lord Rosebery	Curzon	Kirkconnel
1896	Persimmon	H.R.H. The Prince of Wales	St Frusquin	Earwig
1897	Galtee More	Mr J. Gubbins	Velasquez	History
1898	Jeddah	Mr J. W. Larnach	Batt	Dunlop
1899	Flying Fox	Duke of Westminster	Damocles	Innocence
1900	Diamond Jubilee	H.R.H. The Prince of Wales	Simon Dale	Disguise II
1901	Volodyovski	Mr W. C. Whitney	William the Third	Veronese
1902	Ard Patrick	Mr J. Gubbin	Rising Glass	Friar Tuck
1903	Rock Sand	Sir J. Miller	Vinicius	Flotsam
1904	St Amant	Mr L. de Rothschild	John o'Gaunt	St Denis
1905	Cicero	Lord Rosebery	Jardy	Signorino
1906	Spearmint	Major E. Loder	Picton	Troutbeck
1907	Orby	Mr R. Croker	Wool Winder	Slieve Gallion
1908	Signorinetta	Chev. E. Ginistrelli	Primer	Llangwm
1909	Minoru	H.M. King Edward VII	Louviers	William the Fourth
1910	Lemberg	Mr Fairie	Greenback	Charles O'Malley
1911	Sunstar	Mr J. B. Joel	Stedfast	Royal Tender
1912	Tagalie	Mr W. Raphael	Jaeger	Tracery
1913	Aboyeur	Mr A. P. Cunliffe	Louvois	Great Sport
1914	Durbar II	Mr H. B. Duryea	Hapsburg	Peter the Hermit
1915°	Pommern	Mr S.B. Joel	Let Fly	Rossendale
1916°	Fifinella	Mr E. Hulton	Kwang-Su	Nassovian
1917°	Gay Crusader	Mr Fairie	Dansellon	Dark Legend
1918°	Gainsborough	Lady James Douglas	Blink	Treclare
1919	Grand Parade	Lord Glanely	Buchan	Paper Money
1920	Spion Kop	Major G. Loder	Archaic	Orpheus
1921	Humorist	Mr J.B. Joel	Craig an Eran	Lemonora
1922	Captain Cuttle	Lord Woolavington	Tamar	Craigangower
1923	Papyrus	Mr B. Irish	Pharos	Parth
1924	Sansovino	Lord Derby	St Germans	Hurstwood
1925	Manna	Mr H.E. Morriss	Zionist	The Sirdar
1926	Coronach	Lord Woolavington	Lancegaye	Colorado
1927	Call Boy	Mr F. Curzon	Hot Night	Shian Mor
1928	Felstead	Sir H. Cunliffe-Owen	Flamingo	Black Watch

° Run at Newmarket on account of the war.

(Year)	*Jockey*	*Trainer*	*Value to Winner*	*Runners*	*Time (mins. secs.)*	*Starting Price*
(**1878**)	H. Constable	A.Taylor	£5825	22	2 56	100–12
(**1879**)	G. Fordham	J. Hayhoe	£7025	23	3 2	20–1
(**1880**)	F. Archer	R. Peck	£6375	19	2 46	2–1
(**1881**)	F. Archer	J. Pincus	£5925	15	2 50	11–2
(**1882**)	T. Cannon	J. Porter	£4775	14	2 45	11–2
(**1883**)	C. Wood	J. Porter	£5150	12	2 48	11–2
(**1884**)	C. Wood	R. Sherwood	£4900	15	2 46	100–8
	S. Loates	J. Jewitt				100–7
(**1885**)	F. Archer	M.Dawson	£4525	12	2 44	75–40
(**1886**)	F. Archer	J. Porter	£4700	9	2 45	4–9
(**1887**)	J. Watts	M. Gurry	£4525	11	2 43	100–9
(**1888**)	F. Barrett	G. Dawson	£3675	9	2 43	5–6
(**1889**)	T. Loates	G. Dawson	£4050	13	2 44	8–11
(**1890**)	J. Watts	J. Porter	£5940	8	2 49	100–15
(**1891**)	G. Barrett	J. Porter	£5510	11	2 56	10–11
(**1892**)	F. Allsopp	T. Wadlow	£6960	13	2 44	40–1
(**1893**)	T. Loates	J. Jewitt	£5515	11	2 43	4–9
(**1894**)	J. Watts	M. Dawson	£5450	7	2 45	2–9
(**1895**)	S. Loates	M. Dawson	£5450	15	2 43	9–1
(**1896**)	J. Watts	R. Marsh	£5450	11	2 42	5–1
(**1897**)	C. Wood	S. Darling	£5450	11	2 44	1–4
(**1898**)	O. Madden	R. Marsh	£5450	18	2 47	100–1
(**1899**)	M. Cannon	J. Porter	£5450	12	2 42	2–5
(**1900**)	H. Jones	R. Marsh	£5450	14	2 42	6–4
(**1901**)	L. Reiff	J. Huggins	£5670	25	2 40⅘	5–2
(**1902**)	J. H. Martin	S. Darling	£5450	18	2 42⅕	100–14
(**1903**)	D. Maher	S. Blackwell	£6450	7	2 42⅘	4–6
(**1904**)	K. Cannon	A. Hayhoe	£6450	8	2 45⅖	5–1
(**1905**)	D. Maher	P. Peck	£6450	9	2 39⅗	4–11
(**1906**)	D. Maher	P.P. Gilpin	£6450	22	2 36⅘	6–1
(**1907**)	J. Reiff	Colonel McCabe	£6450	9	2 44	100–9
(**1908**)	W. Bullock	Chev. E. Ginistrelli	£6450	18	2 39⅘	100–1
(**1909**)	H. Jones	R. Marsh	£6450	15	2 42⅖	7–2
(**1910**)	B. Dillon	A. Taylor	£6450	15	2 35⅕	7–4
(**1911**)	G. Stern	C. Morton	£6450	26	2 36⅘	13–8
(**1912**)	J. Reiff	D. Waugh	£6450	20	2 38⅘	100–8
(**1913**)	E. Piper	T. Lewis	£6450	15	2 37⅗	100–1
(**1914**)	M. MacGee	T. Murphy	£6450	30	2 38⅖	20–1
(**1915**)	S. Donoghue	C. Peck	£2440	17	2 32⅗	11–10
(**1916**)	J. Childs	R. C. Dawson	£2900	10	2 36⅗	11–2
(**1917**)	S. Donoghue	A. Taylor	£2050	12	2 40⅗	7–4
(**1918**)	J. Childs	A. Taylor	£4000	13	2 33⅕	8–13
(**1919**)	F. Templeman	F. Barling	£6450	13	2 35⅘	33–1
(**1920**)	F. O'Neill	P. P. Gilpin	£6450	19	2 34⅘	100–6
(**1921**)	S. Donoghue	C. Morton	£6450	23	2 36⅕	6–1
(**1922**)	S. Donoghue	F. Darling	£10,625	30	2 34⅗	10–1
(**1923**)	S. Donoghue	B. Jarvis	£11,325	19	2 38	100–15
(**1924**)	T. Weston	G. Lambton	£11,755	27	2 46⅗	9–2
(**1925**)	S. Donoghue	F. Darling	£11,095	27	2 40⅗	9–1
(**1926**)	J. Childs	F. Darling	£10,950	19	2 47⅘	11–2
(**1927**)	E. C. Elliott	J. Watts	£12,615	23	2 34⅖	4–1
(**1928**)	H. Wragg	O. Bell	£11,605	19	2 34⅘	33–1

Year	Winner	Owner	Second	Third
1929	Trigo	Mr W. Barnett	Walter Gay	Brienz
1930	Blenheim	H.H. Aga Khan	Iliad	Diolite
1931	Cameronian	Mr J.A. Dewar	Orpen	Sandwich
1932	April the Fifth	Mr T. Walls	Dastur	Miracle
1933	Hyperion	Lord Derby	King Salmon	Statesman
1934	Windsor Lad	H.H. Maharaja of Rajpipla	Easton	Colombo
1935	Bahram	H.H. Aga Khan	Robin Goodfellow	Field Trial
1936	Mahmoud	H.H. Aga Khan	Taj Akbar	Thankerton
1937	Mid-day Sun	Mrs G.B. Miller	Sandsprite	Le Grand Duc
1938	Bois Roussel	Mr P. Beatty	Scottish Union	Pasch
1939	Blue Peter	Lord Rosebery	Fox Cub	Heliopolis
1940°	Pont l'Evêque	Mr F. Darling	Turkhan	Lighthouse II
1941°	Owen Tudor	Mrs Macdonald-Buchanan	Morogoro	Firoze Din
1942°	Watling Street	Lord Derby	Hyperides	Ujiji
1943°	Straight Deal	Miss D. Paget	Umiddad	Nasrullah
1944°	Ocean Swell	Lord Rosebery	Tehran	Happy Landing
1945°	Dante	Sir E. Ohlson	Midas	Court Martial
1946	Airborne	Mr J.E. Ferguson	Gulf Stream	Radiotherapy
1947	Pearl Diver	Baron G. de Waldner	Migoli	Sayajirao
1948	My Love	H.H. Aga Khan	Royal Drake	Noor
1949	Nimbus	Mrs M. Glenister	Amour Drake	Swallow Tail
1950	Galcador	M.M. Boussac	Prince Simon	Double Eclipse
1951	Arctic Prince	Mr J. McGrath	Sybil's Nephew	Signal Box
1952	Tulyar	H.H. Aga Khan	Gay Time	Faubourg II
1953	Pinza	Sir V. Sassoon	Aureole	Pink Horse
1954	Never Say Die	Mr R.S. Clark	Arabian Night	Darius
1955	Phil Drake	Mme L. Volterra	Panaslipper	Acropolis
1956	Lavandin	M.P. Wertheimer	Montaval	Roistar
1957	Crepello	Sir V. Sassoon	Ballymoss	Pipe of Peace
1958	Hard Ridden	Sir V. Sassoon	Paddy's Point	Nagami
1959	Parthia	Sir H. de Trafford	Fidalgo	Shantung
1960	St Paddy	Sir V. Sassoon	Alcaeus	Kythnos
1961	Psidium	Mrs A. Plesch	Dicta Drake	Pardao
1962	Larkspur	Mr R. Guest	Arcor	Le Cantilien
1963	Relko	M.F. Dupré	Merchant Venturer	Ragusa
1964	Santa Claus	Mr J. Ismay	Indiana	Dilettante II
1965	Sea Bird II	M.J. Ternynck	Meadow Court	I Say
1966	Charlottown	Lady Zia Wernher	Pretendre	Black Prince II
1967	Royal Palace	Mr H.J. Joel	Ribocco	Dart Board
1968	Sir Ivor	Mr R. Guest	Connaught	Mount Athos
1969	Blakeney	Mr A.M. Budgett	Shoemaker	Prince Regent
1970	Nijinsky	Mr C.W. Engelhard	Gyr	Stintino
1971	Mill Reef	Mr P. Mellon	Linden Tree	Irish Ball
1972	Roberto	Mr J.W. Galbreath	Rheingold	Pentland Firth
1973	Morston	Mr A.M. Budgett	Cavo Doro	Freefoot
1974	Snow Knight	Mrs Neil F. Phillips	Imperial Prince	Giacometti
1975	Grundy	Dr C. Vittadini	Nobiliary	Hunza Dancer
1976	Empery	Mr N.B. Hunt	Relkino	Oats
1977	The Minstrel	Mr R. Sangster	Hot Grove	Blushing Groom
1978	Shirley Heights	Lord Halifax	Hawaiian Sound	Remainder Man
1979	Troy	Sir Michael Sobell	Dickens Hill	Northern Baby
1980	Henbit	Mrs A. Plesch	Master Willie	Rankin

° Run over a mile and a half on the July Course,
Newmarket, on account of the war.

(Year)	*Jockey*	*Trainer*	*Value to Winner*	*Runners*	*Time (mins. secs.)*	*Starting Price*
(1929)	J. Marshall	R. Dawson	£11,965	26	2 36⅖	33–1
(1930)	H. Wragg	R. Dawson	£10,636 5s	17	2 38⅕	18–1
(1931)	F. Fox	F. Darling	£12,161 5s	25	2 36⅗	7–2
(1932)	F. Lane	T. Walls	£9730 5s	21	2 43⅕	100–6
(1933)	T. Weston	G. Lambton	£9836 10s	24	2 34	6–1
(1934)	C. Smirke	M. Marsh	£8852	19	2 34	15–2
(1935)	F. Fox	F. Butters	£9216	16	2 36	5–4
(1936)	C. Smirke	F. Butters	£9934 5s	22	2 33⅘*	100–8
(1937)	M. Beary	F. S. Butters	£8441 5s	21	2 37⅗	100–7
(1938)	E. C. Elliott	F. Darling	£8728 15s	22	2 39⅕	20–1
(1939)	E. Smith	J. Jarvis	£10,625 10s	27	2 36⅘	7–2
(1940)	S. Wragg	F. Darling	£5892 10s	16	2 30⅘	10–1
(1941)	W. Nevett	F. Darling	£4473	20	2 32	25–1
(1942)	H. Wragg	W. Earl	£3844	13	2 29⅗	6–1
(1943)	T.H. Carey	W. Nightingall	£4388	23	2 30⅖	100–6
(1944)	W. Nevett	J. Jarvis	£5901	20	2 31	28–1
(1945)	W. Nevett	M. Peacock	£8339	27	2 26⅗	100–30
(1946)	T. Lowrey	R. Perryman	£7915 10s	17	2 44⅗	50–1
(1947)	G. Bridgland	C. Halsey	£9101 5s	15	2 38⅖	40–1
(1948)	W. Johnstone	R. Carver	£13,059 5s	32	2 40	100–9
(1949)	E. C. Elliott	G. Colling	£14,245	32	2 42	7–1
(1950)	W. Johnstone	C.H. Semblat	£17,010 10s	25	2 36⅘	100–9
(1951)	C. Spares	W. Stephenson	£19,386 5s	33	2 39⅖	28–1
(1952)	C. Smirke	M. Marsh	£20,487	33	2 36⅖	11–2
(1953)	G. Richards	N. Bertie	£19,118 10s	27	2 35⅗	5–1
(1954)	L. Piggott	J. Lawson	£16,959 10s	22	2 35⅘	33–1
(1955)	F. Palmer	F. Mathet	£18,702	23	2 39⅘	100–8
(1956)	W. Johnstone	A. Head	£17,282 10s	27	2 36⅖	7–1
(1957)	L. Piggott	N. Murless	£18,659 10s	22	2 35⅖	6–4
(1958)	C. Smirke	J. Rogers	£20,036 10s	20	2 41⅕	18–1
(1959)	W.H. Carr	C. Boyd-Rochfort	£36,078	20	2 36	10–1
(1960)	L. Piggott	N. Murless	£33,052	17	2 35⅗	7–1
(1961)	R. Poincelet	H. Wragg	£34,548	28	2 36½	66–1
(1962)	N. Sellwood	M.V.O'Brien	£34,786	26	2 37.3	22–1
(1963)	Y. Saint-Martin	F. Mathet	£35,338 10s	26	2 39.4	5–1
(1964)	A. Breasley	J.M. Rogers	£72,067	17	2 41.98	15–8
(1965)	T.P. Glennon	E. Pollet	£65,301	22	2 38.41	7–4
(1966)	A. Breasley	G. Smyth	£74,489 10s	25	2 37.63	5–1
(1967)	G. Moore	N. Murless	£61,918	22	2 38.30	7–4
(1968)	L. Piggott	M.V.O'Brien	£58,525 10s	13	2 38.7	4–5
(1969)	E. Johnson	A.M. Budgett	£63,108 6s	26	2 40.3	15–2
(1970)	L. Piggott	M.V. O'Brien	£62,311	11	2 34.6	11–8
(1971)	G. Lewis	I. Balding	£61,625.25	21	2 37.14	100–30
(1972)	L. Piggott	M.V. O'Brien	£63,735.75	22	2 36.09	3–1
(1973)	E. Hide	A.M. Budgett	£66,348.75	25	2 35.92	25–1
(1974)	B. Taylor	P. Nelson	£89,229.25	18	2 35.04	50–1
(1975)	P.Eddery	P.Walwyn	£106,465.50	18	2 35.35	5–1
(1976)	L.Piggott	M.Zilber	£111,825.50	23	2 35.69	10–1
(1977)	L.Piggott	M.V.O'Brien	£107,530	22	2 36.44	5–1
(1978)	G.Starkey	J.Dunlop	£98,410	25	2 35.30	8–1
(1979)	W.Carson	W.R.Hern	£153,980	23	2 36.59	6–1
(1980)	W.Carson	W.R.Hern	£166,820	24	2 34.77	7–1

* A record for the race at Epsom.

Year	Winner	Owner	Second	Third
1981	Shergar	H.H. Aga Khan	Glint of Gold	Scintillating Air
1982	Golden Fleece	Mr R. Sangster	Touching Wood	Silver Hawk
1983	Teenoso	Mr E.B. Moller	Carlingford Castle	Shearwalk
1984	Secreto	Mr L. Miglitti	El Gran Senor	Mighty Flutter
1985	Slip Anchor	Lord Howard de Walden	Law Society	Damister
1986	Shahrastani	H.H. Aga Khan	Dancing Brave	Mashkour
1987	Reference Point	Mr L. Freedman	Most Welcome	Bellotto
1988	Kahyasi	H.H. Aga Khan	Glacial Storm	Doyoun
1989	Nashwan	Sheik H. Al-Maktoum	Terimon	Cacoethes
1990	Quest for Fame	Mr K. Abdulla	Blue Stag	Elmaamul
1991	Generous	Mr F. Salman	Marju	Star of Gdansk
1992	Dr Devious	Mr S.H. Craig	St Jovite	Silver Wisp

APPENDIX II

The Phalaris-Nearco Line

The breeding of thoroughbred racehorses is, to put it mildly, an inexact science. Prominent American horseman, Colonel Bradley, opined: 'If you want the best, you breed the best to the best, and hope for the best'.

E.P. Taylor, the famous Canadian breeder, had studied the Phalaris-Nearco line, noting that back in 1947 Charlie Smirke rode a filly called Lady Angela to win a small race at Epsom. At the time she was not in the same league as her sire Hyperion (the 1933 Derby winner) but in 1952 Taylor spotted her potential as a broodmare. Lady Angela was carrying a foal to be named Nearctic, who was destined to become Canadian Champion, and sire of the legendary Northern Dancer.

The world's most successful stallion sired 605 foals from twenty-one crops including 134 stakes winners. Specifically, Northern Dancer is responsible for seven Epsom Derby winners to date; he is the sire of Nijinsky, The Minstrel and Secreto; and grandsire of Golden Fleece, Shahrastani, Kahyasi, and Generous.

In 1991 Northern Dancer, his sons and grandsons had sired one out of every five stakes winners in the world. Additionally, Northern Dancer-line mares produced 105 stakes winners. His influence has truly altered the course of the thoroughbred racehorse, and he is honoured annually with a major race on Epsom Downs.

This family tree based on a detail from a chart by Michael Church identifies twenty-nine Derby winners in descent from Lord Derby's Phalaris. Twenty-two of these have won since 1961 – a strike rate of 70 per cent.

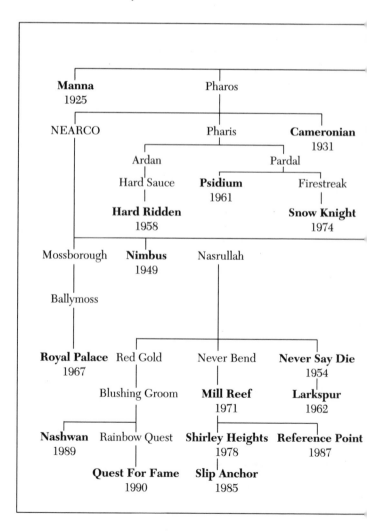

(Year)	Jockey	Trainer	Value to Winner	Runners	Time (mins. secs.)	Starting Price
(**1981**)	W.R.Swinburn	M.Stoute	£149,900	18	2 44.21	10–11
(**1982**)	P.Eddery	M.V.O'Brien	£147,266	18	2 34.27	3–1
(**1983**)	L.Piggott	G.Wragg	£165,080	21	2 49.07	9–2
(**1984**)	C.Roche	D.V.O'Brien	£227,680	17	2 39.12	14–1
(**1985**)	S.Cauthen	H.Cecil	£204,160	14	2 36.23	9–4
(**1986**)	W.R.Swinburn	M.Stoute	£239,260	17	2 37.13	11–2
(**1987**)	S.Cauthen	H.Cecil	£282,024	19	2 33.90	6–4
(**1988**)	R.Cochrane	L.Cumani	£296,500	14	2 33.84	11–1
(**1989**)	W.Carson	W.R.Hern	£296,000	12	2 34.90	5–4
(**1990**)	P.Eddery	R.Charlton	£355,000	18	2 37.26	7–1
(**1991**)	A.Munro	P.Cole	£355,000	13	2 34.00	9–1
(**1992**)	J.Reid	P.Chapple-Hyam	£355,000	18	2 36.19	8–1

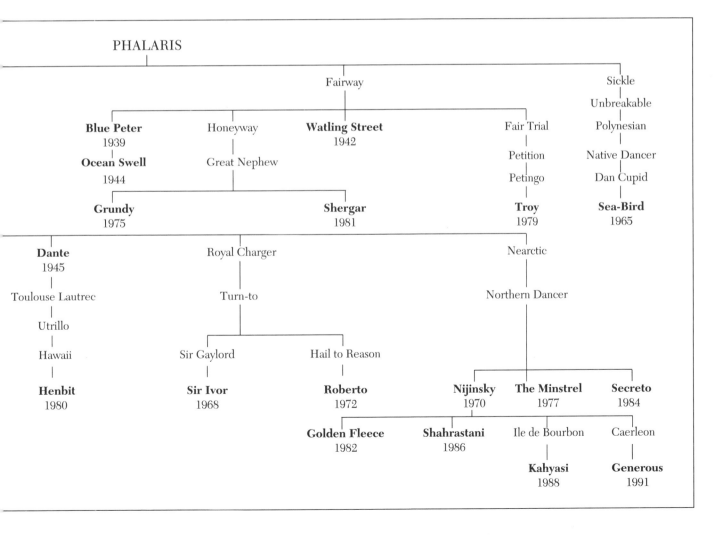

Miscellanea

MOST SUCCESSFUL OWNERS

H.H. Aga Khan IV
Shergar, 1981
Shahrastani, 1986
Kahyasi, 1988

Sir Victor Sassoon
Pinza, 1953
Crepello, 1957
Hard Ridden, 1958
St Paddy, 1960

H.H. Aga Khan III
Blenheim, 1930
Bahram, 1935
Mahmoud, 1936
My Love, 1948
   (half share)
Tulyar, 1952

17th Earl of Derby
Sansovino, 1924
Hyperion, 1933
Watling Street, 1942°

King Edward VII
Persimmon, 1896
Diamond Jubilee, 1900
Minoru, 1909

5th Earl of Rosebery
Ladas II, 1894
Sir Visto, 1895
Cicero, 1905

**1st Duke of
Westminster**
Bend Or, 1880
Shotover, 1882
Ormonde, 1886
Flying Fox, 1899

Sir Joseph Hawley
Teddington, 1851
Beadsman, 1858
Musjid, 1859
Blue Gown, 1868

Mr J. Bowes
Mündig, 1835
Cotherstone, 1843
Daniel O'Rourke, 1852
West Australian, 1853

5th Earl of Jersey
Middleton, 1825
Mameluke, 1827
Bay Middleton, 1836

Lord Egremont
Assassin, 1782
Hannibal, 1804
Cardinal Beaufort, 1805
Election, 1807
Lapdog, 1826

Sir Charles Bunbury
Diomed, 1780
Eleanor, 1801
Smolensko, 1813

3rd Duke of Grafton
Tyrant, 1802
Pope, 1809
Whalebone, 1810

Sir Frank Standish
Spread Eagle, 1795
Didelot, 1796
Archduke, 1799

5th Duke of Bedford
Skyscraper, 1789
Eager, 1791
Fidget colt, 1797

1st Lord Grosvenor
Rhadamanthus, 1790
John Bull, 1792
Daedalus, 1794

° War-substitute race at Newmarket.

• The following owners have won the Derby and the Oaks in the same year: Lord Clermont (1785), Duke of Bedford (1791), Sir F. Standish (1796), Mr J. Gully (1846), Mr J. Merry (1873), M.M. Boussac (1950).
• The following have owned the first two horses in the Derby in the same year: Duke of Bedford (1789), Earl Grosvenor (1790), Lord Jersey (1827), Colonel Peel (1844), H.H. Aga Khan (1936).
• The first woman to own a Derby winner was Lady James Douglas who won a war-substitute race with Gainsborough in 1918.
• The first woman to own an Epsom Derby winner was Mrs G.B. Miller, whose Mid-day Sun, whom she owned in partnership with her mother, Mrs Talbot, won in 1937.

MOST SUCCESSFUL JOCKEYS

L. Piggott
Never Say Die, 1954
Crepello, 1957
St Paddy, 1960
Sir Ivor, 1968
Nijinsky, 1970
Roberto, 1972
Empery, 1976
The Minstrel, 1977
Teenoso, 1983

C. Smirke
Windsor Lad, 1934
Mahmoud, 1936
Tulyar, 1952
Hard Ridden, 1958

S. Donoghue
Pommern, 1915°
Gay Crusader, 1917°
Humorist, 1921
Captain Cuttle, 1922
Papyrus, 1923
Manna, 1925

J. Watts
Merry Hampton, 1887
Sainfoin, 1890
Ladas II, 1894
Persimmon, 1896

F. Archer
Silvio, 1877
Bend Or, 1880
Iroquois, 1881
Melton, 1885
Ormonde, 1886

W. Scott
St Giles, 1832
Mündig, 1835
Attila, 1842
Cotherstone, 1843

J. Robinson
Azor, 1817
Cedric, 1824
Middleton, 1825
Mameluke, 1827
Cadland, 1828
Bay Middleton, 1836

F. Buckle
John Bull, 1792
Daedalus, 1794
Tyrant, 1802
Phantom, 1811
Emilius, 1823

T. Goodisson
Pope, 1809
Smolensko, 1813
Whisker, 1815
Moses, 1822

W. Clift
Waxy, 1793
Champion, 1800
Ditto, 1803
Whalebone, 1810
Tiresias, 1819

J. Arnull
Sergeant, 1784
Rhadamanthus, 1790
Didelot, 1796
Archduke, 1799
Election, 1807

S. Arnull
Diomed, 1780
Assassin, 1782
Sir Peter Teazle, 1787
Sir Harry, 1798

° War-substitute races at Newmarket.

- The oldest winning rider is J. Forth who was over sixty when he won on Frederick in 1829.
- The youngest, at any rate in this century, is L. Piggott who was eighteen when he won on Never Say Die in 1954; the exact age of Parsons, who was only a boy when he won on Caractacus in 1862, is unknown.

MOST SUCCESSFUL TRAINERS

M.V. O'Brien
Larkspur, 1962
Sir Ivor, 1968
Nijinsky, 1970
Roberto, 1972
The Ministrel, 1977
Golden Fleece, 1982

M. Dawson
Thormanby, 1860
Kingcraft, 1870
Silvio, 1877
Melton, 1885
Ladas II, 1894
Sir Visto, 1895

F. Darling
Captain Cuttle, 1922
Manna, 1925
Coronach, 1926
Cameronian, 1931
Bois Roussel, 1938
Pont l'Eveque, 1940°
Owen Tudor, 1941°

J. Scott
Mündig, 1835
Attila, 1842
Cotherstone, 1843
Daniel O'Rourke, 1852
West Australian, 1853

R. Marsh
Persimmon, 1896
Jeddah, 1898
Diamond Jubilee, 1900
Minoru, 1909

R. Robson
Waxy, 1793
Tyrant, 1802
Pope, 1809
Whalebone, 1810
Whisker, 1815
Azor, 1817
Emilius, 1823

John Porter
Blue Gown, 1868
Shotover, 1882
St Blaise, 1883
Ormonde, 1886
Sainfoin, 1890
Common, 1891
Flying Fox, 1899

° War-substitute races at Newmarket.

MOST SUCCESSFUL SIRES

Blandford
Trigo, 1929
Blenheim, 1930
Windsor Lad, 1934
Bahram, 1935

Waxy
Pope, 1809
Whalebone, 1810
Blucher, 1814
Whisker, 1815

Cyllene
Cicero, 1905
Minoru, 1909
Lemberg, 1910
Tagalie, 1912

Sir Peter Teazle
Sir Harry, 1798
Archduke, 1799
Ditto, 1803
Paris, 1806

- Eclipse, Highflyer, Pot-8-os, Touchstone, Stockwell, Polymelus, Hampton, Hurry On and Northern Dancer all sired three Derby winners.

- Sir Peter Teazle sired the first three to finish in the Derby of 1803; Stockwell accomplished the same feat in 1866.

WINNERS
Winners of the triple crown (not counting the war years when substitute races were run):

West Australian, 1853
Gladiateur, 1865
Lord Lyon, 1866
Ormonde, 1886
Common, 1891
Isinglass, 1893

Galtee More, 1897
Flying Fox, 1899
Diamond Jubilee, 1900
Rock Sand, 1903
Bahram, 1935
Nijinsky, 1970

- Pommern (1915), Gay Crusader (1917) and Gainsborough (1918) won war-substitute races and are usually awarded Triple Crown status.

There have been four grey Derby winners: Gustavus (1821), Tagalie (1912), Mahmoud, (1936), Airborne (1946).

The following fillies have won the Derby and the Oaks: Eleanor (1801), Blink Bonny (1857), Signorinetta (1908); Fifinella (1916).
- Other fillies to win the Derby are Shotover (1882) and Tagalie (1912).

Longest-priced winners: Jeddah, 100–1 (1898) and Signorinetta, 100–1 (1908).

Longest-priced placed horse: Terimon, 500–1 (1989).

Fastest time: Mahmoud, 2 minutes 33 ⅘ seconds (1936).

Dead-heats
- Cadland and The Colonel (1828); Cadland won the run off by half a length.
- St Gatien and Harvester (1884); the stakes were divided.

Doubles
- The Prince of Wales (later King Edward VII) won the Derby and the Grand National in 1900.
- G. Blackwell, R.C. Dawson, J. Jewitt, W. Stephenson and M.V. O'Brien have trained winners of the Derby and the Grand National.
- In 1893 H. Barker rode the runner-up in both the Grand National and the Derby.

French-bred Derby winners are Gladiateur (1865), Durbar II (1914), Bois Roussel (1938), Pearl Diver (1947), My Love (1948), Galcador (1950), Phil Drake (1955), Lavandin (1956), Relko (1963), and Sea Bird II (1965).

American-bred Derby winners are Iroquois (1881), Never Say Die (1954), Sir Ivor (1968), Mill Reef (1971), Roberto (1972), Empery (1976), Henbit (1980), Golden Fleece (1982), Teenoso (1983), Secreto (1984) and Shahrastani (1986). Nijinsky (1970) and The Minstrel (1977) were bred in Canada.

Derby winners trained in Ireland are Orby (1907), Hard Ridden (1958), Larkspur (1962), Santa Claus (1964), Sir Ivor (1968), Nijinsky (1970), Roberto (1972), The Minstrel (1977), Golden Fleece (1982) and Secreto (1984).

Exported Derby winner

Diomed (USA)
Saltram (USA)
Spread Eagle (USA)
Gustavus (Prussia)
Middleton (Russia)
Mameluke (USA)
Cadland (France)
Priam (USA)
St Giles (USA)
Dangerous (France)
Phosphorus (Germany)
Bloomsbury (Germany)
Attila (Germany, died en route)
Cossack (France)
The Flying Dutchman (France)
Teddington (Hungary)
Daniel O'Rourke (Hungary)
West Australian (France)
Andover (Russia)
Blue Gown (USA., died en route)
Kingcraft (USA, died en route)
Doncaster (Austria)
George Frederick (USA)
Silvio (France)
St Blaise (USA)
St Gatien (Germany; later to USA)
Harvester (Austria)
Melton (Italy; returned to England)
Ormonde (Argentina; later to USA)
Galtee More (Russia; later to Germany)
Flying Fox (France)
Diamond Jubilee (Argentina)

Ard Patrick (Germany)
Rock Sand (USA; later to France)
Minoru (Russia)
Aboyeur (Russia)
Durbar II (exported from France to USA)
Captain Cuttle (Italy)
Coronach (New Zealand)
Blenheim (USA)
Cameronian (Argentina)
Bahram (USA)
Mahmoud (USA)
Mid-day Sun (New Zealand)
Pont l'Eveque (Argentina)
Watling Street (USA)
Pearl Diver (Japan)
My Love (Argentina)
Nimbus (Japan)
Galcador (Japan)
Arctic Prince (USA)
Tulyar (USA)
Lavandin (Japan)
Hard Ridden (Japan)
Parthia (Japan)
Psidium (Argentina)
Larkspur (Japan)
Sea Bird II (USA)
Sir Ivor (USA)°
Nijinsky (USA)
Snow Knight (Canada)
Grundy (Japan)
Empery (USA)°
The Minstrel (USA)
Secreto (USA)°
Shahrastani (USA)°
Dr Devious (Japan)

° Bred in America.

The oldest mare to breed a Derby winner was Horatia, who was twenty-five when she produced Paris, winner of the 1806 Derby.

The smallest Derby field was four runners in 1794.

The largest Derby field was thirty-four runners in 1862.

Illustration Acknowledgments

The publisher gratefully acknowledges permission given by the following to reproduce illustrations and photographs:

Black and white
The Bowes Museum 17; Gerry Cranham 92, 97, 107, 109 (top and bottom); Mary Evans Picture Library 7, 13, 30, 32, 40, 45, 90, 124, 130, 132, 133, 135, 136, 139; Hulton Deutch 26, 50; Munnings Museum 6; Jacqueline O'Brien 75; Press Association 66, 69, 71 (top and bottom), 72 (top and bottom), 78, 88, 112, 113, 116, 122; George Selwyn 67, 73, 77 (top and bottom), 79 (top and bottom), 94, 101, 103, 105, 111, 141; Sheepdown 2, 14, 15, 20, 21, 22, 23, 25, 28–29, 31, 36, 37, 38 (top and bottom), 42, 44, 47, 49, 55, 57, 59, 62, 63, 83, 85, 126, 128, 129; United Racecourses Limited 18, 46, 48, 52, 54, 64, 82, 86, 87, 91, 96, 143.

Colour
Gerry Cranham 18 (top left, top right and bottom), 19 (top and bottom), 20 (top and bottom), 21, 24 (top left, top right and bottom); The Garrick Club (E.T. Archive) 17 (top); Tim Graham 22, 23 (top and bottom); Louvre 1 (bottom); Sheepdown 1 (top), 4 (top and bottom), 5, 6 (top), 8 (top), 9, 12–13, 15 (bottom); United Racecourses Limited 2–3, 6 (bottom), 7, 8 (bottom), 10–11, 14 (top and bottom), 15 (top), 16 (top and bottom), 17 (bottom).

Index